THE
REPRODUCTIVE
SYSTEM

THE HUMAN BODY

THE
REPRODUCTIVE
SYSTEM

EDITED BY KARA ROGERS, SENIOR EDITOR, BIOMEDICAL SCIENCES

Britannica®
Educational Publishing

IN ASSOCIATION WITH

ROSEN
EDUCATIONAL SERVICES

Published in 2011 by Britannica Educational Publishing
(a trademark of Encyclopædia Britannica, Inc.)
in association with Rosen Educational Services, LLC
29 East 21st Street, New York, NY 10010.

Distributed exclusively by Rosen Educational Services.
For a listing of additional Britannica Educational Publishing titles, call toll free (800) 237-9932.

First Edition

Britannica Educational Publishing
Michael I. Levy: Executive Editor
J.E. Luebering: Senior Manager
Marilyn L. Barton: Senior Coordinator, Production Control
Steven Bosco: Director, Editorial Technologies
Lisa S. Braucher: Senior Producer and Data Editor
Yvette Charboneau: Senior Copy Editor
Kathy Nakamura: Manager, Media Acquisition
Kara Rogers: Senior Editor, Biomedical Sciences

Rosen Educational Services
Heather M. Moore Niver: Senior Editor
Nelson Sá: Art Director
Cindy Reiman: Photography Manager
Matthew Cauli: Designer, Cover Design
Introduction by Cathy Vanderhoof

Library of Congress Cataloging-in-Publication Data

The reproductive system / edited by Kara Rogers.
    p. cm. — (The human body)
Includes bibliographical references and index.
ISBN 978-1-61530-139-3 (library binding)
1. Generative organs Popular works. 2. Human reproduction Popular works. I. Rogers, Kara.
QP251.R44465 2011
612.6—dc22

2010006081

Manufactured in the United States of America

CONTENTS

INTRODUCTION 10

CHAPTER 1: ANATOMY OF THE HUMAN REPRODUCTIVE SYSTEM 19

The Male Reproductive System 20
 External Genitalia 21
 The Penis 23
 The Scrotum 26
 The Testes 27
 Structures of the Sperm Canal 31
 Accessory Organs 35
The Female Reproductive System 38
 External Genitalia 38
 Internal Structures 40

CHAPTER 2: HORMONES AND REPRODUCTIVE MATURITY 52

Sex Hormones 52
 Androgens 52
 Estrogens 57
 Progesterone 61
 Gonadotropins 62
Puberty 65
 Reproductive Organs and Secondary Sex Characteristics 66
 Normal Variations 70
 Physical and Behavioral Interactions 71
Menstruation 74
 Phases of the Menstrual Cycle 76
 Hormonal Control of the Menstrual Cycle 78

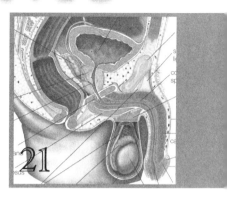

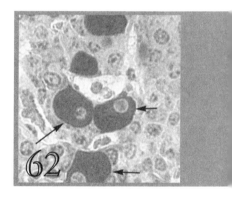

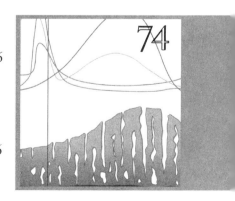

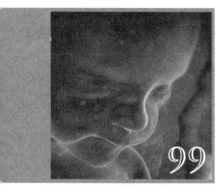

Ovulation and the Fertile
Phase 80
Menarche 81
Normal Menstruation 82
Menopause 82

**CHAPTER 3: REPRODUCTION AND
PREGNANCY 87**
Sexual Intercourse 87
Sperm and Ova 89
Fertilization 92
Development of the Reproductive
Organs 95
Implantation 97
Pregnancy 98
Development of the Placenta 99
Changes to Reproductive
Tissues 104
Pregnancy Tests 109
Prenatal Care and Testing 109
Multiple Birth 113
Twins and Twinning 113
Other Multiple Births 116

**CHAPTER 4: DISORDERS OF
REPRODUCTIVE DEVELOPMENT
AND FUNCTION 118**
Genetic and Congenital
Abnormalities 118
Abnormalities in Males 119
Abnormalities in Females 122
Intersexuality 124
Disorders of Sexual Maturity 133
Precocious Puberty 133
Delayed Puberty 136
Disorders Affecting Menstruation 138
Dysmenorrhea 138
Menorrhagia 139

Metrorrhagia 140
Amenorrhea 141
Oligomenorrhea 142
Dysfunctional Uterine
    Bleeding 143
Premenstrual Syndrome 143
Stein-Leventhal Syndrome 145
Disorders of the Testes and Penis 148
Hydrocele 148
Priapism 149

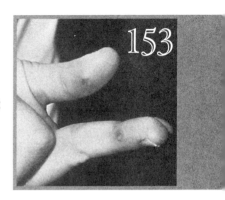

**Chapter 5: Infections and
Cancers of the
Reproductive System 151**

Sexually Transmitted Diseases 151
Syphilis and Gonorrhea 152
Genital Herpes 154
AIDS 155
Chlamydia 158
Trichomoniasis and
    Candidiasis 158
Genital Warts 158
Chancroid and Granuloma 159
Cytomegalovirus and
    Hepatitis B 159
Pubic Lice 160
Other Infections of the Reproductive
    System 160
Puerperal Fever 160
Tuberculosis 161
Balanitis, Posthitis, and
    Epididymitis 162
Orchitis 162
Vesiculitis 164
Leukorrhea 164
Vaginitis 165
Vulvitis 166
Cervicitis 168

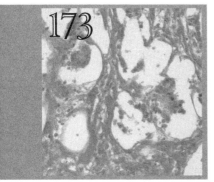

Mastitis 169
Pelvic Inflammatory Disease 171
Hyperplasia and Major Cancers of the
    Reproductive Organs 172
    Benign Prostatic Hyperplasia 173
    Testicular Cancer 174
    Prostate Cancer 174
    Vulvar Cancer 175
    Cervical Cancer 175
    Uterine and Ovarian Cancer 176

**CHAPTER 6: INFERTILITY AND
    DISORDERS OF PREGNANCY 178**

Infertility 178
    Female Infertility 180
    Male Infertility 185
    Assistive Reproductive
    Technologies and Artificial
    Insemination 186
Abnormal Changes in Pregnancy 192
    Ectopic Pregnancy 192
    Miscarriage 197
Disorders of the Placenta 199
    Placenta Praevia 199
    Placentae Abruptio 200
    Placenta Accreta 200
    Other Abnormalities of
    Placenta 201
Other Disorders of Pregnancy 202
    Anomalies of the Umbilical
    Cord 202
    Hydramnios 203
    Oligohydramnios 205
    Hydatidiform Mole 205
    Choriocarcinoma 206
    Gestational Diabetes 207
    Preeclampsia and Eclampsia 208

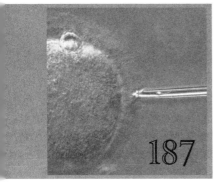

Chapter 7: Issues Concerning Birth Control and Abortion 211
History of Birth Control 212
Early Advocates 214
The Population Explosion 217
Birth Control and Health 218
Family Planning 219
Methods of Birth Control 221
    Abstinence 221
    Breast-Feeding 221
    Coital Techniques 222
    Barrier Methods 223
    Periodic Abstinence 223
    Hormonal Contraceptives 224
    Intrauterine Devices 227
    Voluntary Sterilization 229
The Legality of Birth Control 230
The Ethics of Birth Control 231
The Significance of Birth Control 238
Abortion 240
    Procedures 240
    Legality of Abortion 242
    A Divisive Issue 244

Conclusion 246
Glossary 248
Bibliography 251
Index 253

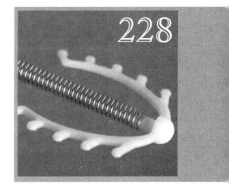

INTRODUCTION

As far back as the biblical story of Adam and Eve, people have understood that human reproduction is the result of sexual union between a man and a woman. Over the centuries, however, theories on exactly how it occurs varied wildly. The early Greek physicians Hippocrates and Galen believed that the male and female reproductive organs were opposite counterparts of each other in form but similar in function, both producing semen or "seeds." Conversely, the Greek philosopher Aristotle posited that the male contributed the human essence and the woman provided only the physical matter that nurtured that essence into an infant. Even as late as the 17th century, scientists continued to argue over whether the human being was formed from an egg or from a miniature human "animalcule" in the sperm.

Today it is known that reproduction occurs through the joining of an egg, contributed by the female, and a sperm, contributed by the male. Much more is known, too, about how that initial fertilized egg develops during pregnancy. In fact, scientists' understanding is now so complete that doctors fertilize eggs outside the body, or "in vitro," to help treat certain types of infertility. Pregnancy can even be prevented through a variety of birth control methods. But as science advances in the understanding of human reproduction, it also leads to new ethical and societal issues that must be resolved.

This book explores both the science and the social issues surrounding the human reproductive system. The differences between the male and female reproductive organs are highlighted, in addition to the different hormones controlling their development and function. The book outlines the process of reproduction and how the fetus develops, as well as issues that can interfere with those processes. Ethical debates range from birth control to infertility treatments.

Sexual reproduction is a trait shared by humans and most other complex life-forms, which means that the male and the female each have a distinct role to play in the process. Each individual's gender determines not only the physical characteristics of his or her reproductive organs, but also secondary sexual characteristics that are controlled by male and female reproductive hormones. The physical structure of the organs is present from birth, but the process of sexual maturation typically takes place in the early to mid-teens for boys as well as girls. The male reproductive organs include the external penis and scrotum as well as a variety of internal organs for the production of sperm and seminal fluid. Female reproductive organs are mostly internal and include the ovaries, where eggs develop and are stored; the fallopian tubes, which deliver them to the uterus; and the uterus itself, where the fertilized egg develops into a viable fetus until delivery through the birth canal.

In both boys and girls, puberty occurs between approximately 11 and 16 years of age. The process is generated in both sexes by the release of hormones, with estrogen secreted by the ovaries in girls and testosterone secreted by the testes in boys. During this period the sexual organs reach maturity and the individual is capable of reproduction. Other changes occur, too, giving rise to secondary sex characteristics. Boys and girls both develop pubic and underarm hair. Boys begin to display chest and facial hair, whereas girls develop breast tissue. Boys also experience a sudden voice change to a deeper register when the larynx lengthens, which is caused by the male hormone testosterone. For girls the most definitive indication of sexual maturity is the first menstruation, called menarche.

Menstruation is in essence the body's response to a potential pregnancy that never occurred. Each month the ovaries release one or occasionally multiple eggs. The release of the ovum, or egg, sets off a series of hormonal responses. The inner wall of the uterus, called the endometrium, begins to thicken and swell with fluid as it prepares to nourish a fertilized embryo. If the egg is not fertilized, the endometrial tissue breaks down and flows out as menstruation. Conversely, if sperm is present and fertilizes the egg within a few days after ovulation, pregnancy occurs. Many forms of birth control are based on changing the levels of the hormones occurring during the ovulation cycle, with the result that changes in menstruation may also occur.

The study of human reproduction, however, is essentially the study of pregnancy: how it occurs and what happens during gestation. A new life is created when an active sperm enters the nucleus of a fertile egg. This normally happens when the male deposits semen, typically containing millions of sperm cells per cubic centimeter, in the female's vagina. The sperm cells then "swim" up to meet the egg in the fallopian tube on its way to the uterus. One of these sperm cells penetrates the outer wall of the ovum and enters the cell nucleus. The sperm and egg cells are the only cells in the human body with only one set of chromosomes, rather than a paired set. When the sperm fertilizes the egg, their chromosomes become paired, forming a new individual with a unique genetic makeup created by the combination of DNA from both parent cells.

Once the egg is fertilized, it begins the process of cell division and growth. By the time the fertilized egg, now called a zygote, has arrived in the uterus, it is a multi-celled blastocyst. Within about five to six days after conception, the blastocyst has embedded itself into the uterine wall and begins to develop specialized cells to allow for embryonic growth and development. Twins or other multiple births may occur if more than one egg has been released and fertilized, in which case the twins are fraternal, or if the early cell divisions result in two separate zygotes, in which case the twins are identical and share the same DNA.

During the period of pregnancy, the fetus is essentially sharing the mother's blood supply through the placenta. Thus doctors strongly discourage smoking, drinking alcohol, and taking most kinds of drugs during pregnancy because they may lead to low birth weight, birth defects, premature birth, or other problems. Even drug addiction on the part of the newborn is possible.

Although most pregnancies and births proceed normally and the reproductive system performs properly, there are many potential disorders of both the male and female reproductive systems, as well as possible risks of pregnancy. This book provides an overview of those disorders, describing how they alter the normal, healthy function of the reproductive system. There are also diseases and infections that may affect the reproductive organs. Many of these conditions are preventable, particularly sexually transmitted diseases, such as syphilis, gonorrhea, chlamydia, genital herpes, and AIDS.

Some individuals also experience difficulty either conceiving or carrying a child to term. These are both generally treated under the broad category of infertility and may be caused by either partner. There may be problems with the viability of the eggs, particularly as a woman reaches the end of her reproductive years, or a woman may fail to ovulate regularly. There may also be issues with the uterine environment that make it difficult for the embryo to become implanted or develop. In some cases, miscarriage, also known as spontaneous abortion, may occur for unknown reasons. In the male, sperm count may be low, or the sperm may not be active in moving up from the vagina to the fallopian tubes, conditions that may also be affected by age. Some infertility issues may also be caused by preventable activities, such as smoking, sexually transmitted diseases, alcohol consumption, and drug use.

Today many infertile couples can receive help with conceiving and having children. Treatments include hormonal injections to stimulate the release of multiple eggs; artificial insemination, in which active sperm from either the husband or another male donor is inserted into the woman's vagina by syringe; and in vitro fertilization (IVF), in which egg and sperm are removed from the female and male, respectively, combined outside the body, and reinserted into the uterus to be carried to term. All these techniques are relatively recent, with the first successful birth of a human child from IVF occurring in 1978. Today, however, infertility treatment is relatively commonplace with a reasonably high success rate. One side effect has been a dramatic increase in the incidence of multiple births, particularly from IVF in which multiple embryos may be used to maximize the likelihood of at least one embryo successfully implanting in the uterus.

IVF, and even more recently surrogate motherhood using IVF, has also engendered ethical controversy. The Roman Catholic Church has opposed IVF on several grounds: the destruction of human embryos not used for implantation; the possibility of in vitro fertilization by a donor other than the husband, thus removing reproduction from the marital context; and the severing of an essential connection between the conjugal act and procreation. IVF has also raised a number of unresolved moral issues concerning the freezing (cryopreservation) of ovaries, eggs, sperm, or embryos for future pregnancies.

Perhaps just as controversial, however, has been the development of methods to prevent pregnancy, more commonly known as birth control. The ability to prevent pregnancy has advanced in parallel with improvements in scientists' understanding of how pregnancy occurs. The earliest examples of birth control were abstinence (still the only 100 percent effective solution other than sterilization) or the male withdrawing from intercourse before ejaculation (coitus interruptus). Arabic medical texts from the 10th century suggest a variety of contraceptive methods, most of questionable scientific value. By the 1500s early condoms were in use, preventing the sperm from entering the vagina, and vaginal barriers, such as diaphragms and caps, were known by the early 19th century. Simple intrauterine devices, preventing implantation of the fertilized embryo, were in use by the mid-1800s. By the early 20th century, an understanding of the hormonal effect on fertility allowed for the development of oral contraceptives, but they were only finally available by about mid-century, thanks largely to the advocacy of Margaret Sanger in the United States and Marie Stopes in Britain.

The dissemination of information about and devices and drugs for birth control was frequently opposed by religious authorities and prohibited by civil ones, often under the guise of anti-pornography legislation. Although in much of the West, less restrictive attitudes and regulations generally prevail, in some societies today there are still strict limits, particularly on the most contentious of all issues—abortion.

Abortion, the artificial termination of pregnancy by either pharmacological or physical intervention, is a complex issue, particularly within the context of religion. Conflicting views often arise in parallel with differing religious beliefs as to when human life begins, which may be with the formation of a viable embryo or with the later development of a viable fetus. Thus, the primary theme that transcends most religious concern over abortion is its association with the taking of life, namely that of an unborn fetus.

At the end of the 19th century, almost every country in the world had laws criminalizing abortion. In the mid-20th century, however, social and legal perspectives on abortion became much more divided. In 1973, in the well-known court case *Roe v. Wade*, the unduly restrictive state regulation of abortion was ruled unconstitutional by the U.S. Supreme Court. The court found that the criminalization of abortion in most cases deprived a woman of her right to privacy, thereby infringing on the Fourteenth Amendment of the Constitution.

Today as much as 70 percent of the world's population lives in countries where abortion is legally available. Still, many individuals and organizations are opposed to the practice of abortion. In the United States the issue remains highly polarizing, with protests at clinics providing abortion services and litigation in the courts and legislative bodies common at the state and federal levels. Debates include whether certain procedures should be prohibited, whether a waiting period should be mandated, whether federal medical insurance should cover abortion procedures, and whether parents should be provided notification if a minor seeks an abortion.

Ironically, as birth control has become more widely available and more reliable, the need for fertility treatments has also increased because individuals often delay childbearing until they are older, when fertility issues are more common. Advances in understanding of the human reproductive system have led to a whole new set of issues that must be addressed on both scientific and societal levels. This volume's thorough and thought-provoking overview will enable readers to develop an informed perspective of these issues.

CHAPTER 1

ANATOMY OF THE HUMAN REPRODUCTIVE SYSTEM

The human reproductive system consists of a network of organs and signaling molecules that interact and communicate to give rise to the human ability to produce and bear live offspring. It is distinguished from all other organ systems of the human body by the fact that it is composed of two anatomically different organ plans, one for the female and one for the male. It is also a slow-developing system, with the reproductive organs obtaining full maturity at some point during adolescence, the transitional phase of growth and development between childhood and adulthood.

Provided all organs are present, normally constructed, and functioning properly, the seven essential features of human reproduction are (1) liberation of an ovum, or egg, at a specific time in the reproductive cycle; (2) internal fertilization of the ovum by spermatozoa, or sperm cells; (3) transport of the fertilized ovum to the uterus, or womb; (4) implantation of the blastocyst, the early embryo developed from the fertilized ovum, in the wall of the uterus; (5) formation of a placenta and maintenance of the unborn child during the entire period of gestation; (6) birth of the child and expulsion of the placenta; and (7) suckling and care of the child, with an eventual return of the maternal organs to virtually their original state.

For this biological process to be carried out, certain organs and structures are required in both the male and the female. The source of the ova (the female germ cells) is the female ovary; that of sperm (the male germ cells) is the testis. In females, the two ovaries are situated in the pelvic cavity. In males, the two testes are enveloped in a sac of skin, the scrotum, lying below and outside the abdomen. Besides producing the germ cells, or gametes, the ovaries and testes are the source of hormones that cause full development of secondary sexual characteristics and the proper functioning of the reproductive tracts. These tracts comprise the fallopian tubes, the uterus, the vagina, and associated structures in females and the penis, the sperm channels (epididymis, ductus deferens, and ejaculatory ducts), and other related structures and glands in males. The function of the fallopian tube is to convey an ovum, which is fertilized in the tube, to the uterus, where gestation (development before birth) takes place. The function of the male ducts is to convey sperm from the testis, to store them, and, when ejaculation occurs, to eject them with secretions from the male glands through the penis.

At copulation, or sexual intercourse, the erect penis is inserted into the vagina, and sperm contained in the seminal fluid (semen) are ejaculated into the female genital tract. Sperm then pass from the vagina through the uterus to the fallopian tube to fertilize the ovum in the outer part of the tube. Females exhibit a periodicity in the activity of their ovaries and uterus, which starts at puberty and ends at menopause. The periodicity is manifested by menstruation at intervals of about 28 days. Important changes occur in the ovaries and uterus during each reproductive, or menstrual, cycle. Periodicity, and subsequently menstruation, is suppressed during pregnancy and lactation.

THE MALE REPRODUCTIVE SYSTEM

The male gonads are the testes, the source of sperm and of male sex hormones called androgens. The other genital

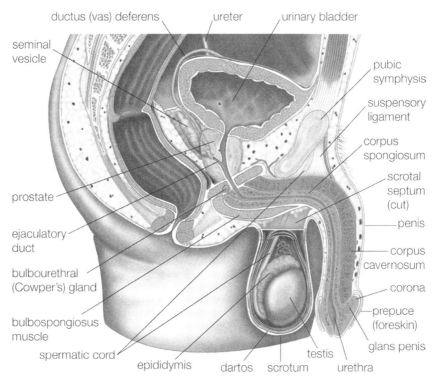

ductus (vas) deferens   ureter   urinary bladder

seminal vesicle

pubic symphysis

suspensory ligament

corpus spongiosum

prostate

scrotal septum (cut)

penis

ejaculatory duct

corpus cavernosum

bulbourethral (Cowper's) gland

corona

prepuce (foreskin)

bulbospongiosus muscle

glans penis

spermatic cord   epididymis   dartos scrotum   urethra

testis

Organs of the male reproductive system. Encyclopædia Britannica, Inc.

organs are the epididymides; the ductus, or vasa, deferentia; the seminal vesicles; the ejaculatory ducts; and the penis; as well as certain accessory structures, such as the prostate and the bulbourethral (Cowper) glands. The principal functions of these structures are to transport the sperm from the testes to the exterior, to allow their maturation on the way, and to provide certain secretions that help form the semen.

EXTERNAL GENITALIA

The two testes, or testicles, which usually complete their descent into the scrotum from their point of origin on the back wall of the abdomen in the seventh month after conception, are suspended in the scrotum by the spermatic cords. Each testis is enclosed in a fibrous sac, the tunica albuginea. The sac is lined internally by the tunica vasculosa, containing a network of blood vessels, and is covered by the tunica vaginalis, which is a continuation of the membrane that lines the abdomen and pelvis. The tunica albuginea has extensions into each testis that act as partial partitions to divide the testis into lobules.

Each lobule contains one or more convoluted, narrow tubes, known as seminiferous tubules, where sperm are formed. The tubules, if straightened, would extend about about 28 inches (70 cm). The multistage process of sperm formation, which takes about 60 days, occurs in the lining of the tubules, starting with the spermatogonia, or primitive sperm cells, in the outermost layer of the lining. Spermatozoa (sperm) leaving the tubules are incapable of independent motion, but they undergo a further maturation process in the ducts of the male reproductive tract. The process may be continued when, after ejaculation, they

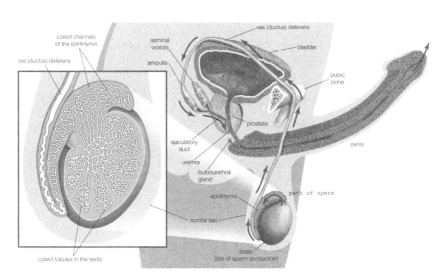

Structures involved in the production and transport of semen. Encyclopædia Britannica, Inc.

pass through the female tract. Maturation of the sperm in the female tract is called capacitation. Each sperm is a slender elongated structure with a head, a neck, a middle piece, and a tail. The head contains the cell nucleus. When the sperm is fully mature, it is propelled by the lashing movements of the tail.

Each testis is supplied with blood by the testicular arteries, which arise from the front of the aorta just below the origin of the renal (kidney) arteries. Each artery crosses the rear abdominal wall, enters the spermatic cord, passes through the inguinal canal, and enters the upper end of each testis at the back. The veins leaving the testis and epididymis form a network, which ascends into the spermatic cord. The lymph vessels, which also pass through the spermatic cord, drain to the lateral and preaortic lymph nodes. Nerve fibres to the testis accompany the vessels, passing through the renal and aortic nerve plexuses, or networks.

The Penis

The penis, the male organ of copulation, is partly inside and partly outside the body. The inner part, attached to the bony margins of the pubic arch (that part of the pelvis directly in front and at the base of the trunk), is called the root of the penis. The second, or outer, portion is free, pendulous, and enveloped all over in skin. It is known as the body of the penis. The organ is composed chiefly of cavernous or erectile tissue that becomes engorged with blood to produce considerable enlargement and erection. The penis is traversed by a tube, the urethra, which serves as a passage both for urine and for semen.

The body of the penis, sometimes referred to as the shaft, is cylindrical in shape when flaccid but when erect is somewhat triangular in cross section, with the angles

Penis

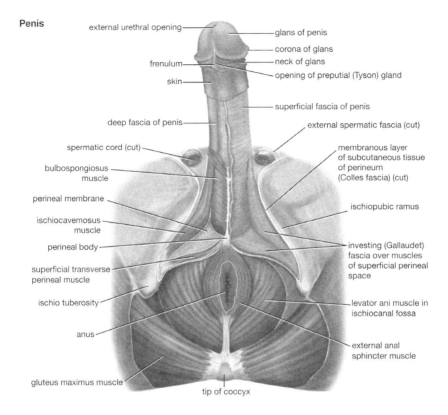

external urethral opening

glans of penis

corona of glans

frenulum

neck of glans

skin

opening of preputial (Tyson) gland

superficial fascia of penis

deep fascia of penis

external spermatic fascia (cut)

spermatic cord (cut)

membranous layer of subcutaneous tissue of perineum (Colles fascia) (cut)

bulbospongiosus muscle

perineal membrane

ischiopubic ramus

ischiocavemosus muscle

perineal body

investing (Gallaudet) fascia over muscles of superficial perineal space

superficial transverse perineal muscle

ischio tuberosity

levator ani muscle in ischiocanal fossa

anus

external anal sphincter muscle

gluteus maximus muscle

tip of coccyx

The human penis. Encyclopædia Britannica, Inc.

rounded. This condition arises because the right corpus cavernosum and the left corpus cavernosum, the masses of erectile tissue, lie close together in the dorsal part of the penis, while a single body, the corpus spongiosum, which contains the urethra, lies in a midline groove on the undersurface of the corpora cavernosa. The dorsal surface of the penis is that which faces upward and backward during erection.

The slender corpus spongiosum reaches beyond the extremities of the erectile corpora cavernosa and at its outer end is enlarged considerably to form a soft, conical, sensitive structure called the glans penis. The base of the glans has a projecting margin, the corona, and the groove where the corona overhangs the corpora cavernosa is referred to as the neck of the penis. The glans is traversed by the urethra, which ends in a vertical, slitlike, external opening. The skin over the penis is thin and loosely adherent and at the neck is folded forward over the glans for a variable distance to form the prepuce or foreskin. A median fold, the frenulum of the prepuce, passes to the undersurface of the glans to reach a point just behind the urethral opening. The prepuce can usually be readily drawn back to expose the glans.

The root of the penis comprises two crura, or projections, and the bulb of the penis. The crura and the bulb are attached respectively to the edges of the pubic arch and to the perineal membrane (the fibrous membrane that forms a floor of the trunk). Each crus is an elongated structure covered by the ischiocavernosus muscle, and each extends forward, converging toward the other, to become continuous with one of the corpora cavernosa. The oval bulb of the penis lies between the two crura and is covered by the bulbospongiosus muscle. It is continuous with the corpus spongiosum. The urethra enters it on the flattened deep aspect that lies against the perineal membrane, traverses its substances, and continues into the corpus spongiosum.

The two corpora cavernosa are close to one another, separated only by a partition in the fibrous sheath that encloses them. The erectile tissue of the corpora is divided by numerous small fibrous bands into many cavernous spaces, relatively empty when the penis is flaccid but engorged with blood during erection. The structure of the tissue of the corpus spongiosum is similar to that of the corpora cavernosa, but there is more smooth muscle and elastic tissue. A deep fascia, or sheet of connective tissue, surrounding the structures in the body of the penis is prolonged to form the suspensory ligament, which anchors the penis to the pelvic bones at the midpoint of the pubic arch.

The penis has a rich blood supply from the internal pudendal artery, a branch of the internal iliac artery, which supplies blood to the pelvic structures and organs, the buttocks, and the inside of the thighs. Erection is brought about by distension of the cavernous spaces with blood, which is prevented from draining away by compression of the veins in the area.

The penis is amply supplied with sensory and auto-nomic (involuntary) nerves. Of the autonomic nerve fibres the sympathetic fibres cause constriction of blood vessels, and the parasympathetic fibres cause their dilation. It is usually stated that ejaculation is brought about by the sympathetic system, which at the same time inhibits the desire to urinate and prevents the semen from entering the bladder.

THE SCROTUM

The scrotum is a pouch of skin lying below the pubic sym-physis and just in front of the upper parts of the thighs. It contains the testes and lowest parts of the spermatic cord. A scrotal septum or partition divides the pouch into two compartments and arises from a ridge, or raphe, visible on the outside of the scrotum. The raphe turns for-ward onto the undersurface of the penis and is continued back onto the perineum (the area between the legs and as far back as the anus). This arrangement indicates the bilateral origin of the scrotum from two genital swellings that lie one on each side of the base of the phallus, the pre-cursor of the penis or clitoris in the embryo. The swellings are also referred to as the labioscrotal swellings because in females they remain separate to form the labia majora and in males they unite to form the scrotum.

The skin of the scrotum is thin, pigmented, devoid of fatty tissue, and more or less folded and wrinkled. There are some scattered hairs and sebaceous glands on its surface. Below the skin is a layer of involuntary muscle, the dartos, which can alter the appearance of the scrotum. On exposure of the scrotum to cold air or cold water, the dartos contracts and gives the scrotum a shortened, corrugated appearance, whereas warmth causes the scrotum to become smoother, flaccid, and less closely tucked in around the testes. Beneath the dartos muscle are layers of fascia continuous with those forming the coverings of each of the two spermatic cords, which suspend the testes within the scrotum and contain each ductus deferens, the testicular blood and lymph vessels; the artery to the cremaster muscle (which draws the testes upward); the artery to each ductus deferens; the genital branch of the genitofemoral nerve; and the testicular network of nerves.

The scrotum is supplied with blood by the external pudendal branches of the femoral artery, which is the chief artery of the thigh, and by the scrotal branches of the internal pudendal artery. The veins follow the arteries. The lymphatic drainage is to the lymph nodes in the groin.

THE TESTES

The testes are the two sperm-producing organs in males. They also produce androgens, the male hormones. In humans the testes occur as a pair of oval-shaped organs and are contained within the scrotal sac.

In humans each testis weighs about 0.875 ounce (25 grams) and is 1.6–2.0 inches (4–5 cm) long and 0.8–1.2 inches (2–3 cm) in diameter. Each is divided by partitions of fibrous tissue from the tunica albuginea into 200 to

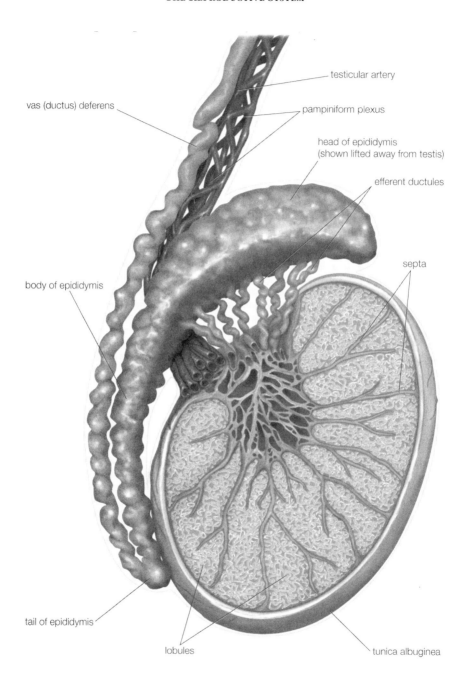

Human male testis, epididymis, and ductus deferens. Encyclopædia Britannica, Inc.

400 wedge-shaped sections, or lobes. Within each lobe are 3 to 10 seminiferous tubules. The partitions between the lobes and the seminiferous tubules both converge in one area near the anal side of each testis to form what is called the mediastinum testis.

The testes contain germ cells that differentiate into mature spermatozoa, supporting cells called Sertoli cells, and testosterone-producing cells called Leydig (interstitial) cells. The germ cells migrate to the fetal testes from the embryonic yolk sac. The Sertoli cells, which are interspersed between the germinal epithelial cells within the seminiferous tubules, are analogous to the granulosa cells in the ovary, and the Leydig cells, which are located beneath the tunica albuginea, in the septal walls, and between the tubules, are analogous to the hormone-secreting interstitial cells of the ovary. The Leydig cells are irregularly shaped; commonly have more than one nucleus; and frequently contain fat droplets, pigment granules, and crystalline structures. They vary greatly in number and appearance among the various animal species. Leydig cells are surrounded by numerous blood and lymphatic vessels, as well as by nerve fibres.

The embryonic differentiation of the primitive, indifferent gonad into either the testes or the ovaries is determined by the presence or absence of genes carried on the Y chromosome. Testosterone and its potent derivative, dihydrotestosterone, play key roles in the formation of male genitalia in the fetus during the first trimester of gestation but do not play a role in the actual formation of the testes. The testes are formed in the abdominal cavity and descend into the scrotum during the seventh month of gestation, when they are stimulated by androgens. About 2 percent of newborn boys have an undescended testis at birth, but this condition often corrects itself by the age of three months. The production of testosterone by the fetal testes is stimulated by human chorionic gonadotropin, a hormone secreted by the placenta. Within a few weeks following birth, testosterone secretion ceases, and the cells within the testes remain undeveloped during early childhood. During adolescence, gonadotropic hormones from the pituitary gland at the base of the brain stimulate the development of tissue, and the testes become capable of producing sperm and androgens.

The seminiferous tubules constitute about 90 percent of the testicular mass. In the young male the tubules are simple and composed of undeveloped sperm-producing cells (spermatogonia) and the Sertoli cells. In the older male the tubules become branched, and spermatogonia are changed into the fertile sperm cells after a series of transformations called spermatogenesis. The Sertoli cells found in both young and adult males mechanically support and protect the spermatogonia.

Each seminiferous tubule of the adult testis has a central lumen, or cavity, which is connected to the epididymis and spermatic duct (ductus deferens). Sperm cells originate as spermatogonia along the walls of the seminiferous tubules. The spermatogonia mature into spermatocytes, which mature into spermatids that mature into spermatozoa as they move into the central lumen of the seminiferous tubule. The sperm migrate, by short contractions of the tubule, to the mediastinum testis and are then transported through a complex network of canals (rete testis and efferent ductules) to the epididymis for temporary storage. The sperm move through the epididymis and the spermatic duct to be stored in the seminal vesicles for eventual ejaculation with the seminal fluid. Healthy men produce about one million sperm daily.

In animals that breed seasonally, such as sheep and goats, the testes regress completely during the nonbreeding season and the spermatogonia return to the state found in the young, sexually immature males. Frequently in these animals the testes are drawn back into the body cavity except in the breeding season, when they again descend and mature, a process known as recrudescence.

The principal androgen produced by the testes is testosterone. Testosterone produced locally in the testes and follicle-stimulating hormone (FSH) produced distally in the pituitary gland stimulate the process of spermatogenesis. Testosterone production and spermatogenesis slowly decrease in older men, whereas in women ovarian function ceases abruptly at the time of menopause.

STRUCTURES OF THE SPERM CANAL

The epididymis, ductus deferens (or vas deferens), and ejaculatory ducts form the sperm canal. Together they extend from the testis to the urethra, where it lies within the prostate gland.

Epididymis

The epididymis is either of a pair of elongated crescent-shaped structures attached to each testis. Sperm cells produced in the testes are transported to the epididymes, where they mature and are stored. Each epididymis has three regions, called, respectively, the head, body, and tail. The head is the uppermost and largest part of the epididymis. It lies on the top surface of the testis. The body is attached to the anal side of the testis and extends the length of the gland. The smallest region is the tail, which begins at the point of separation of the epididymis from the testis. Sperm cells mature primarily in the head and body of the epididymis and are stored in the tail.

The epididymis receives sperm from the tubules in the mediastinum testis. Leading from the mediastinum to the head of the epididymis are 15–20 small, tightly coiled ducts called the ductuli efferentes. The cells lining the ductuli have pigment granules, secretory granules, and cilia (hair-like structures). In the head region of the epididymis, all the ductuli efferentes connect to one large vessel, the ductus epididymidis. The lining of the duct is thick and has tufts of large nonmotile cilia. The duct is also extremely coiled, being about 13 to 16 feet (4 to 5 metres) long when stretched out. The ductus epididymidis extends through both the body and the tail region of the epididymis. In the tail region it becomes thicker, less coiled, and larger in diameter. As it emerges from the end of the epididymis, it straightens out to form the ductus deferens. There is some evidence that the ductules and the first portion of the duct of the epididymis remove extraneous debris from the testicular secretions entering these tubes. The blood supply to the epididymis is by a branch from the testicular artery given off before that vessel reaches the testis.

During ejaculation, sperm are propelled through the ductuli efferentes and ductus epididymidis in two ways. First, the muscle tissue, by contracting, narrows the ducts, propelling the sperm. Second, the cilia located in the ductuli efferentes can propel sperm by their continual swaying motions. As sperm pass through the various ducts, they acquire small amounts of fluids that help to keep them alive. These secretions include high concentrations of potassium, sodium, and a substance known as glycerylphosphorylcholine, which is an energy source for sperm.

Ductus Deferens

The ductus deferens, or vas deferens, is the continuation of the duct of the epididymis. There are two ductus deferentes, identical in structure and function, which emerge from the two epididymides. Each appears as a thick-walled tube.

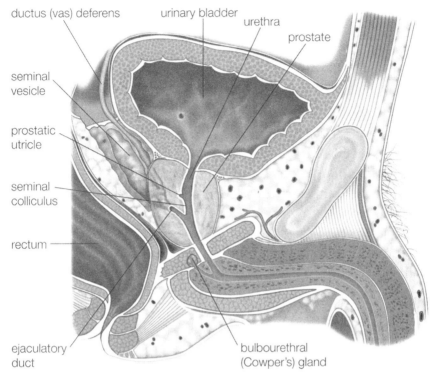

Sagittal section of the male reproductive organs, showing the prostate gland, seminal vesicles, and ductus (vas) deferens. Encyclopædia Britannica, Inc.

The channel of the ductus deferens is slightly larger than that of the ductus epididymidis. The tissue lining the inside wall is a moist and folded layer of mucous membrane. Surrounding the mucous membrane are three layers of circular and longitudinal muscle fibres. These fibres cause the ducts to contract and thus allow the sperm and fluids to be transported. The ductus deferens begins at the tail of the epididymis, in the lower region of the scrotal sac, the pouch of thin skin that covers the testes and epididymides. It extends into the pelvic region. While ascending to the level of the bladder, the ductus deferens is surrounded by a network of arteries, veins (pampiniform plexus), and nerve fibres, and the whole is covered by layers of connective tissue. (This complex tubular structure, called the spermatic cord, also serves to suspend the testes.) At the level of the bladder, each duct separates from its sheath of connective tissue and travels back over the top of the bladder. The two ducts turn downward at the rear of the bladder, and their channels enlarge to form the two ampullae attached to the bladder's outside left and right walls.

The ampullae act as storage chambers for the semen and contribute secretions to it. The yellow secretions of the ampullae include ergothioneine, a substance that reduces chemical compounds, and fructose, a sugar and nutrient. Both secretions moisten the sperm and help to keep them viable. The inside cavities of the ampullae have several meshlike partitions and folds. The walls of the ampulla are thinner than the rest of the sperm canal, and the channel is usually larger. The size of the ampulla varies with different animal species. For example, in the stallion the ampullae are relatively large, whereas in man they are only about twice the size of the ductus deferentes. The ampullae join the ducts of the seminal vesicles to form the ejaculatory ducts.

Ejaculatory Ducts

The ejaculatory ducts are two hollow tubes, each formed by union of the ampulla of a ductus deferens and the excretory duct of a seminal vesicle. The ducts, which open into the urethra about halfway through the prostate gland, function to mix the sperm stored in the ampulla with fluids secreted by the seminal vesicles and to transport these substances to the prostate.

The two ejaculatory ducts lie on each side of the midline and are formed by the union of the duct of the seminal vesicle, which contributes secretions to the semen, with the end of the ductus deferens at the base of the prostate.

Each duct is about 0.8 inch long (about 2 cm) and passes between a lateral and the median lobe of the prostate to reach the floor of the prostatic urethra. This part of the urethra has on its floor (or posterior wall) a longitudinal ridge called the urethral crest. On each side is a depression, the prostatic sinus, into which open the prostatic ducts. In the middle of the urethral crest is a small elevation, the colliculus seminalis, on which the opening of the prostatic utricle is found. The prostatic utricle is a short diverticulum or pouch lined by mucous membrane, which may correspond to the vagina or uterus in the female. The small openings of the ejaculatory ducts lie on each side of or just within the opening of the prostatic utricle. The ejaculatory ducts are thin-walled and lined by columnar cells.

ACCESSORY ORGANS

The accessory organs of the male reproductive tract are those tissues that support the function and activity of the system. The male accessory organs include the prostate gland, the seminal vesicles, and the bulbourethral glands. These structures provide secretions to form the bulk of the seminal fluid of an ejaculate.

Prostate Gland

The prostate gland is a chestnut-shaped organ located directly beneath the bladder in the male. The gland surrounds the urethra, the duct that serves for the passage of both urine and semen. The prostate is of a firm consistency, surrounded by a capsule of fibrous tissue and smooth muscle. The gland is rounded at the top and narrows to form a blunt point at the bottom, or apex. The diameter in the broadest area is about 1.6 inches (4 cm). It measures about 1.2 inches (3 cm) in height and 0.8 inch (2 cm) front to back. The two ejaculatory ducts converge and narrow in the centre of the prostate and unite with the urethra, which then continues to the lower segment of the prostate and exits near the apex.

The prostate is a conglomerate of 30 to 50 tubular or saclike glands that secrete fluids into the urethra and ejaculatory ducts. The secretory ducts and glands are lined with a moist, folded mucous membrane. The folds permit the tissue to expand while storing fluids. Beneath this layer is connective tissue composed of a thick network of elastic fibres and blood vessels. The tissue surrounding the secretory ducts and glands, which is known as interstitial tissue, contains muscle, elastic fibres, and collagen fibres that give the prostate gland support and firmness. The capsule enclosing the prostate is also composed of interstitial tissue. The gland is imperfectly divided into three lobes. Two lobes at the side form the main mass and are continuous behind the urethra. In front of the urethra they are connected by an isthmus of fibromuscular tissue devoid of glands. The third, or median, lobe is smaller and variable in size and may lack glandular tissue.

The prostate contributes 15–30 percent of the seminal plasma (or semen) secreted by the male. The fluid from the prostate is clear and slightly acidic. It is composed of several protein-splitting enzymes: fibrolysin, an enzyme that reduces blood and tissue fibres; citric acid and acid phosphatase, which help to increase the acidity; and other constituents, including ions and compounds of sodium, zinc, calcium, and potassium.

Normally the prostate reaches its mature size at puberty, between ages 10 and 14. Around age 50, the size of the prostate and the amount of its secretions commonly decrease. Increase in size after midlife, often making urination difficult, may occur as a result of inflammation or malignancy. A group of short glands that are closest to the urethra and discharge mucus into its channel are particularly susceptible to simple enlargement. Prostate cancer is almost exclusively confined to glands in an outer zone of tissue that has a lining of tall columnar cells that secrete prostatic fluid under the influence of androgens from the testis. Males who secrete inadequate amounts of androgen may maintain normal function of the prostate with injections of androgen.

Seminal Vesicles

The seminal vesicles are two structures, about 2 inches (5 cm) in length, lying between the rectum and the base of the bladder. Their secretions form the bulk of semen. Essentially, each vesicle consists of a much-coiled tube with numerous diverticula or outpouches that extend from the main tube, the whole being held together by connective tissue. At its lower end the tube is constricted to form a straight duct or tube that joins with the corresponding ductus deferens to form the ejaculatory duct. The vesicles are close together in their lower parts, but they are separated above where they lie close to the deferent ducts. The seminal vesicles have longitudinal and circular layers of smooth muscle, and their cavities are lined with mucous membrane, which is the source of the secretions of the organs. These secretions are ejected by muscular contractions during ejaculation. The activity of the vesicles is dependent on the production of androgen by the testes. The secretion is thick, sticky, and yellowish; contains the sugar fructose; and is slightly alkaline.

Bulbourethral Glands

The bulbourethral glands, often called Cowper glands, are pea-shaped glands located beneath the prostate gland at the beginning of the internal portion of the penis. The glands, which measure only about 0.4 inch (1 cm) in diameter, have slender ducts that run forward and toward the centre to open on the floor of the spongy portion of the urethra. They are composed of a network of small tubes, or tubules, and saclike structures. Fibres of muscle and elastic tissue between the tubules give the glands muscular support. Cells within the tubules and sacs contain droplets of mucus, a thick protein compound. The fluid excreted by these glands is clear and thick and acts as a lubricant. It is thought to function as a flushing agent that washes out the urethra before the semen is ejaculated and may also help make the semen less watery and provide a suitable living environment for the sperm.

THE FEMALE REPRODUCTIVE SYSTEM

The female gonads, or sexual glands, are the ovaries. The ovaries are the source of ova (eggs) and of the female sex hormones (i.e., estrogens and progestogens). The fallopian, or uterine, tubes conduct ova to the uterus, which lies within the lesser or true pelvis. The uterus connects through the cervical canal with the vagina. The vagina opens into the vestibule about which lie the external genitalia, collectively known as the vulva.

EXTERNAL GENITALIA

The female external genitalia include the structures placed about the entrance to the vagina and external to the hymen, the membrane across the entrance to the vagina. They are the mons pubis (also called the mons veneris), the labia majora and minora, the clitoris, the vestibule of the vagina, the bulb of the vestibule, and the greater vestibular glands.

The mons pubis is the rounded eminence, made by fatty tissue beneath the skin, lying in front of the pubic symphysis. A few fine hairs may be present in childhood; later, at puberty, they become coarser and more numerous. The upper limit of the hairy region is horizontal across the lower abdomen.

The labia majora are two marked folds of skin that extend from the mons pubis downward and backward to merge with the skin of the perineum. They form the lateral boundaries of the vulval or pudendal cleft, which receives the openings of the vagina and the urethra. The outer surface of each labium is pigmented and hairy; the inner surface is smooth but possesses sebaceous glands. The labia majora contain fat and loose connective tissue and sweat glands. They correspond to the scrotum in the male and contain tissue resembling the dartos muscle. The round ligament ends in the tissue of the labium. The labia minora are two small folds of skin, lacking fatty tissue, that extend backward on each side of the opening into the vagina. They lie inside the labia majora and are about 1.5 inches (4 cm) in length. In front, an upper portion of each labium minus passes over the clitoris—the structure in the female corresponding to the penis (excluding the urethra) in the male—to form a fold, the prepuce of the clitoris, and a lower portion passes beneath the clitoris to form its frenulum. The two labia minora are joined at the back across the midline by a fold that becomes stretched at childbirth. The labia minora lack hairs but possess sebaceous and sweat glands.

The clitoris is a small erectile structure composed of two corpora cavernosa separated by a partition. Partially concealed beneath the forward ends of the labia minora, it possesses a sensitive tip of spongy erectile tissue, the glans clitoridis. The external opening of the urethra is about 1 inch (2.5 cm) behind the clitoris and immediately in front of the vaginal opening.

The vestibule of the vagina is the cleft between the labia minora into which the urethra and vagina open. The hymen vaginae lies at the opening of the vagina, a thin fold of mucous membrane that varies in shape. After rupture of the hymen, the small rounded elevations that remain are known as the carunculae hymenales. The bulb of the vestibule, corresponding to the bulb of the penis, is two elongated masses of erectile tissue that lie one on each side of the vaginal opening. At their posterior ends lie the greater vestibular glands, small mucous glands that open by a duct in the groove between the hymen and each labium minus. They correspond to the bulbourethral glands of the male. The blood supply and nerve supply of the female external genital organs are similar to those supplying corresponding structures in the male.

INTERNAL STRUCTURES

The internal structures of the female reproductive system include the vagina, the uterus, the fallopian tubes, and the ovaries. These structures fulfill diverse roles in the overall function of the system and are fundamental to the female's ability to bear offspring.

The Vagina

The vagina (or "sheath") is the canal that extends from the cervix (outer end) of the uterus within the lesser pelvis down to the vestibule between the labia minora. The orifice of the vagina is guarded by the hymen. The vagina lies behind the bladder and urethra and in front of the rectum and anal canal. Its walls are collapsed: The anterior wall is some 3 inches (7.5 cm) in length, whereas the posterior wall is about 0.6 inch (1.5 cm) longer. The vagina is directed obliquely upward and backward. The axis of the vagina forms an angle of over 90° with that of the uterus. This angle varies considerably depending on conditions in the bladder, in the rectum, and during pregnancy.

The cervix of the uterus projects for a short distance into the vagina and is normally pressed against its posterior wall. Therefore, there are recesses in the vagina at the back, on each side, and at the front of the cervix. These are known as the posterior fornix (behind the cervix and the largest), the lateral fornices (at the sides), and the anterior fornix (at the front of the cervix). The upper part of the posterior wall of the vagina is covered by peritoneum (a serous membrane), which is folded back onto the rectum to form the recto-uterine pouch. The lower part of the posterior vaginal wall is separated from the anal canal by a mass of tissue known as the perineal body.

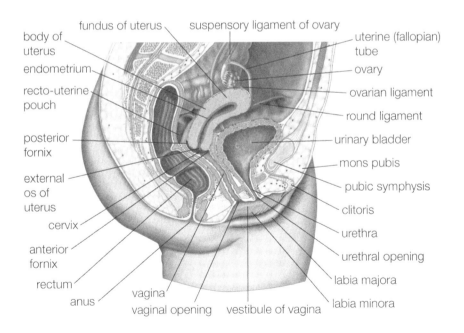

Organs of the female reproductive system. Encyclopædia Britannica, Inc.

The vagina has a mucous membrane and an outer smooth muscle coat closely attached to it. The mucous membrane has a longitudinal ridge in the midline of both the anterior and posterior walls. The ridges are known as the columns of the vagina; many rugae, or folds, extend from them to each side. The furrows between the rugae are more marked on the posterior wall and become especially pronounced before the birth of a child. The membrane undergoes little change during the menstrual cycle (except in its content of glycogen, a complex starchlike carbohydrate). This is in contradistinction to the situation in many mammals in which marked exfoliation (shedding of the surface cells) can occur. No glands are present in the vaginal lining, and mucus present has been secreted by the glands in the cervical canal of the uterus. The smooth muscle coat consists of an outer longitudinal layer and a less developed inner circular layer. The lower part of the vagina is surrounded by the bulbospongiosus muscle, a striped muscle attached to the perineal body.

The blood supply to the vagina is derived from several adjacent vessels, there being a vaginal artery from the internal iliac artery and vaginal branches from the uterine, middle rectal, and internal pudendal arteries, all branches of the internal iliac artery. The nerve supply to the lower part of the vagina is from the pudendal nerve and from the inferior hypogastric and uterovaginal plexuses.

The Uterus

The uterus, or womb, is shaped like an inverted pear. It is a hollow, muscular organ with thick walls, and it has a glandular lining called the endometrium. In an adult the uterus is 3 inches (7.5 cm) long, 2 inches (5 cm) in width, and 1 inch (2.5 cm) thick, but it enlarges to four to five times this size in pregnancy. The narrower, lower end forms the cervix, which projects into the vagina. The cervix is made of fibrous connective tissue and is of a firmer consistency than the body of the uterus. The two fallopian tubes enter the uterus at opposite sides, near its top. The part of the uterus above the entrances of the tubes is called the fundus, and the part below is known as the body. The body narrows toward the cervix, and a slight external constriction marks the juncture between the body and the cervix.

The uterus does not lie in line with the vagina but is usually turned forward (anteverted) to form approximately a right angle with it. The position of the uterus is affected by the amount of distension in the urinary bladder and in the rectum. Enlargement of the uterus in pregnancy causes it to rise up into the abdominal cavity, so that there is closer alignment with the vagina. The nonpregnant uterus is anteflexed, or curved gently forward. The uterus is supported and held in position by the other pelvic organs, the muscular floor or diaphragm of the pelvis, certain ligaments (bands of fibrous connective tissue), and folds of peritoneum. Among the supporting ligaments are two double-layered broad ligaments, each of which contains a fallopian tube along its upper free border and a round ligament, corresponding to the gubernaculum testis of the male, between its layers. Two ligaments—the cardinal (Mackenrodt) ligaments—at each side of the cervix are also important in maintaining the position of the uterus.

The cavity of the uterus is remarkably small in comparison with the size of the organ. Except during pregnancy, the cavity is flattened, with front and rear walls touching, and is triangular. The triangle is inverted, with its base at the top, between the openings of the two fallopian tubes, and with its apex at the isthmus of the uterus, the opening into the cervix. The canal of the cervix is flattened from front to back and is somewhat larger in its middle part. It is traversed by two longitudinal ridges and has oblique folds stretching from each ridge in an arrangement like the branches of a tree. The cervical canal is about 1 inch (2.5 cm) long. Its opening into the vagina is called the external os of the uterus. The external os is small, almost circular, and often depressed. After childbirth, the external os becomes bounded by lips in front and in back and is thus more slitlike.

The cervical canal is lined by a mucous membrane containing numerous glands that secrete a clear, alkaline mucus. The upper part of this lining undergoes cyclical changes resembling, but not as marked as, those occurring in the body of the uterus. Numerous small cysts (nabothian cysts) are found in the cervical mucous membrane. It is from this region that cervical smears are taken to detect early changes indicative of cancer.

The uterus is composed of three layers of tissue. On the outside is a serous coat of peritoneum, which partially covers the organ. In front it covers only the body of the cervix. Behind, it covers the body and the part of the cervix that is above the vagina and is prolonged onto the posterior vaginal wall. From there it is folded back to the rectum. At the side the peritoneal layers stretch from the margin of the uterus to each side wall of the pelvis, forming the two broad ligaments of the uterus.

The middle layer of tissue (myometrium) is muscular and comprises the greater part of the bulk of the organ. It is firm and consists of densely packed, unstriped, smooth muscle fibres. Blood vessels, lymph vessels, and nerves are also present. The muscle is more or less arranged in three layers of fibres running in different directions. The outermost fibres are arranged longitudinally. Those of the middle layer run in all directions without any orderly arrangement; this layer is the thickest. The innermost fibres are longitudinal and circular in their arrangement.

The innermost layer of tissue in the uterus is the mucous membrane, or endometrium. It lines the uterine cavity as far as the isthmus of the uterus, where it becomes continuous with the lining of the cervical canal. The endometrium contains numerous uterine glands that open into the uterine cavity and are embedded in the cellular framework or stroma of the endometrium. Numerous blood vessels and lymphatic spaces are also present. The appearances of the endometrium vary considerably at the different stages in reproductive life. It begins to reach full development at puberty and thereafter exhibits dramatic changes during each menstrual cycle. It undergoes further changes before, during, and after pregnancy, during menopause, and in old age. These changes are for the most part hormonally induced and controlled by the activity of the ovaries.

To understand the nature of the changes in the endometrium during each menstrual cycle, it is usual to consider the endometrium to be composed of three layers. They blend imperceptibly but are functionally distinct: The inner two layers are shed at menstruation, and the outer or basal layer remains in position against the innermost layer of the myometrium. The three layers are called, respectively, the stratum compactum, the stratum spongiosum, and the stratum basale epidermidis. The stratum compactum is nearest to the uterine cavity and contains the lining cells and the necks of the uterine glands. Its stroma is relatively dense. Superficial blood vessels lie beneath the lining cells. The large middle layer, the stratum spongiosum, contains the main portions of uterine glands and accompanying blood vessels. The stromal cells are more loosely arranged and larger than in the stratum compactum. The stratum basale epidermidis lies against the uterine muscle. It contains blood vessels and the bases of the uterine glands. Its stroma remains relatively unaltered during the menstrual cycle.

The menstrual cycle extends over a period of about 28 days (normal range 21–34 days), from the first day of one menstrual flow to the first day of the next. It reflects the cycle of changes occurring in the ovary, which is itself under the control of the anterior lobe of the pituitary gland. The menstrual cycle is divided into four phases: menstrual, postmenstrual, proliferative, and secretory. The secretory phase reaches its climax about a week after ovulation (the rupture and release of a mature ovum, or egg, from the ovary). Ovulation occurs in midcycle, about 14 days before the onset of the next menstrual flow. The endometrium has been prepared and has been stimulated to a state of active secretion for the reception of a fertilized ovum. The stage has been set for the attachment of the blastocyst, derived from a fertilized ovum, to the endometrium and for its subsequent embedding. This process is called implantation, and its success depends on the satisfactory preparation of the endometrium in both the proliferative and secretory phases. When implantation occurs, a hormone from certain cells of the blastocyst causes prolongation of the corpus luteum and its continued activity. This causes suppression of menstruation and results in the maintenance of the endometrium and its further stimulation by progesterone, with consequent increased thickening. The endometrium of early pregnancy is known as the decidua. In a cycle in which fertilization of the ovum has not taken place, the secretory phase terminates in menstruation.

The endometrium needs to be in a certain state of preparedness before implantation can occur. When this stage has been passed, menstruation occurs. Repair then reestablishes an endometrium capable of being stimulated again to the critical stage when implantation can occur.

The uterus is supplied with blood by the two uterine arteries, which are branches of the internal iliac arteries, and by ovarian arteries, which connect with the ends of the uterine arteries and send branches to supply the uterus. The nerves to the uterus include the sympathetic nerve fibres, which produce contraction of uterine muscle and constriction of vessels, and parasympathetic (sacral) fibres, which inhibit muscle activity and cause dilation of blood vessels.

The Fallopian Tubes

The fallopian, or uterine, tubes carry ova from the ovaries to the cavity of the uterus. Each opens into the abdominal cavity near an ovary at one end and into the uterus at the other. Three sections of the tubes are distinguished: the funnel-shaped outer end, or infundibulum; the expanded and thin-walled intermediate portion, or ampulla; and the cordlike portion, the isthmus, that opens into the uterus. The infundibulum is fringed with irregular projections called fimbriae. One fimbria, somewhat larger than the others, is usually attached to the ovary. The opening into the abdomen is at the bottom of the infundibulum and is small.

Fertilization of the ovum usually occurs in the ampulla of the tube. Normally, the fertilized ovum is transported to the uterus, but occasionally it may adhere to the tube and start developing as an ectopic pregnancy, or tubal pregnancy. The tube is unable to support this pregnancy, and the conceptus may be extruded through the abdominal opening or may cause rupture of the tube, with ensuing hemorrhage.

The fallopian tube is covered by peritoneum except on its border next to the broad ligament. There are inner circular and outer longitudinal layers of smooth muscle fibres continuous with those of the uterus. The inner lining has numerous longitudinal folds that are covered with ciliated columnar and secretory cells. Muscular contraction, movement of the hairlike cilia, and the passage of the watery secretions all probably assist in the transport of sperm to the ampulla and of a fertilized ovum toward the uterus.

The Ovaries

The ovaries are the female reproductive organs in which sex cells (ova, or eggs) are produced. The usually paired ovaries of female vertebrates produce both the sex cells and the hormones necessary for reproduction. In some invertebrate groups, such as coelenterates (cnidarians), formation of ovaries is associated with the seasons. Many invertebrates have both ovaries and testes in one animal, and some species undergo sex reversal.

The primary function of the ovaries is to nurture and prepare oocytes (eggs) for the process of ovulation. Once an ovum is released, it migrates down a fallopian tube to the uterus. While in the fallopian tube, an ovum may be penetrated and fertilized by a sperm. If an ovum becomes fertilized, it implants in the wall of the uterus. The processes of ovulation and fertilization are controlled largely by cells in the ovaries that produce and secrete hormones. These hormones also are essential for female sexual development and are necessary to sustain a pregnancy. They also regulate the menstrual cycle.

The ovaries of newborns and young girls are a mass of elongated tissue located in the pelvic girdle. As the female reaches adolescence, the ovaries gradually enlarge and change their shape. The adult ovaries are almond-shaped, and their surface is usually uneven and has areas of scar tissue. Averaging 1.6 inches (4 cm) long, 0.8 inch (2 cm) wide, and 0.6 inch (1.5 cm thick), the two ovaries weigh 0.14–0.3 ounce (4–8 grams). They are held in place by several ligaments, including the broad ligament, the suspensory ligament, and the ovarian ligament. Each ovary consists of an outer cortex, which contains the follicles, oocytes, and some interstitial cells, and an inner medulla, which contains additional interstitial cells, fibrous tissue, blood vessels, lymphatic ducts, and nerves.

The follicles, which are hollow balls of cells, contain immature ova (eggs) and are present in the ovaries at birth. There are usually 150,000 to 500,000 follicles at that time. By the beginning of a woman's reproductive life, the number of immature follicles has fallen to about 34,000, and this number continues to fall thereafter. As a woman ages, the follicles gradually diminish in number until, at menopause and the cessation of reproductive function, the few remaining follicles degenerate. During the active childbearing years, normally between ages 13 and 50, only 300 to 400 of the follicles undergo maturation. At the beginning of each menstrual cycle, known as the early follicular phase, several follicles enlarge and migrate from the cortex toward the outer surface of the ovary. The cells lining the follicle multiply to form a layer known as the zona granulosa, within which a cavity forms. The stromal and interstitial cells that surround the follicle arrange themselves concentrically to form a theca (an enclosing sheath) around the zona granulosa. One or sometimes more of the follicles are selected for further growth and maturation. The mature follicles, known as Graafian follicles, may reach about 1.2 inches (30 mm) in diameter before they rupture.

The interstitial cells, especially those in the theca, produce mainly the hormones known as androgens. Within the granulosa cells these androgens are converted to estrogens (estradiol and estrone), the major ovarian hormones. The fluid in the cavity bathing the oocyte contains high concentrations of estrogens and other steroid hormones (progesterone and androgens), as well as enzymes and bioactive proteins. This phase of the menstrual cycle, during which follicular development occurs, lasts about two weeks.

At the end of the follicular phase of the menstrual cycle, one or occasionally two (or even more) mature follicles at the surface of the ovary rupture and release the ovum. The ovum then enters a fallopian tube to be carried to the uterus. After the follicle ruptures, the granulosa and theca cells fill the lumen of the follicle, forming the corpus luteum. The corpus luteum produces large amounts of progesterone for about two weeks. If at the end of that time the ovum has not been fertilized, the corpus luteum involutes (becomes smaller) and becomes a whitish scar mass, known as a corpus albicans. As the corpus luteum disappears, progesterone levels fall, and the uterine lining is shed through the process of menstruation, thereby passing the unfertilized ovum from the body. However, if fertilization occurs, the corpus luteum continues to produce large amounts of progesterone for several months and will remain in the ovary until the end of the pregnancy. Progesterone helps the fertilized ovum secure itself to the uterus and develop into an embryo. The processes of follicular development, ovulation, and formation and function of the corpus luteum are controlled by gonadotropins known as follicle-stimulating hormone (FSH) and luteinizing hormone (LH), both of which are secreted from the pituitary gland.

The ovaries secrete both estrogen and progesterone into the bloodstream, and thus they are important endocrine glands. Before the onset of puberty, the ovaries are quiescent, or inactive, and the cortex of each ovary contains only immature follicles. Puberty begins with pulsatile nocturnal secretion of gonadotropin-releasing hormone

(GnRH) from the hypothalamus. GnRH activates the gonadotroph cells of the anterior pituitary, resulting in pulses of secretion of moderate quantities of FSH and of significant quantities of LH. In time, pulsatile secretion of GnRH and pulsatile secretion of the gonadotropins occur continuously. Increasing secretion of gonadotropins leads to increasing production of estrogens by the ovaries, which in turn stimulates the development of secondary sex characteristics and the maturation of ovarian follicles. Increased estrogen secretion normally occurs between ages 8 and 14 in girls.

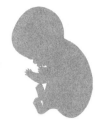

CHAPTER 2

HORMONES AND REPRODUCTIVE MATURITY

The sex hormones, together with the hypothalamus and the pituitary gland, form a complex regulatory system that influences sexual activity and the maturation and maintenance of the reproductive organs. The secretion of the various sex hormones, particularly testosterone and estrogen, increases significantly during adolescence. These changes give rise to puberty, a stage of rapid growth and sexual development. The cycle of physical changes that ensues ultimately culminates in reproductive maturity.

SEX HORMONES

The sex hormones are those produced by the testes and ovaries. This distinction is not exclusive, however, because the cortex region of the adrenal gland also secretes sex hormones (albeit to a lesser extent than do the ovaries or the testes), and the ovaries under abnormal conditions may produce adrenal steroids.

ANDROGENS

Androgens are hormones that primarily influence the growth and development of the male reproductive system. The predominant and most active androgen is testosterone, which is produced by the male testes. The other androgens, which support the functions of testosterone, are produced mainly by the adrenal cortex—the outer portion of the adrenal glands—and only in relatively small quantities. The adrenal production of androgens is of importance to several physiological processes. Certain adrenal androgens—androstenedione, dehydroepiandrosterone (DHEA), and dehydroepiandrosterone sulfate (DHEA sulfate)—can be converted to testosterone in other tissues.

Only a small amount of androgen is secreted before puberty. In both girls and boys, puberty is associated with an increase in adrenal androgen production. This "adrenarche" contributes to pubertal maturation, particularly growth of axillary and pubic hair. Androgens also are needed for the development of the male reproductive system. Males that have been castrated prior to adolescence and sexual maturity require injections of testosterone to develop functioning adult reproductive organs. Androgens given to normal males tend to increase the size of the reproductive organs. In contrast, castration performed on males that have already reached maturity causes the organs to shrink and to stop functioning. Androgens also are necessary for the formation of sperm cells and for the maintenance of sexual interest and behaviour.

Other effects of androgens on the male body are diversified. The growth of pubic hair and of facial and chest hair and the regression of scalp hair, or baldness, are influenced by androgens. During adolescence, androgens lengthen and thicken the male vocal cords, causing voice deepening, and they enhance bone growth and increase the number and thickness of muscle fibres in the male body. Other growth patterns that androgens stimulate are kidney weight and size, the increase of protein in bone tissue, the regeneration of red blood cells (erythrocytes), the presence of pigments in the skin, and the increased activity of sweat and sebaceous (oil-producing) glands.

Testosterone is the major hormone responsible for development of the male sex organs and masculine characteristics. It was first isolated from testicular extracts in 1935. Its discovery followed that of an androgen called androsterone, which was isolated from urine in 1931. However, testosterone proved to be more potent than androsterone, which was later shown to be a biochemical product (a metabolite) of testosterone.

A healthy man produces about 1.8×10^{-4} ounces (5 mg) of testosterone daily. Testosterone serves as a circulating prohormone for a more active androgen called dihydrotestosterone. Testosterone is converted to dihydrotestosterone in most tissues that are sensitive to androgens, including the testes, prostate gland, hair follicles, and muscles. Although testosterone has androgenic actions, its conversion to dihydrotestosterone is critical to the development of external genitalia in boys. Testosterone is also converted to estradiol in adipose tissue (and to a lesser extent in some other tissues), which is the most important source of estrogen in men. Furthermore, testosterone is interconvertible with androstenedione, which can be converted into estrogens. When androstenedione is formed in adipose tissue, it may be converted to a form of estrogen called estrone.

Testosterone has several major physiological actions. For example, it directs the development of the embryonic Wolffian ducts into the vas deferens (ductus deferens) and seminal vesicles and stimulates the formation of muscle and bone. Dihydrotestosterone is responsible for sperm maturation during spermatogenesis, for the formation of the prostate gland and external genitalia, and for sexual maturation at puberty.

The production of testosterone by the testes is stimulated by luteinizing hormone (LH), which is produced by the anterior pituitary and acts via receptors on the surface of the Leydig cells. The secretion of LH is stimulated by gonadotropin-releasing hormone (GnRH), which is released from the hypothalamus. Testosterone, in turn, provides negative feedback inhibition on the secretion of GnRH and LH. These three hormones constitute the hypothalamic-pituitary-testes axis. When serum testosterone concentrations decrease, the secretion of GnRH and LH increase. In contrast, when serum testosterone concentrations increase, the secretion of GnRH and LH decrease. These mechanisms maintain serum testosterone concentrations within a narrow range. In addition, the secretion of GnRH and the secretion of LH must be pulsatile to maintain normal testosterone production. Continuous administration of GnRH results in a decrease in the secretion of LH and therefore a decrease in the secretion of testosterone. Testosterone also inhibits the secretion of follicle-stimulating hormone (FSH), which is also inhibited by inhibin, a polypeptide hormone produced by the Sertoli cells.

Similar to other steroid hormones, testosterone in the serum exists in one of two forms. Most testosterone in the serum is bound to a protein known as sex hormone-binding globulin and to a protein called albumin, while the remaining amount (about 1 percent) is free, or unbound. Free testosterone is in equilibrium with bound testosterone so that when free testosterone enters cells, some bound testosterone is immediately freed. In the cytoplasm of target cells, testosterone or dihydrotestosterone binds to specific androgen receptors, and the hormone-receptor complexes enter the cell nucleus, where they modulate protein synthesis by influencing the rate at which particular genes are transcribed. Gene transcription is the process by which DNA (deoxyribonucleic acid) codes for certain proteins by producing specific molecules of messenger RNA (ribonucleic acid) that direct the synthesis of those proteins.

Testosterone can be manufactured by chemical and microbiological modification of inexpensive steroids, such as diosgenin. It is used clinically to treat testicular insufficiency, to suppress lactation (milk production), and to treat certain types of breast cancer.

Women produce about one-twelfth as much androgen as men. Androgens are essential precursors of estrogens, and no estrogens can be produced without them. Whether androgens have physiological actions in women is less clear. Some evidence suggests that androgens contribute to bone growth and libido. Mild androgen excess in women results in excess hair growth (hirsutism) that occurs all over the body but is most often noted on the face. With increasing androgen excess, menstrual periods become irregular (oligomenorrhea) and eventually cease (amenorrhea), and women are virilized. The manifestations of virilism include frontal balding, deepening of the voice, acne, clitoral enlargement, and increased muscle mass.

In women about half of the daily production of androgen comes from the ovaries in the form of testosterone and the less active androstenedione. The remainder comes from the adrenal glands, mostly as DHEA and DHEA sulfate, which are converted to androstenedione and testosterone in other tissues. The tissues capable of these conversions include the skin, fat, muscle, and brain. Some of these tissues are also capable of converting androstenedione to the more potent testosterone. Some of the testosterone produced in this way returns to the circulation to act at distant sites, but high concentrations may accumulate in key local areas such as hair follicles.

In women excess production of androgen can occur as a result of adrenal disorders, ovarian disorders, ingestion or injection of androgens, and perhaps disorders of fat or other nonendocrine tissues. The adrenal causes of excess production of androgens are Cushing syndrome, congenital adrenal hyperplasia, and adrenal tumours. Tumours (including cancers) of the interstitial cells and other cells of the ovary are a rare cause of androgen excess in women. A far more common cause of excess production of androgens in women is polycystic ovary syndrome (PCOS; also called Stein-Leventhal syndrome). This syndrome is characterized by excess androgens and the presence of a menstrual disorder.

ESTROGENS

Estrogens are hormones that primarily influence the female reproductive tract in its development, maturation, and function. There are three major hormones—estradiol, estrone, and estriol—among the estrogens, and estradiol is the predominant one of the three..

The major sources of estrogens are the ovaries and the placenta (the temporary organ that serves to nourish the fetus and remove its wastes). Additional small amounts of estrogens are secreted by the adrenal glands and by the male testes. It is believed that the egg follicle and interstitial cells in the ovaries are the actual production sites of estrogens in the female. Estrogen levels in the bloodstream seem to be highest during the egg-releasing period (ovulation) and after menstruation, when tissue called the corpus luteum replaces the empty egg follicle.

Cholesterol is the parent molecule from which all ovarian steroid hormones are formed. Cholesterol is converted to pregnenolone, and pregnenolone is converted to progesterone. The steps in the conversion of progesterone

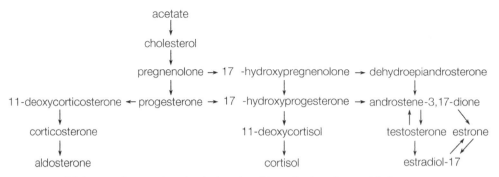

Major pathways involved in the biosynthesis of steroid hormones.
Encyclopædia Britannica, Inc.

to the main estrogens—estradiol and estrone—include the intermediate formation of several androgens: dehydroepiandrosterone, androstenedione, and testosterone. Androgens are converted to estrogens through the action of an enzyme known as aromatase. Although the ovaries are the richest source of aromatase, some aromatase is present in adipose tissue, which is also an important source of estrogen in postmenopausal women. Estradiol, the most potent estrogen, is synthesized from testosterone. Estrone can be formed from estradiol, but its major precursor is androstenedione. Estriol, the weakest of the estrogens, is formed from both estrone and estradiol.

Once secreted into the blood, estrogens bind reversibly to sex hormone–binding globulin. Thus, similar to testosterone, some of the hormone in serum is bound and some is free, or unbound. At its target tissues, the free estrogen penetrates the cell surface and then binds to a protein known as an estrogen receptor in the cytoplasm of the cells. In the case of estrogens, there are two types of cytoplasmic receptors—estrogen receptor-alpha and estrogen receptor-beta—that have a different tissue distribution but similar capacities to activate DNA synthesis. The estrogen-receptor complexes activate DNA synthesis by entering the cell nucleus, where they influence the rate of transcription of particular genes and thereby modulate protein synthesis.

In females, estrogens affect the ovaries, vagina, fallopian tubes, uterus, and mammary glands. In the ovaries, estrogens help to stimulate the growth of the egg follicle. They also stimulate the pituitary gland in the brain to release hormones that assist in follicular development. Once the egg is released, it travels through the fallopian tubes on its way to the uterus. In the fallopian tubes estrogens are responsible for developing a thick muscular wall and for the contractions that transport the egg and sperm cells.

Estrogens also build and maintain the endometrium, the mucous membrane that lines the uterus. They increase the endometrium's size and weight, cell number, cell types, blood flow, protein content, and enzyme activity. Estrogens also stimulate the muscles in the uterus to develop and contract, contractions having a crucial role in helping the wall to slough off dead tissue during menstruation and during the delivery of a child and placenta. The cervix secretes mucus that enhances sperm transport, and estrogens are thought to regulate the flow and thickness of these mucous secretions. The growth of the vagina to its adult size, the thickening of the vaginal wall, and the increase in vaginal acidity that reduces bacterial infections are also correlated to estrogen activities. The young female uterus, if deprived of estrogens, does not develop into its adult form, and the adult uterus that does not receive estrogens begins to show tissue degeneration.

In the breasts the actions of estrogens are complexly interrelated with those of other hormones, and their total significance is not easily defined. However, estrogens are responsible for growth of the breasts during adolescence, pigmentation of the nipples, and the eventual cessation of the flow of milk.

Actions of estrogens related to bone development and bone maintenance include the stimulation of bone formation and the closure of bone epiphyses, which causes linear growth to cease at the end of puberty, and the maintenance of bone throughout the reproductive years, which limits bone resorption and preserves bone strength.

Estrogens tend to decrease serum cholesterol concentrations and increase serum triglyceride concentrations. The overall effect of these changes, perhaps in conjunction with direct effects of estrogens on blood vessels, is to protect against atherosclerosis (the deposition of fats, cholesterol, calcium, and other substances in the arteries) before menopause. Estrogens also increase the serum concentrations of binding proteins that transport other substances, including the binding proteins for cortisol, thyroxine, and iron, as well as sex hormone-binding globulin.

Estrogens influence the structural differences between the male and female bodies. Usually, the female has smaller, shorter bones, a broader pelvis, and narrower shoulders. The female body is more curved and contoured because of fatty tissue that covers the muscles, breasts, buttocks, hips, and thighs. The body hair is finer and less pronounced, and the scalp hair usually is more permanent. The voice box is smaller and the vocal cords shorter, giving a higher-pitched voice than in males. In addition, estrogens suppress the activity of sebaceous (oil-producing) glands and thereby reduce the likelihood of acne in the female. In experimental animals, loss of estrogens diminishes the mating desires and other sexual behaviour patterns.

In the male, traces of estrogens are present in the blood and urine. Estrogens seem to be most evident in the male during puberty and old age. Their function in the male and their interplay with the male hormones are not completely known.

PROGESTERONE

Progesterone is a hormone secreted by the female reproductive system that functions mainly to regulate the condition of the inner lining (endometrium) of the uterus. Progesterone is produced by the ovaries, placenta, and adrenal glands. In the ovaries the site of production is the corpus luteum tissue, which begins to form prior to an egg's release and continues to grow into the empty follicular space once the egg has left the follicle (a capsule of tissue around the egg). The released egg, if fertilized by the male sperm cell, becomes implanted in the uterus, and a placenta forms. The placenta then produces progesterone during the period of pregnancy. If the egg is unfertilized, progesterone is secreted by the ovaries until a few days before menstruation, at which time the level of progesterone drops sufficiently to stop the growth of the uterine wall and to cause it to start to break down, and menstruation ensues.

Progesterone prepares the wall of the uterus so the lining is able to accept a fertilized egg and the egg can be implanted and develop. It also inhibits muscular contractions of the uterus that would probably cause the wall to reject the adhering egg. Progesterone is known to affect other female organs as well. In the ovaries, progesterone and estrogens are responsible for the release of an egg during ovulation. If the egg is fertilized, these hormones are influential in the prevention of further egg release until the pregnancy has terminated. This dual action ordinarily prevents the release and fertilization of more than one egg at one time, but two or more eggs are occasionally released.

Many oral contraceptives are composed of a synthetic chemical similar to progesterone that inhibits egg growth and release in the ovaries and thereby prevents fertilization. In the fallopian tubes progesterone is thought to stop the muscular contractions in the tube once the egg has been transported. During pregnancy, progesterone also stimulates development of the glands in the breasts that are responsible for milk production.

GONADOTROPINS

Gonadotropins are hormones secreted from the anterior pituitary gland that act on the ovaries and the testes. Gonadotrophs, cells that constitute about 10 percent of the pituitary gland, secrete the two primary gonadotropins: LH (also known as interstitial-cell stimulating hormone, or ICSH) and FSH. The amount and rate of

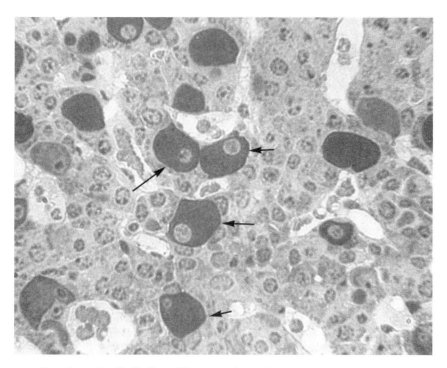

Gonadotroph cells (indicated by arrows) constitute about 10 percent of the pituitary gland and secrete hormones called gonadotropins, which include luteinizing hormone (LH) and follicle-stimulating hormone (FSH). Uniformed Services University of the Health Sciences (USUHS)

secretion of these hormones vary widely at different ages and different times during the menstrual cycle in women.

Secretion of LH and FSH is low in both males and females prior to puberty. The start of this stage of development is marked by the onset of nocturnal pulses of gonadotropin-releasing hormone (GnRH; also known as luteinizing hormone-releasing hormone). GnRH is a neurohormone consisting of 10 amino acids that is produced in the arcuate nuclei of the hypothalamus. Its primary function is to stimulate the synthesis and secretion of LH and FSH from the anterior pituitary gland. The effects of GnRH on the secretion of LH and FSH are not exactly parallel. For example, following puberty, more LH than FSH is secreted. These variations are probably caused by modulating factors such as the serum concentrations of steroid hormones (the general term used to describe the substances secreted by the adrenal cortex, testes, and ovaries).

Characteristic of all releasing hormones and most striking in the case of GnRH is the phenomenon of pulsatile secretion. Under normal circumstances, GnRH is released in pulses at intervals of about 90 to 120 minutes. To increase serum gonadotropin concentrations in patients with GnRH deficiency, the releasing hormone must be administered in pulses. In contrast, constant administration of GnRH suppresses gonadotropin secretion, which has therapeutic benefits in certain patients, such as children with precocious puberty and men with prostate cancer.

The neurons that secrete GnRH have connections to an area of the brain known as the limbic system, which is heavily involved in the control of emotions and sexual activity. In rats that are deprived of their pituitary gland and ovaries but are given physiological amounts of estrogen, injection of GnRH results in changes in posture characteristic of the receptive female stance for sexual intercourse.

Biochemically, FSH and LH are characterized as glycoproteins. In women, FSH operates in conjunction with LH to stimulate the maturation of cells lining the spherical egg-containing structures known as Graafian follicles. In menstruating women, there is a preovulatory surge in serum FSH and LH concentrations. The preovulatory surge of LH is essential for rupture of the Graafian follicle, after which the egg enters the fallopian tube and travels to the uterus. The empty Graafian follicle becomes filled with progesterone-producing cells, transforming it into a corpus luteum. LH stimulates the production of progesterone by the corpus luteum. Inhibin, a hormone secreted by the Graafian follicles of the ovaries and by the Sertoli cells of the testes, inhibits the secretion of FSH from the pituitary gonadotrophs. The secretion of both LH and FSH increases 10- to 15-fold in postmenopausal women. In women, FSH also stimulates the synthesis of estrogens.

In men, LH stimulates the development of the interstitial cells of the testes, and FSH promotes the development of the tubules of the testes and the development of sperm. The latter function is accomplished in large part by acting on the Sertoli cells in the testes. Although in the male the presence of FSH is necessary for the maturation of spermatozoa, additional FSH may not be required for months because testosterone can maintain this activity. In the female, however, there is a rhythmic, or cyclical, increase and decrease of FSH, which is essential for monthly ovulation. The production of LH is cyclical in nature as well, especially in the female.

Another type of gonadotropin found in women is human chorionic gonadotropin (HCG), which is produced by the placenta during pregnancy. The detection of HCG forms the basis of pregnancy tests.

Patients with diseases involving the anterior pituitary gland often have gonadotropin deficiency. Thus, the disappearance of menstrual periods may be the first sign of a pituitary tumour or other pituitary disease in women. In men the most common symptoms of gonadotropin deficiency are loss of libido and erectile dysfunction. Isolated deficiencies of both LH and FSH do occur but only rarely. In men isolated LH deficiency ("fertile eunuch") is characterized by symptoms and signs of androgen deficiency, however, there is sufficient secretion of FSH to permit the maturation of sperm. Some pituitary tumours produce an excess of LH or FSH, whereas other pituitary tumours produce the hormonally inactive alpha chain subunit of the glycoprotein hormones.

Hypogonadism, in which the functional activity of the gonads is decreased and sexual development is inhibited, can be caused by a congenital deficiency of GnRH. Patients with this type of hypogonadism typically respond to pulsatile treatment with the hormone. Many of these patients also have deficiencies of other hypothalamic-releasing hormones. A subset of patients with hypogonadism have isolated GnRH deficiency and loss of the sense of smell (anosmia), a disorder called Kallmann syndrome that is usually caused by a mutation in a gene that directs the formation of the olfactory (sense of smell) system and the formation of parts of the hypothalamus. Abnormalities in the pulsatile secretion of GnRH result in subnormal fertility and abnormal or absent menstruation.

PUBERTY

Puberty is the stage or period of life when a child transforms into an adult normally capable of procreation. The timing of puberty varies from person to person and from country to country owing to genetic, environmental, and other factors but usually occurs between ages 11 and 16. Among moderately prosperous British or North American children, puberty on the average peaks at about age 12 for girls and age 14 for boys. The rapidity with which a child passes through the several stages of puberty also varies. In girls the interval from the first indication of puberty to complete maturity may vary from 18 months to 6 years. In boys a similar variation occurs, with male genitalia taking anywhere between 2 and 5 years to attain full development.

In puberty both girls and boys experience a swift increase in body size, a change in shape and composition of the body, and a rapid development of the reproductive organs and other characteristics marking sexual maturity. Nocturnal pulses of GnRH play a major role in the development of the reproductive organs during this stage of life. These pulses are initiated at least in part by increasing body size, which may cause an increase in the secretion of leptin (from the Greek *leptos*, meaning "thin"; a protein hormone important for regulation of reproduction, metabolism, and body weight), which in turn stimulates the secretion of GnRH. Numerous factors may delay maturation or prevent normal growth, including hormonal disorders, metabolic defects, hereditary conditions, and inadequate nutrition.

REPRODUCTIVE ORGANS AND SECONDARY SEX CHARACTERISTICS

The adolescent spurt in skeletal and muscular dimensions is closely related to the rapid development of the reproductive system that takes place at this time. The acceleration of penis growth begins on average at about age 12 ½ years but sometimes as early as 10 ½ and sometimes as late as 14 ½. The completion of penis development usually occurs at about age 14 ½ but in some boys is at 12 ½ and in others at 16 ½. A few boys do not begin their spurts in height or penis development until the earliest maturers have entirely completed theirs. At ages 13, 14, and 15 there is an enormous variability among any group of boys, who range all the way from practically complete maturity to absolute preadolescence. The same is true of girls aged 11, 12, and 13.

The psychological and social importance of this difference in the tempo of development, as it has been called, is great, particularly in boys. Boys who are advanced in development are likely to dominate their contemporaries in athletic achievement and sexual interest alike. Conversely, the late developer all too often loses out in the rough and tumble of the adolescent world, and he may begin to wonder whether he will ever develop his body properly or be as well endowed sexually as those others whom he has seen developing around him. An important part of the educator's and the doctor's task at this time is to provide information about growth and its variability to preadolescents and adolescents and to give sympathetic support and reassurance to those who need it.

Although not exactly the same for each boy or girl, the sequence of events is much less variable than the age at which the events occur. The first sign of puberty in the boy is usually an acceleration of the growth of the testes and scrotum with reddening and wrinkling of the scrotal skin. Slight growth of pubic hair may begin about the same time but is usually a trifle later. The spurts in height and penis growth begin on average about a year after the first testicular acceleration. Concomitantly with the growth of the penis, and under the same stimulus, the seminal vesicles, the prostate, and the bulbourethral glands, all of which contribute their secretions to the seminal fluid, enlarge and develop. The time of the first ejaculation of seminal fluid is to some extent culturally as well as biologically determined but as a rule is during adolescence and about a year after the beginning of accelerated penis growth.

Axillary (armpit) hair appears on average some two years after the beginning of pubic hair growth. There is enough variability and dissociation in these events, so that a very few children's axillary hair actually appears first. In boys, facial hair begins to grow at about the time that the axillary hair appears. There is a definite order in which the hairs of moustache and beard appear: first at the corners of the upper lip, then over all the upper lip, then at the upper part of the cheeks, in the midline below the lower lip, and, finally, along the sides and lower borders of the chin. The remainder of the body hair appears from about the time of first axillary hair development until a considerable time after puberty. The ultimate amount of body hair that an individual develops seems to depend largely on heredity, but whether because of the kinds and amounts of hormones secreted or because of variations in the reactivity of the end organs is unknown.

Breaking of the voice occurs relatively late in adolescence. The change in pitch accompanies enlargement of the larynx and lengthening of the vocal cords, caused by the action of testosterone on the laryngeal cartilages. There is also a change in quality that distinguishes the voice (more particularly the vowel sounds) of both male and female adults from that of children. This is caused by the enlargement of the resonating spaces above the larynx, as a result of the rapid growth of the mouth, nose, and maxilla (upper jaw).

In the skin, particularly of the armpits and the genital and anal regions, the sebaceous and apocrine sweat glands develop rapidly during puberty and give rise to a characteristic odour. The changes occur in both sexes but are more marked in the male. Enlargement of the pores at the root of the nose and the appearance of comedones (blackheads) and acne, while likely to occur in either sex, are considerably more common in adolescent boys than girls because the underlying skin changes are the result of androgenic activity.

During adolescence the male breast undergoes changes, some temporary and some permanent. The diameter of the areola, which is equal in both sexes before puberty, increases considerably, though less than it does in girls. In some boys (between a fifth and a third of most groups studied) there is a distinct enlargement of the breast (sometimes unilaterally) about midway through adolescence. This usually regresses again after about one year.

In girls the start of breast enlargement—the appearance of the "breast bud"—is as a rule the first sign of puberty, but the appearance of pubic hair precedes it in about one-third. The uterus and vagina develop simultaneously with the breast. The labia and clitoris also enlarge. Menarche, the first menstrual period, is a late event in the sequence. Although it marks a definitive and probably mature stage of uterine development, it does not usually signify the attainment of full reproductive function. The early cycles may be more irregular than later ones and in some girls, but by no means all, are accompanied by discomfort. They are often anovulatory (that is, without the shedding of an egg). Thus there is frequently a period of adolescent sterility lasting 12 to 18 months after menarche, but it cannot be relied on in the individual case. Similar considerations may apply to the male, but there is no reliable information about this. On average, girls grow 2.4 inches (about 6 cm) more after menarche, but gains of up to twice this amount may occur. The gain is practically independent of whether menarche occurs early or late.

Normal Variations

Children vary a great deal both in the rapidity with which they pass through the various stages of puberty and in the closeness with which the various events are linked together. At one extreme one may find a perfectly healthy girl who has not yet menstruated even though her breasts and pubic hair are characteristic of the adult and she is already two years past her peak height velocity. At the other extreme, a girl may have passed all the stages of puberty within the space of two years.

In girls the interval from the first indication of puberty to complete maturity varies from 18 months to six years. The period from the moment when the breast bud first appears to menarche averages 2 ½ years, but it may be as little as six months or as much as 5 ½ years. The rapidity with which a child passes through puberty seems to be independent of whether puberty is occurring early or late. Menarche invariably occurs after peak height velocity has been passed.

In boys a similar variability of maturation occurs. The male genitalia may take between two and five years to attain full development, and some boys complete the whole process before others have moved from the first to the second stage.

The height spurt occurs relatively later in boys than in girls. Thus there is a difference between the average boy and girl of two years in age of peak height velocity but of only one year in the first appearance of pubic hair. Indeed, in some girls the acceleration in height is the first sign of puberty, but this is never so in boys. A small boy whose genitalia are just beginning to develop can be unequivocally reassured that an acceleration in height is soon to take place, but a girl in the corresponding situation may already have had her height spurt.

The differential effects on the growth of bone, muscle, and fat at puberty increase considerably the difference in body composition between the sexes. Boys have a greater increase not only in stature but especially in breadth of shoulders, whereas girls have a greater relative increase in width of hips. These differences are produced chiefly by the changes that occur during puberty, but other sex differentiations arise before that time. Some, like the external genital difference itself, develop during fetal life. Others develop continuously throughout the whole growth period by a sustained differential growth rate. An example of this is the greater relative length and breadth of the forearm in the male when compared with whole arm length or whole body length.

Part of the sex difference in pelvic shape antedates puberty. Girls at birth already have a wider pelvic outlet. Thus the adaptation for childbearing is present from an early age. The changes at puberty are concerned more with widening the pelvic inlet and broadening the much more noticeable hips.

Physical and Behavioral Interactions

The concept of developmental age, as opposed to chronological age, is important. To measure developmental age, there must be some way to determine how far along his or her own path to maturity a given child has gone. Therefore, there is need of a measure in which everyone at maturity ends up the same (not different as in height). The usual measure used is skeletal maturity or bone age. This is measured by taking an X-ray of the hand and wrist. The appearances of the developing bones can be rated and formed into a scale of development. Although the scale is applicable to boys and girls of all genetic backgrounds, girls on average reach any given score at a younger age than do boys, and blacks on average, at least in the first few years after birth, reach a given score younger than do whites. Other areas of the body may be used if required.

Skeletal maturity is closely related to the age at which adolescence occurs, that is, to maturity measured by some sex character developments. Thus the range of the chronological age within which menarche may normally fall is about 10 to 16 ½, but the corresponding range of bone age for menarche is only 12 to 14 ½. Evidently, the physiological processes controlling progression of skeletal development are in most instances closely linked with those that initiate the events of adolescence. Furthermore, children tend to be consistently advanced or delayed during their whole growth period, at any rate after about age three.

There is little doubt that being an early or a late maturer may have considerable repercussions on behaviour in some children. There is little enough solid information on the relation between emotional and physiological development, but what there is supports the common sense notion that emotional attitudes are clearly related to physiological events.

The rate of maturing and the age of puberty onset depend on a complex interaction of genetic and environmental factors. Where the environment is conducive to good health, most variability in age at menarche in a population results from genetic differences. In many societies puberty occurs later in children who are deprived of adequate nutrition, and, in most societies investigated, children with many siblings grow more slowly than children with few.

During the last hundred years there has been a striking tendency for children to become progressively larger at all ages. This is known as the "secular trend." The magnitude of the trend in Europe and America is such that it dwarfs the differences between socioeconomic classes.

The data from Europe and America agree: From about 1900, or a little earlier, to the present, children in average economic circumstances have increased in height at age five to seven by about 0.4 to 0.8 inch (1 to 2 cm) per decade, and at age 10 to 14 by 0.8 to 1.2 inches (2 to 3 cm) each decade. Preschool data show that the trend starts directly after birth and may, indeed, be relatively greater from age two to five than subsequently. The trend started, at least in Britain, as early as 1850.

Most of the trend toward greater size in children reflects a more rapid maturation; only a minor part reflects a greater ultimate size. The trend toward earlier maturing is best shown in the statistics on age at menarche. The trend is between three and four months per decade since 1850 in average sections of western European populations. Prosperous persons show a trend of about half of this magnitude, having never been so delayed in menarche as the poor. The causes of the secular trend are probably multiple. Certainly, better nutrition is a major one and perhaps in particular more protein and calories in early infancy. A lessening of disease may also have contributed. Some authors have supposed that the increased psychosexual stimulation consequent on modern urban living has contributed, but there is no positive evidence for this.

MENSTRUATION

Menstruation is the periodic discharge from the vagina of blood, secretions, and disintegrating mucous membrane that had lined the uterus. The biological significance of the process in humans can best be explained by reference to the reproductive function in other mammals. In many species of wild sheep, for example, there is only one breeding season in the year, during which a cycle of changes takes place in the reproductive organs, characterized by

The menstrual cycle

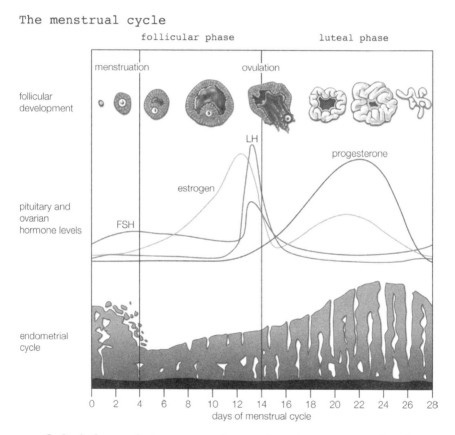

Cyclical changes during a woman's normal ovulatory menstrual cycle. Encyclopædia Britannica, Inc.

ripening and release of ova from the ovaries, increased blood supply to the genital tract, growth of the uterus, and proliferation of its lining. There is a discharge of blood and mucus from the uterus and vagina, and this is the time when coition may take place. Pregnancy normally follows, but if the ewe is not served by the ram the changes retrogress until the next breeding season. This cycle of changes is termed the estrous cycle.

In many domesticated sheep there is more than one estrous cycle in the breeding season. If the ewe does not become pregnant in the first cycle, there is a short resting phase, after which ovulation is repeated and another cycle of activity of the reproductive system takes place. After each breeding period, with its succession of estrous cycles, there is a relatively long resting phase. In most female primates, including women, there is no resting phase. An unbroken series of estrous cycles occurs throughout the year, and pregnancy can occur in any one of them.

In some animals a variety of external stimuli act through the central nervous system on the hypothalamic region of the brain. The hypothalamus controls the release from the pituitary gland of the gonadotropins that induce ripening of ovarian follicles. These hormones are carried to the ovaries by way of the bloodstream. In primates the hypothalamic mechanism normally is independent of external stimuli, and regular discharge of ova into the tubes leading to the uterus occurs even in the absence of coitus. Under the influence of the pituitary gonadotropic hormones, the ovary produces estrogens—chiefly estradiol (the most potent of the estrogens)—and progesterone, which cause growth and increased vascularity of the uterus and vagina. It is as though the ovary prepares the uterus for the reception of the ovum that is released in the particular cycle.

PHASES OF THE MENSTRUAL CYCLE

The normal menstrual cycle is typically divided into a follicular phase of about 14 days, during which the endometrium proliferates, and a luteal phase of about 14 days, which culminates with the endometrial lining being sloughed off. Thus, the two phases are separated by ovulation on the one hand and by menstruation on the other hand. The phases vary in length by several days in different women and sometimes in the same woman. Variations in cycle length are most common in the first years after menarche (the first menstrual cycle) and just before menopause (when menstruation ceases).

Although it is customary to call the first day of the menstrual period the first day of the cycle, menstruation is the end, rather than the beginning, of a process. On this basis the cycle is described as starting with about five days of menstruation, followed by a proliferative phase that lasts to about the 14th day, and then a secretory phase that lasts until the next menstruation. The external manifestation of menstruation depends on cyclical change in the lining of the body of the uterus.

In puberty, the onset of menarche is marked by the maturation of the hypothalamus, pituitary, and ovaries, at which point the cyclic hypothalamic-pituitary-ovarian activity characteristic of adult women begins. During the first days of the menstrual cycle, secretion of FSH increases, causing the maturation of follicles. As follicles mature, they secrete more estradiol, which is paralleled by an increase in the secretion of LH. Increased secretion of LH stimulates the secretion of more estradiol and a small amount of progesterone that then trigger a transient surge in LH secretion and to a lesser extent FSH secretion, causing rupture of the mature Graafian follicle.

The Graafian follicle contains the ovum, which is a cell about 0.006 inch (0.14 mm) in diameter, surrounded by a group of smaller cells, called granulosa cells. The granulosa cells multiply, with the ovum situated in the wall of the rounded structure that they form, and secrete estradiol. This hormone causes proliferative changes in the endometrium, so that the glands become taller and the whole endometrium becomes thicker and more vascular.

At about mid-cycle ovulation, or rupture of the Graafian follicle, occurs. The ovum is discharged out of the follicle and from the surface of the ovary, to be received into the fallopian tube, down which it is carried to the uterus. After ovulation the granulosa cells lining the follicle from which the ovum has been extruded accumulate yellow lipid and are therefore called lutein cells, from the Latin word *luteus*, meaning "saffron-yellow." The altered follicle is called corpus luteum. The surge in LH secretion that occurs at ovulation can be readily detected in the urine, providing a means whereby women can determine if they have ovulated and therefore are potentially fertile.

The follicular phase of the cycle ends at the time of ovulation. Serum LH, FSH, and estradiol concentrations then decrease considerably, and the corpus luteum begins to produce some estrogen and large quantities of progesterone. This is known as the luteal phase of the menstrual cycle. During this time, the endometrial glands are distended with secretion and become tortuous, while the stromal cells are swollen. The appearance of the endometrium at the end of the menstrual cycle is indistinguishable from that of early pregnancy, and this endometrial change is a preparation for the reception of the ovum. If it is fertilized, the ovum liberated at mid-cycle reaches the uterine cavity at a time when the endometrium is in the secretory phase, and the ovum embeds itself in the endometrium and starts its growth. If the ovum is not fertilized, the corpus luteum degenerates (luteolysis) and estradiol and progesterone production decreases. The decreasing serum estrogen and progesterone concentrations result in constriction of uterine arteries, thus interrupting the delivery of oxygen and nutrients to the endometrium. The endometrium is then sloughed off. The endometrium contains plasmin, an enzyme that dissolves blood clots, so that the menstrual discharge is normally fluid. The total blood loss does not ordinarily exceed 1.69 U.S. fluid ounces (50 ml). After menstruation the endometrium regenerates from the residual basal layer during the proliferative phase of the next cycle.

The changing serum estrogen and progesterone concentrations during the menstrual cycle have several other effects. Basal body temperature fluctuates little during the follicular phase of the menstrual cycle but increases abruptly after ovulation. This increase parallels the postovulatory increase in serum progesterone concentrations and is caused by an effect of progesterone on the temperature-regulating centres in the brain. The decrease in serum estradiol and progesterone concentrations near the end of the cycle may be accompanied by changes in mood and activity and by an increase in fluid retention. The changes initiated by the decrease in secretion of estradiol and progesterone comprise the symptoms of premenstrual syndrome, although the relationship between hormonal changes and these symptoms is unclear.

HORMONAL CONTROL OF THE MENSTRUAL CYCLE

The ovarian hormones circulate in the blood and are excreted in modified forms in the urine. Estimation of the urinary output by chemical methods gives an indication of the blood levels and of the total production of these substances. There are several natural estrogens, and numerous synthetic modifications of these and of progesterone have been devised. Many are active when taken by mouth and are used for treatment of hormonal disorders and as oral contraceptives.

The previously mentioned cyclic events in the ovary depend on gonadotropic hormones secreted by the anterior lobe of the pituitary gland. FSH is secreted in the greatest amount in the first half of the menstrual cycle, and LH has its peak of secretion at mid-cycle. The sequential action of FSH and LH causes ripening of the follicle and ovulation. In some animals a hormone known as luteotropic hormone (LTH; or prolactin) is necessary for maintenance of the corpus luteum, but in women under treatment for infertility, ovulation has been successfully induced with FSH and LH alone. Multiple births, as the result of multiple ovulation, have occurred after excessive doses of FSH have been given.

The pituitary gland stimulates the ovary to produce estrogens and progesterone, but there is a "negative feedback" by which the estrogens inhibit the output of FSH from the pituitary gland (and probably stimulate the output of LH). In addition, progesterone is believed to inhibit the further output of LH. In this process, in which the pituitary first stimulates the ovary, and the ovary then inhibits the pituitary, the basic rhythm is under the control of the hypothalamus. Nevertheless, ovulation can be inhibited by oral contraceptives, which contain estrogens and progestogens—modifications of progesterone.

The anterior lobe of the pituitary gland is connected by its stalk to the hypothalamic region of the brain. The anterior lobe secretes many important hormones, including those that control the activity of the adrenal and thyroid glands and the release of growth hormone and the gonadotropic hormones. From the hypothalamus substances are carried in the veins in the pituitary stalk that cause release of hormones from the pituitary, including FSH and LH, but also a factor that inhibits release of LTH. The higher brain centres no doubt affect hypothalamic function, which explains the temporary disturbances of menstruation that may follow emotional stress.

OVULATION AND THE FERTILE PHASE

The release of a mature egg from the ovary during ovulation enables the egg to be fertilized by the male sperm cells. The egg erupts from the ovary on the 14th to 16th day of the approximately 28-day menstrual cycle. An unfertilized egg is passed from the reproductive tract during menstrual bleeding, which starts about two weeks

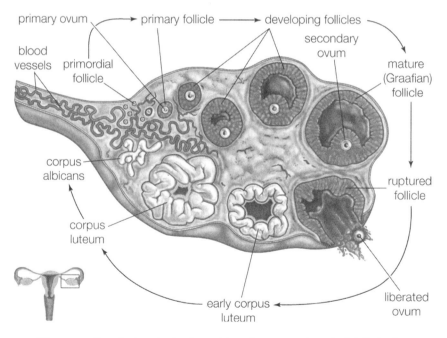

The steps of ovulation, beginning with a dormant primordial follicle that grows and matures and is eventually released from the ovary into the fallopian tube. Encyclopædia Britannica, Inc.

after ovulation. Occasionally, cycles occur in which an egg is not released, which are called anovulatory cycles.

Prior to eruption from the ovary, an egg first must grow and mature. Until stimulated to grow, the primary egg cell passes through a period of dormancy that may last several years. The egg cell is surrounded by a capsule of cells that form the follicle. The follicular wall serves as a protective casing around the egg and provides a suitable environment for egg development. As the follicle ripens, the cell wall thickens and a fluid is secreted to surround the egg. The follicle migrates from within the ovary's deeper tissue to the outer wall. Once the follicle reaches the surface of the ovary, the follicular wall thins. Pressure caused by the follicle and fluid against the ovary's surface causes bulging of the ovarian wall. When the follicle ruptures, the egg and fluid are released along with some torn patches of tissue. The cells, fluid, and egg are directed into the nearby fallopian tube.

After the egg leaves the ovary, the walls of the follicle again close, and the space that was occupied by the egg begins to fill with the corpus luteum. The progesterone secreted by the corpus luteum helps to keep the uterine wall receptive to a fertilized egg. If the egg is unfertilized, the corpus luteum stops secreting progesterone about nine days after ovulation. If the egg becomes fertilized, progesterone continues to be secreted, first by the corpus luteum and then by the placenta, until the child is born. Progesterone blocks the release of more hormones from the pituitary gland, so that further ovulation does not normally occur during pregnancy.

Menarche

The first menstruation, or menarche, usually occurs between 11 and 13 years of age, but in a few otherwise normal children menstruation may begin sooner or may be delayed. If the menstrual periods have not started by age 16, gynecological investigation is indicated. Menarche is preceded by other signs of estrogenic activity, such as enlargement of the breasts and the uterus and growth of pubic hair. The ovarian response to gonadotropic hormones may be erratic at first, so that irregular or heavy bleeding sometimes occurs, but this irregularity nearly always disappears spontaneously.

NORMAL MENSTRUATION

Each menstrual period lasts for about five days, but the duration and amount of the flow vary considerably even in perfect health. In some women there may be premonitory symptoms such as pelvic discomfort, soreness of the breasts (because of the response of these organs to estrogens), and emotional tension. Ovarian hormones cause retention of sodium and water in the tissue fluids. In part this may cause premenstrual tension, sometimes called premenstrual syndrome, which is sometimes relieved by diuretics, drugs that increase the production of urine.

When the menstrual flow starts, the uterus contracts to expel the blood and disintegrating endometrium. These contractions may be painful, especially in young women who have never been pregnant. Menstrual discomforts vary greatly in degree from woman to woman and from time to time but ordinarily do not interfere with normal activities.

MENOPAUSE

Menopause is the permanent cessation of menstruation that results from the loss of ovarian function and therefore represents the end of a woman's reproductive life. At the time of menopause, the ovaries contain few follicles; have decreased in size; and consist mostly of atretic (shrunken) follicles, some interstitial cells, and fibrous tissue. Estrogen production decreases by 80 percent or more, and this along with the loss of follicles results in marked increases in the secretion of luteinizing hormone (LH) and follicle-stimulating hormone (FSH). Menstrual periods may cease abruptly or may be irregular for a year or so before ceasing. In a similar fashion, menopausal symptoms may occur abruptly or gradually. While menopausal symptoms may begin when the woman is still menstruating, they are more likely to begin after menstruation ceases.

Menopause occurs in most women between 45 and 55 years of age, but it may begin as early as age 40 or be delayed to the late 50s. The age of onset is probably determined by the hereditary background of the individual, however, good nutrition and health habits tend to postpone onset. Premature menopause, which takes place spontaneously before the age of 40, occurs in about 8 percent of women. Menopause may be induced by removing the ovaries by surgery or destroying them with X-rays or radium.

The natural life of the ovaries is about 35 years, and thus the decline of ovarian function is a normal result of aging, although it is accelerated as menopause approaches. During the reproductive years, follicles in the ovaries mature and release their ova (mature eggs) periodically under hypothalamic-pituitary stimulation. In the years immediately preceding menopause, however, first some follicles and later all follicles fail to rupture and release their ova. The failure to ovulate results in a disturbed menstrual pattern. A woman may miss a period or two and suspect pregnancy, but a medical examination will establish the proper diagnosis. The continued decline in ovarian activity may provoke prolonged intervals between periods or irregular bleeding episodes. The length of the periods may vary, and the flow may become either more scant or more profuse. In a small minority the periods cease abruptly.

As the ovaries decline in function, they produce smaller and smaller amounts of the hormone estrogen, thereby initiating subtle rearrangements in the hormonal activity of the glands that control reproductive function. Estrogen deficiency, during menopause and in general, causes the uterus and breasts to decrease in size and the vaginal mucosa to become atrophic and dry. In addition, sexual intercourse often becomes painful (dyspareunia).

A common symptom of declining estrogen production during menopause is "hot flashes," which are characterized by a sensation of warmth of the face and upper body, flushing of the skin, sweating, tachycardia (accelerated heart rate), irritability, and headache. A hot flash typically lasts a few minutes and may be followed by a sensation of cold and even shivering. About 75 percent of women have hot flashes at the time of menopause, and about 30 percent may still have hot flashes five years later. The frequency of hot flashes varies from one or two per day to one per hour. Hot flashes may be a source of embarrassment and may interfere with sleep. They seem to be caused by sudden autonomic nerve activation that stimulates the dilation of blood vessels that supply the skin, leading to an increase in skin temperature.

Other physiological symptoms associated with menopause include decreased libido and dryness and atrophy of the skin. Some symptoms may be caused in part by rearrangements in the hormonal activity of the adrenal and thyroid glands, because the metabolic activities of these glands are interrelated and are associated with some actions of estrogen. Many women complain of weight gain during menopause, and occasionally this is related to decreased thyroid function. However, menopause is not necessarily associated with unusual changes in physical appearance and fitness. Many menopausal women experience psychological symptoms, such as changes in mood, depression, and feeling as though they lack well-being. Nervousness, headaches, and dizziness are common complaints. A fear of aging or an altered pattern of life may precipitate psychological symptoms.

Important consequences of menopause are osteopenia, a minor reduction in bone mass, and osteoporosis, a severe reduction in bone mass that is associated with a tendency to sustain fractures from minor stresses. In women (and men) bone density is maximal at about 30 years of age, after which it gradually decreases, except for a period of accelerated bone loss that occurs at the time of and for several years after menopause. This acceleration is associated with decreased production of estrogen and other sex hormones at the onset of menopause.

Another important consequence of menopause is an increased risk of heart disease. Increased risk of cardiovascular diseases such as atherosclerosis, a chronic condition affecting the arteries, is attributed to decreased levels of estrogen that lead to increased serum cholesterol and triglyceride concentrations and changes in vascular function and the production of blood clotting factors.

The administration of estrogen is effective for treating many problems associated with menopause, including hot flashes, breast atrophy, vaginal dryness, and psychological symptoms. Estrogen is also effective for increasing libido. In addition, estrogen increases bone density, thereby decreasing the risk of fracture. Although estrogen therapy causes a decrease in serum cholesterol concentrations, it does not appear to reduce the frequency of cardiovascular disease, and it may actually increase the risk of developing it. Estrogen therapy increases the risk of uterine cancer, which can be avoided if estrogen is given in conjunction with a progestin, and it slightly increases the risk of breast cancer.

There are important practical aspects of estrogen therapy in menopausal women. It can be given orally or applied to the skin (transdermal estrogen) or to the vagina. Estrogen that is applied to the skin is absorbed into the circulation and has effects throughout the body. It is less active in the liver than oral estrogen and therefore has fewer effects on serum lipids, hormone-binding proteins, and blood clotting factors that are produced in the liver. Estrogen that is applied to the vagina is not well absorbed and acts mostly on local tissues. Because of the risks of irregular vaginal bleeding and uterine cancer, any woman who has not had a hysterectomy (removal of the uterus) who is given estrogen should also be given a progestin. The two hormones are usually given together continuously, which results in uterine atrophy. They also can be given cyclically, with estrogen administered most of the time and progestin administered for 7 to 10 days each month, in which case there often will be vaginal bleeding after the progestin is stopped.

There is no reason to treat menopausal women who have no symptoms. Bone loss can be minimized or prevented by exercise, good general nutrition, vitamin D and calcium supplementation, and avoidance of smoking and drugs such as bisphosphonates, which block the resorption of bone.

REPRODUCTION AND PREGNANCY

The process of reproduction begins with intercourse and concludes with the birth of live offspring at the end of pregnancy. However, there are many steps in between, including fertilization—the uniting of sperm and ovum (egg)—and implantation—the embedding of the fertilized ovum in the wall of the female uterus. Following implantation, a woman's body undergoes a series of changes that are characteristic of pregnancy, including the development of the maternal placenta, the temporary tissue that nourishes the developing conceptus (the fertilized ovum that becomes the fetus). Prenatal care and testing is used to assess the health of the developing fetus during pregnancy, thereby helping to ensure successful reproduction.

SEXUAL INTERCOURSE

Sexual intercourse, also known as coitus (or copulation), is a reproductive act in which the male reproductive organ enters the female reproductive tract. If the reproductive act is complete, sperm cells are passed from the male body into the female, in the process fertilizing the female egg and forming a new organism. In some vertebrates, such as fish, eggs are laid outside of the body and fertilized externally.

To accomplish internal copulation, certain body and organic adaptations are necessary. In the human male, the penis serves both excretory and reproductive functions.

During intercourse, the blood flow is temporarily increased and trapped in the penis so that it becomes enlarged and elevated, a condition known as erection. Erection changes the normally soft and flaccid organ to one of greater size and rigidity to permit easier penetration into the reproductive tract of the female. Sexual intercourse both culminates and terminates in orgasm, a process in which the male expels semen—containing sperm cells, which may unite with and fertilize the female egg, and a seminal plasma that contains cell nutrients, water, salts, and metabolites—into the female's vaginal canal.

The male's ability to produce and secrete semen, as well as to function sexually, depends on the androgen hormones, which circulate in the male's body. In the female reproductive system, an external opening leads to the vagina, which in turn communicates with the uterus (or womb), where the fetus develops. In humans, a pattern of physiological events occurs during sexual arousal and intercourse. These events may be identified as occurring in a sequence of four stages: excitement, plateau, orgasm, and resolution. The basic pattern is similar in both sexes, regardless of the specific sexual stimulus.

In the excitement stage, the body prepares for sexual activity by tensing muscles and increasing heart rate. In the male, blood flows into the penis, causing it to become erect; in the female, the vaginal walls become moist, the inner part of the vagina becomes wider, and the clitoris enlarges. In the plateau stage, breathing becomes more rapid and the muscles continue to tense. The glans at the head of the penis swells and the testes enlarge in the male; in the female, the outer vagina contracts and the clitoris retracts.

At orgasm the neuromuscular tension built up in the preceding stages is released in a few seconds. In the woman, the vagina begins a series of regular contractions;

in the man, the penis also contracts rhythmically to expel the sperm and semen (ejaculation). The succeeding resolution stage brings a gradual return to the resting state that may take several hours. In the male, the penis shrinks back to its normal size; in the female, the vagina and other genital structures also return to their pre-excitement condition. The resolution stage in men contains a refractory period of several minutes to a few hours, during which the man is incapable of further sexual arousal. Women have no such refractory period and can quickly become aroused again from any point in the resolution stage.

In some animals, such as sheep and migratory birds, copulation occurs only seasonally. During the breeding season, hormones are produced in both the male and female species that prepare their reproductive systems for copulation. In the nonbreeding seasons, the hormone levels drop so that the animals are incapable of fertilized breeding and do not have the desire to engage in copulation.

SPERM AND OVA

Sperm and ova (eggs) are known as sex cells, or gametes. Sperm, or spermatozoa, are the male reproductive cells. Sperm are produced by most animals. With the exception of nematode worms, decapods (e.g., crayfish), diplopods (e.g., millipedes), and mites, sperm are flagellated; that is, they have a whiplike tail. In higher vertebrates, especially mammals, sperm are produced in the testes. The sperm unite with (fertilize) an ovum (egg) of the female to produce a new offspring. Mature sperm have two distinguishable parts, a head and a tail.

The head of the sperm varies in shape for each animal species. In man it is flattened and almond shaped and is approximately four to five micrometres long and two to three micrometres wide. (There are about 25,000 micrometres in an inch.) The head portion is mainly a cell nucleus and consists of genetic substances, called chromosomes, which are responsible for transmitting specific characteristics of an individual, such as the colour of eyes, hair, and skin. In each body cell of a normal human, there are 46 chromosomes, which are responsible for the individual's general physical makeup. The sperm cells have only 23 chromosomes, or half of the usual number. When a sperm cell unites with an ovum, which also has 23 chromosomes, the resulting 46 chromosomes determine the offspring's characteristics. The sperm cells also carry the X or Y chromosome that determines the sex of the future child.

Covering the head of the sperm is a cap known as the acrosome, which contains chemical substances that help sperm to enter an ovum. Only one sperm fertilizes each ovum, even though 300,000,000 to 400,000,000 sperm are contained in an average ejaculation. Each ovum and sperm produced has slightly different genetic information carried in the chromosomes, which accounts for the differences and similarities between children of the same parents.

A small middle portion of the sperm contains the mitochondria. The tail of the sperm, sometimes called the flagellum, is a slender, hairlike bundle of filaments that connects to the head and middle portion. The tail is about 50 micrometres long, and its thickness of one micrometre near the mitochondria gradually diminishes to less than one-half micrometre at the end of the tail. The tail gives the sperm cell movement. It whips and undulates so that the cell can travel to the ovum. Sperm deposited in the reproductive tract of the female travel through the tract until they fertilize an ovum or die. Sperm cells may live in the human body for two or three days after mating. Sperm may also be stored in a frozen state for months or years and still retain their capacity to fertilize ova when thawed.

The ovum is a single cell released from either of the ovaries. The outer surface of each ovary is covered by a layer of cells (germinal epithelium). The germinal epithelium surrounds the immature egg cells, which are present in the ovaries from the time of birth. A hollow ball of cells, the follicle, encompasses each ovum. Within the follicle the ovum gradually matures. It takes about four months for a follicle to develop once it is activated. Some follicles lie dormant for 40 years before they mature, whereas others degenerate and never develop. During child-bearing years, 300 to 400 follicles mature and emit eggs capable of being fertilized. By the time a woman reaches menopause, most remaining follicles have degenerated.

Follicle-stimulating hormone (FSH), secreted into the bloodstream by the pituitary, causes ovum growth. As the ovum develops, the walls of the follicle expand by adding new cells. The follicle and ovum slowly migrate through the tissue of the ovary until they cause a bulge in the surface of the organ. The hollow cavity between the ovum and the follicular wall usually contains a fluid secreted by the follicular cells, which keeps the ovum moist and provides a suitable growing environment. When the follicle ruptures, the ovum is released from the ovary (ovulation). This process of liberation is prompted by the secretion of luteinizing hormone (LH) from the pituitary gland. The released ovum is captured and guided by the fallopian tubes. Muscular contractions of the fallopian tubes move the ovum to the cavity of the uterus.

The ovum itself has a central nucleus that contains the female's genetic material. Surrounding the nucleus is a cell plasma, or yolk, that contains nutritional elements essential to the developing ovum cell. If an ovum does not become fertilized within 24 hours of its eruption, it begins to degenerate. Once fertilized, the ovum undergoes a series of cell divisions. If at an early stage of its development, the fertilized ovum splits into two parts that continue to grow, identical twins will result. Incomplete division will result in conjoined twins (formerly known as Siamese twins), born physically joined. Fraternal twins result when two separate ova are released and independently fertilized.

FERTILIZATION

Fertilization is the union of a spermatozoal nucleus (of paternal origin) with an ovum nucleus (of maternal origin) to form the primary nucleus of an embryo. In all organisms the essence of fertilization is, in fact, the fusion of the hereditary material of the two different sex cells. The most primitive form of fertilization, found in microorganisms and protozoans, consists of an exchange of genetic material between two cells.

In humans, both the sperm and the ovum migrate for considerable distances to achieve their union. Many actively motile sperm are deposited in the vagina, pass through the uterus, and invade the uterine (fallopian) tube, where they surround the ovum. The ovum has arrived there after extrusion from its follicle, or capsule, in the ovary. After it enters the tube, the ovum loses its outer layer of cells as a result of action by substances in the sperm and from the lining of the tubal wall. Loss of the outer layer of the ovum allows a number of sperm to penetrate the ovum's surface. Only one sperm, however, normally becomes the fertilizing organism. Once it has entered the substance of the ovum, the nuclear head of this sperm separates from its tail. The tail gradually disappears, but the head with its nucleus survives. As it travels toward the nucleus of the ovum (at this stage called the

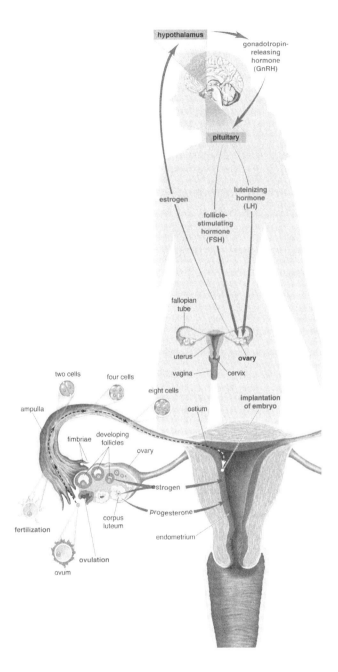

Major structures and hormones involved in the initiation of pregnancy. Also seen is the development of an egg cell (ovum) from follicle to embryo. Encyclopædia Britannica, Inc.

female pronucleus), the head enlarges and becomes the male pronucleus. The two pronuclei meet in the centre of the ovum, where their threadlike chromatin material organizes into chromosomes.

Originally, the female nucleus has 44 autosomes (chromosomes other than sex chromosomes) and two (X, X) sex chromosomes. Before fertilization a type of cell division called a reduction division brings the number of chromosomes in the female pronucleus down to 23, including one X-chromosome. The male gamete also has 44 autosomes and two (X, Y) sex chromosomes. As a result of a reducing division occurring before fertilization, it, too, has 23 chromosomes, including either an X or a Y sex chromosome at the time that it merges with the female pronucleus.

After the chromosomes merge and divide in a process termed mitosis, the fertilized ovum, or zygote, as it is now called, divides into two equal-sized daughter cells. The mitotic division gives each daughter cell 44 autosomes, half of which are of maternal and half of paternal origin. Each daughter cell also has either two X-chromosomes, making the new individual a female, or an X- and a Y-chromosome, making it a male. The sex of the daughter cells is determined, therefore, by the sex chromosome from the male parent.

Fertilization occurs in the uterine tube. How long the zygote remains in the tube is unknown, but it probably reaches the uterine cavity about 72 hours after fertilization. It is nourished during its passage by the secretions from the mucous membrane lining the tube. By the time it reaches the uterus, which may take up to seven days, it has become a mulberry-like solid mass called a morula. A morula is composed of 60 or more cells. As the number of cells in a morula increases, the zygote forms a hollow bubble-like structure, the blastocyst.

DEVELOPMENT OF THE REPRODUCTIVE ORGANS

The sex of a child is determined at the time of fertilization of the ovum by the sperm. The differences between a male and a female are genetically determined by the chromosomes that each possesses in the nuclei of the cells. Once the genetic sex has been determined, there normally follows a succession of changes that will result, finally, in the

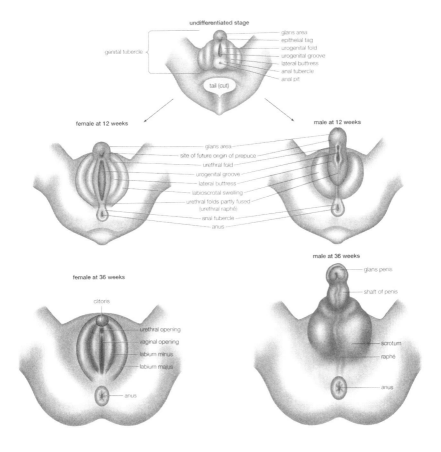

Differentiation of the external genitalia in the human embryo and fetus. Encyclopædia Britannica, Inc.

development of an adult male or female. There is, however, no external indication of the sex of an embryo during the first eight weeks of its life within the uterus. This is a neutral or indifferent stage during which the sex of an embryo can be ascertained only by examination of the chromosomes in its cells.

The next phase, one of differentiation, begins first in gonads that are to become testes and a week or so later in those destined to be ovaries. Embryos of the two sexes are initially alike in possessing similar duct systems linking the undifferentiated gonads with the exterior and in having similar external genitalia, represented by three simple protuberances. The embryos each have four ducts, the subsequent fate of which is of great significance in the eventual anatomical differences between men and women. Two ducts closely related to the developing urinary system are called mesonephric, or wolffian, ducts. In males each mesonephric duct becomes differentiated into four related structures: a duct of the epididymis, a ductus deferens, an ejaculatory duct, and a seminal vesicle. In females the mesonephric ducts are largely suppressed. The other two ducts, called the paramesonephric or müllerian ducts, persist, in females, to develop into the fallopian tubes, the uterus, and part of the vagina. In males they are largely suppressed. Differentiation also occurs in the primitive external genitalia, which in males become the penis and scrotum and in females the vulva (the clitoris, labia, and vestibule of the vagina).

At birth the organs appropriate to each sex have developed and are in their adult positions but are not functioning. Various abnormalities can occur during development of sex organs in embryos, leading to hermaphroditism, pseudohermaphroditism, and other chromosomally induced conditions.

IMPLANTATION

Implantation is the adherence of the blastocyst to a surface in the reproductive tract, usually to the uterine wall (the endometrium). The uterus has thick walls that support blastocyst attachment, and the uterus itself provides a suitable environment for blastocyst growth and development into a new offspring.

The blastocyst cells that will become the embryo (the embryonic disk) form a thickened layer on one side. Elsewhere, the walls of the structure consist of a single layer of cells, the trophoblast, which has a special ability to attach to and invade the uterine wall. The trophoblast plays an important role later in the development of the placenta or afterbirth. The blastocyst makes contact with the uterine lining about the fifth or sixth day after conception. After contact the blastocyst collapses to form a rounded disk with the embryonic mass on the surface and the trophoblast against the endometrium (uterine lining). The part of the trophoblast that is in contact with the endometrium grows into and invades the maternal tissue. Concomitant disintegration of the endometrium allows the conceptus to sink into the uterine lining.

By the 11th day after fertilization, the entire blastocyst is buried in the endometrium. Proliferation of the trophoblast over the part of the collapsed bubble that is opposite the embryo is part of the implantation procedure that helps to cover the blastocyst. After a few days, a cavity forms that bears the same relation to the embryonic disk that the blastocyst cavity did before; this cavity will become the fluid-filled chorionic cavity containing the embryo. Ultimately, it will contain the amniotic fluid that surrounds the fetus, the fetus itself, and the umbilical cord. The product of conception—first the fertilized ovum and then the developing child and the placenta—normally remains implanted in the human uterus for nine months.

The female hormone progesterone, secreted by the corpus luteum in the ovary, influences the readiness of the uterine wall for implantation. It increases the blood supply in the wall, water content, and secretion of glycogen, a nutrient for the surrounding tissue and developing ovum. If the uterus is not first prepared by progesterone, the fertilized ovum will not attach itself. Progesterone also inhibits muscular contractions in the uterine wall that would tend to reject the adhering blastocyst.

PREGNANCY

Pregnancy consists of a series of changes that take place in a woman's organs and tissues to accommodate a developing conceptus. The entire process from fertilization to birth takes an average of 266–270 days, or about nine months. The due date of a pregnancy is typically set from the time of a woman's last menstruation. This method of estimation is highly accurate, with an astonishing 90 percent of babies being born within two weeks of the projected date.

The blastocyst that implants into the uterine lining gradually grows into an embryo and then a fetus. A placenta and umbilical cord develop for nutrient and waste exchange between the circulations of mother and fetus, and a protective fluid-filled amniotic sac encloses and cushions the fetus. Early in pregnancy, higher estrogen and progesterone levels halt menstruation, cause nausea (often with vomiting, or morning sickness), and enlarge the breasts and prepare them for lactation.

As the fetus grows, so does the uterus, displacing other organs. Normal weight gain in pregnancy is 20–25 lbs

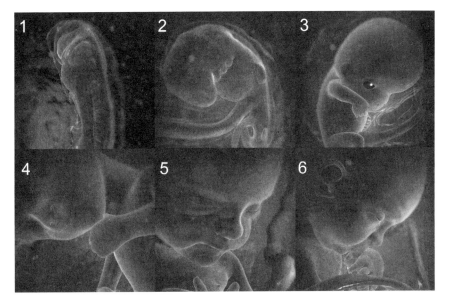

From fertilization to birth, embryonic development takes place over about nine months. 3D4Medical.com/Getty Images

(9–11.5 kg). The fetus's nutritional needs require the mother to take in more calories and especially protein, water, calcium, and iron. Folic-acid supplements are recommended during early pregnancy to prevent neural tube defects. Smoking, alcohol, and many legal and illegal drugs can cause congenital disorders (birth defects) and should be avoided during pregnancy. Ultrasound imaging is often used to monitor structural and functional progress of the growing fetus.

DEVELOPMENT OF THE PLACENTA

Pregnancy, if it occurs, maintains the corpus luteum by means of the hormones produced by the young placenta. The corpus luteum is not essential in human pregnancy after the first few weeks because of the takeover of its functions by the placenta. Gradually the placenta, or afterbirth, begins to elaborate progesterone and estrogen itself. By the 70th day of pregnancy, the placenta is unquestionably able to replace the corpus luteum without endangering the pregnancy during the transfer of function. At the end of pregnancy, the corpus luteum has usually regressed until it is no longer a prominent feature of the ovary.

Following implantation, the body stalk, which will become the umbilical cord, begins to separate the embryo from the syncytiotrophoblast, the outer layer of the trophoblast lying against the endometrium. The inner lining of the trophoblast is called cytotrophoblast. As the syncytiotrophoblast advances into the endometrium, it surrounds minute branches of the uterine arteries that contain maternal blood. Erosion of the endometrium about these blood sinuses allows them to open into the small cavities in the trophoblast. The cytotrophoblast, which lines the cavity, forms fingers of proliferating cells extending into the syncytiotrophoblast. After the placenta is developed, these fingers will be the cores of the root-like placental villi, structures that will draw nutrients and oxygen from the maternal blood that bathes them. This is the first step in uteroplacental circulation, which supplies the fetus with all of the sustenance necessary for life and growth and removes waste products from it.

During the third week of pregnancy, the syncytiotrophoblast forms a single layer of cells covering the growing villi and lining the syncytial lacunae or small cavities between the villi. The conceptus is buried in the endometrium, and its whole surface is covered at this time by developing villi. The greater part of the chorionic wall is now cytotrophoblast. Fingers of cytotrophoblast in the form of cell masses extend into the syncytial layer. Soon thereafter, a layer of connective tissue, or mesoderm, grows into the villi, which now form branches as they spread out into the blood-filled spaces in the endometrium adjacent to the conceptus.

By the end of the third week, the chorionic villi that form the outer surface of the chorionic sac are covered by a thick layer of cytotrophoblast and have a connective tissue core within which embryonic blood vessels are beginning to develop. The vessels, which arise from the yolk sac, connect with the primitive vascular system in the embryo. As growth progresses the layer of cytotrophoblast begins to regress. It disappears by the fifth month of pregnancy.

The layer of endometrium closest to the encroaching conceptus forms, with remnants of the invading syncytiotrophoblast, a thin plate of cells known as the decidua basalis, the maternal component of the mature placenta, which is cast off when the placenta is expelled. The fetal part of the placenta—the villi and their contained blood vessels—is separated from the decidua basalis by a lake-like body of fluid blood. This pool was created by coalescence of the intervillous spaces. The intervillous spaces in turn were formed from the syncytial lacunae in the young conceptus. Maternal blood enters this blood mass from the branches of the uterine arteries. The pool is drained by the uterine veins. It is so choked by intermingling villi and their branches that its continuity is lost on gross inspection.

The chorionic cavity contains the fluid in which the embryo floats. As its shell or outer surface becomes larger, the decidua capsularis, which is that part of the endometrium that has grown over the side of the conceptus away from the embryo (i.e., the abembryonic side) after implantation, becomes thinner. After 12 weeks or so, the villi on the side directed toward the uterine cavity disappear, leaving the smooth chorion, now called the chorion laeve. The chorion frondosum is that part of the conceptus that forms as the villi grow larger on the side of the chorionic shell next to the uterine wall. The discus-shaped placenta develops from the chorion frondosum and the decidua basalis.

At term, the normal placenta is a disk-shaped structure about 6 to 7 inches (approximately 16 to 20 cm) in diameter, about 1.2 to 1.6 inches (3 to 4 cm) in thickness at its thickest part, and weighing between 1.1 and 2.2 pounds (500 and 1,000 grams). It is thinner at its margins, where it is joined to the membrane-like chorion that spreads out over the whole inner surface of the uterus and contains the fetus and the amniotic fluid. The amnion, a thinner membrane, is adherent to and covers the inner surface of the chorion. The inner or fetal surface of the placenta is shiny, smooth, and traversed by a number of branching fetal blood vessels that come together at the point—usually the centre of the placenta—where the umbilical cord attaches. The maternal or uterine side of the placenta, covered by the thin, flaky decidua basalis, a cast-off part of the uterine lining, is rough and purplish-red, and has a raw appearance.

When the placenta is cut across, its interior is seen to be made of a soft, crepelike or spongy matrix from which semisolid or clotted blood, caught when it is separated from the uterine wall to which it was attached, can be squeezed. Detailed examination shows that the villi and their branches form an arborescent (treelike) mass within the huge blood lake of the intervillous space. Anchoring villi extend outward from the fetal side and fuse with the decidua basalis to hold the organ's shape. Others, algae-like, float freely in the blood lake. Dividing partitions, formed from the trophoblast shell, project into the intervillous space from the decidual side. They divide the placenta into 15 or 20 compartments, which are called cotyledons.

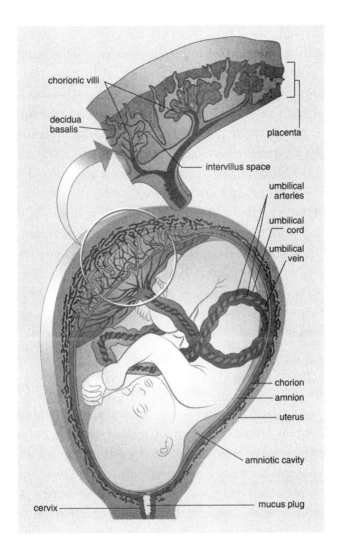

Full-term fetus in the uterus. The amnion, formed from the inner embryonic membrane, encloses the fetus. The space between the amnion and fetus (amniotic cavity) is filled with the watery amniotic fluid. The outermost embryonic membrane, the chorion, has developed fingerlike projections (villi) on its outer surface, which have enlarged and penetrated the decidua basalis layer of the uterus. The chorionic villi and the decidua basalis form the placenta. Maternal blood fills the spaces around the villi (intervillous spaces). Oxygen and nutrients diffuse into the villi and pass on to the fetus via the umbilical vein. Waste materials that leave the fetus via the umbilical arteries diffuse out of the villi into the mother's blood. © Merriam-Webster, Inc.

Maternal blood flows from the uterine vessels into the trophoblast-lined intervillous blood lake. Within each villus is a blood vessel network that is part of the fetal circulatory system. Blood within the villous vessel is circulated by the fetal heart. The blood vessel wall, the connective tissue of the villous core, and the syncytiotrophoblast covering the villus lie between the fetal and the maternal bloodstreams. This is known as the placental barrier. As pregnancy progresses, the fetal blood vessels become larger, the connective tissue stretches over them, and the syncytiotrophoblastic layer becomes fragmentary. As a result, the placental barrier becomes much thinner. Normally, blood cells and bacteria do not pass through it, but nutrients, water, salt, viruses, hormones, and many other substances, including many drugs, can filter across it.

CHANGES TO REPRODUCTIVE TISSUES

Pregnancy causes many changes to take place in a woman's reproductive tissues. The most visible of these changes affects the uterus. In a woman in her later teens who is not pregnant, the uterus measures about 2.75 inches (about 7 cm) in length and weighs approximately one ounce (about 30 grams). The corpus, the bulbous larger portion of the uterus that merges with the cervix, comprises approximately three-fourths of the organ in an unpregnant woman. During the first few weeks of pregnancy, the shape of the uterus is unchanged, but the organ becomes gradually softer. By the 14th week it forms a flattened or oblate spheroid. The fibrous cervix becomes remarkably softer and acquires a protective mucus plug within its cavity, but otherwise it changes little before labour. The lower part of the corpus, the isthmus, first becomes elongated and then, as the uterine contents demand more space, stretches and unfolds to form a bowl-shaped formation called the lower uterine segment. The fibrous nature of the cervix causes it to resist this unfolding action.

The uterine wall is stretched and thinned during pregnancy by the growing fetus and by the fluid that surrounds it. The greater size of the uterus as a result of pregnancy also results from a marked increase in the number of muscle fibres, blood vessels, nerves, and lymphatic vessels in the uterine wall. There is also a five- to tenfold increase in the size of the individual muscle fibre and marked enlargement in the diameters of the blood and lymph vessels. Thus, by term, the uterus has been converted into an elastic, fluid-filled cylinder. In a pregnant woman at term, the uterus measures approximately 12 inches (about 30 cm) in length, weighs 2.6 pounds (approximately 1,200 grams), and has a capacity of 4.2 to 5.3 quarts (4,000 to 5,000 ml).

As pregnancy progresses, the uterus rises out of the pelvis and fills the abdominal cavity. It is top-heavy near term so that it falls forward and, because of the large bowel on the left side, rotates to the right. It presses on the diaphragm and pushes the other organs aside. The uterus may sink downward in the pelvis several weeks before term in a process that is known as lightening or dropping. This occurs as the fetal head descends into the pelvis. In some women, particularly those who have borne children, lightening does not occur until the onset of labour. Lightening may be impossible in women who have an abnormally small pelvis, an oversized fetus, or a fetus lying in an abnormal position.

Several changes occur in the ovaries during pregnancy. For example, in the first few months following conception the ovary that contains the functioning corpus luteum is considerably larger than the other ovary. During pregnancy, both ovaries usually are studded with fluid-filled egg sacs as a result of chorionic gonadotropin stimulation.

By the end of pregnancy, most of these follicles have gradually regressed and disappeared.

The blood supply to both ovaries is increased during pregnancy. Both glands frequently reveal plaques of bright red fleshy material on their surfaces, which, if examined microscopically, demonstrate the typical cellular change of pregnancy, called a decidual reaction. In this reaction, cells develop that look like the cells in the lining of the pregnant uterus. They result from the high hormone levels that occur during pregnancy and disappear after the pregnancy terminates.

The pinkish tan colour of the lining of the vagina gradually takes on a bluish cast during the early months of pregnancy as a result of the dilation of the blood vessels in the vaginal wall. Later, the vaginal wall tends to become a purplish red colour as the blood vessels become further engorged. The cells of the vaginal mucosa increase in size. Added numbers of these cells peel off the surface of the mucosa and mix with the increased vaginal fluid. This produces a profuse vaginal secretion. Thickening, softening, and relaxation of the loosely folded, succulent lining of the vagina and the sodden tissues beneath it greatly increase distensibility and capacity of the vaginal cavity, a process that partially prepares the birth canal for the passage through it of the large fetal mass.

Changes in the external genitalia are similar to those in the vagina. The tissues become first softened and more succulent and later extremely fragile, as an increasing amount of blood and fluid collects in them. They take on a purplish red colour because of increased blood supply. Darkening of the vulvar skin, frequently seen during pregnancy, is particularly common among women of Mediterranean ethnic groups.

The pelvic blood vessels and lymph channels become larger and longer. They develop new branches adequate to transport the greatly increased amounts of blood and tissue fluid that accumulate in the uterus and the other pelvic organs during pregnancy. Congestion and engorgement of blood in the pelvis, both within and without the uterus, are characteristic of pregnancy.

Changes in the muscles, ligaments, and other supporting tissues of the pelvis begin early in pregnancy and become progressively more pronounced as pregnancy continues. These changes are induced by the greatly increased hormonal levels in the mother's blood that characterize pregnancy. Before labour starts, the pelvic supporting tissues must have sufficient elasticity and strength to permit the uterus to grow out of the pelvis and yet support it. The muscles must be soft and elastic enough during delivery so that they can stretch apart and not obstruct the baby's birth. Softening and greater elasticity is brought about not only by the growth of new tissue but also by congestion and retained fluid within the tissues themselves.

The bones forming the mother's pelvis show relatively few changes during pregnancy. Loosening of the joint between the pubic bones in front and of the joints between the sacrum and the pelvis in back occurs as a response to the hormone called relaxin, which is produced by the ovary. Although relaxin, which causes marked separation of the pelvic joints in some animals, usually has too slight an effect in human beings to be noticed, softening of the attachments between the bones may be sufficient to cause a few women considerable distress. The strain on the joint between the sacrum and the spine becomes greater near term when the woman tilts her pelvis forward and bends the upper part of her body backward to compensate for the weight of the heavy uterus. When relaxation is excessive, the woman suffers from backache and difficulty in walking. If it is extreme, she may have a waddling gait. Relaxation of the pelvic joints does not disappear quickly after delivery, accounting for much of the backache that women with new babies experience.

The mother's bones show no structural change if her calcium reserve and intake are normal. If her reserve and intake are inadequate, the fetus may draw so much calcium from her bones that the bones become soft and deformed. This condition is rarely seen, except in areas of the world where extreme poverty and serious calcium deficiency are major problems.

The earliest changes in the breasts during pregnancy are an exaggeration of the frequently experienced premenstrual discomfort and fullness. The sensation is so specific for pregnancy that many women who have been pregnant before are made aware of their condition by the feeling that they have in their breasts. As pregnancy progresses the breasts become larger, the lightly pigmented area (areola) around each nipple becomes first florid or dusky in colour and then appreciably darker. During the later months the areola takes on a hue that is deep bronze or brownish black, depending on the woman's natural pigmentation. The veins beneath the skin over the breast become enlarged and more prominent. The small oily or sebaceous glands (glands of Montgomery) about the nipple become prominent.

These changes are caused by the greatly increased levels of estrogen and progesterone in the woman's blood. These ovarian hormones also prepare the breast tissue for the action of the lactogenic (milk-causing) hormone, prolactin, produced by the pituitary gland. During the later part of pregnancy a milky fluid, colostrum, exudes from the ducts or can be expressed from them.

After delivery the decrease in estrogen and progesterone levels presumably permits the pituitary gland to release prolactin, which causes the breast to secrete milk. It is thought that the high hormonal levels inhibit the action or secretion of prolactin before delivery. Prolactin continues to be produced, and lactation usually continues, as long as the mother feeds her baby at the breast.

PREGNANCY TESTS

Pregnancy tests are procedures aimed at determining whether a woman is pregnant. Pregnancy tests are based on a detectable increase in human chorionic gonadotropin (HCG) in the blood serum and urine during early pregnancy. HCG is the principal hormone produced by the chorionic layers of the placenta. Levels of HCG increase significantly following implantation of the fertilized ovum in the uterine wall.

In home pregnancy tests, which are qualitative (determining whether HCG is present), a small amount of urine is applied to a chemical strip. The result is usually indicated by some visible change in the strip (whether this is a change in colour or the appearance of a symbol depends on how the test is manufactured). A positive home pregnancy test should be confirmed with a laboratory test and pelvic examination by a doctor. Pregnancy tests performed in a laboratory on a sample of blood or urine are quantitative and therefore are more accurate than a home pregnancy test. Laboratory tests using a sample of blood also have a high degree of sensitivity and can be used to detect increased levels of HCG early in the implantation process.

PRENATAL CARE AND TESTING

An adequate maternal diet is necessary to ensure proper fetal development as well as to maintain the health of the mother. The physiological adjustments of a pregnant woman's body are significant, and nutritional requirements increase as a result. In addition to an awareness of the substances that are of benefit during pregnancy, a knowledge of which substances are harmful and should be avoided is equally important. Alcohol has been found to be teratogenic (causing developmental malformations in the fetus). Intake of large to moderate quantities of alcohol during pregnancy is responsible for fetal alcohol syndrome, which is characterized by impaired growth and development, facial abnormalities, cardiac defects, and skeletal and joint malformations. The effects of limited intake of alcohol are not as well known, but avoidance of any amount of alcohol throughout pregnancy is recommended.

Smoking of tobacco during pregnancy is believed to lower the birth weight of the fetus and is associated with placenta praevia, abruptio placentae, and elevated maternal blood pressure. Sudden infant death syndrome, delayed mental development in childhood, and spontaneous abortion also have been linked to smoking. Limiting the use of caffeine also is encouraged. Although not believed to have teratogenic effects, excessive caffeine intake may account for low birth weight in infants. Over-the-counter medications as well as prescription drugs can adversely affect fetal development and should not be taken unless a health care provider is consulted.

Ultrasound

The use of high-frequency sound waves to produce a graphic image of the growing fetus—ultrasonography—is a ubiquitous tool in prenatal medicine, furnishing information on the morphological and functional status of the fetus. It is commonly used to estimate the gestational age of the fetus, identify fetal number, assess growth,

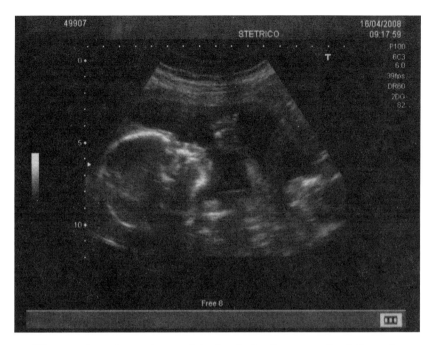

Ultrasounds produce an image of the developing fetus, revealing information such as age, growth, and heart activity. Cristian Baitg/Photographer's Choice/Getty Images

determine fetal heart activity, and provide a general survey of fetal anatomy. The presentation of the fetus and placenta and the volume of amniotic fluid also can be determined using ultrasound.

Theoretical risks of ultrasound are involved because of the nature of this technique (i.e., sound waves are reflected off tissues). Studies to date have revealed no evidence of tissue damage when diagnostic ultrasound is used, however, and the benefits of this procedure seem to outweigh the risks.

Amniocentesis

In the procedure of amniocentesis, amniotic fluid is aspirated (withdrawn) from the uterus by a needle inserted through a woman's abdomen, using ultrasound to circumnavigate the fetus and placenta. Although not all birth defects can be detected by this procedure, spinal cord defects and a host of genetic abnormalities such as Down syndrome and autosomal recessive diseases such as Tay-Sachs disease and cystic fibrosis can be screened for by amniocentesis. It can also be used to determine the sex of the fetus and to identify sex-linked diseases. This test is generally performed about the 16th week of pregnancy, and results take several weeks to obtain. Of the potential risks associated with this procedure, the most significant one is that of fetal loss, which may result from disruption of the placenta.

Chorionic Villi Sampling

The technique of retrieving a sample of villi from the chorion (outer embryonic membrane) within the uterus is similar to amniocentesis but can be carried out much earlier in pregnancy, between the 8th and 12th weeks of gestation. The test can be performed through either the abdomen or the vagina and cervix. The latter technique is carried out using ultrasonic visualization, and a thin catheter is inserted through the vagina into the uterus; a sample of villi from the chorion is then extracted and examined. If unfavourable results are received, termination of the pregnancy can be accomplished at an earlier stage than would be possible with amniocentesis. This procedure does carry a slightly higher risk of fetal loss than does amniocentesis, possibly because it is carried out at an earlier stage in fetal development. With this technique there is also concern that fetal limb reduction or malformation may result, but reports are inconclusive.

Alpha-fetoprotein screening

Shed by the yolk sac and fetal liver, alpha-fetoprotein can be used to screen for neural tube defects such as anencephaly and spina bifida (developmental abnormality in which spinal cord is not fully enclosed). The measurement of elevated levels of alpha-fetoprotein in a woman's blood between the 16th and 18th weeks of pregnancy are associated with this abnormality. Because other circumstances such as multiple pregnancies, underestimation of gestational age, and fetal death are associated with high levels of alpha-fetoprotein, ultrasound should be used to help rule out these different causes. Abnormally low levels of alpha-fetoprotein have been linked to a significant incidence of Down syndrome. A high rate of false-positive results is associated with this test, and so it is not routinely recommended. This procedure has been reserved primarily for those women with a family history of neural tube defects.

MULTIPLE BIRTH

Multiple birth is the delivery of more than one offspring in a single birth event. In most mammals the litter size is fairly constant and roughly correlates with, among other features, body size, gestation period, life span, type of uterus, and number of teats. For example, a large mammal with a normal pregnancy of more than 150 days, a life span of more than 20 years, a simple (or unicornuate) uterus, and two breasts rarely bears more than one young (a singleton) at a birth. Most primates, humans included, fit into this category, so multiple births among them are exceptional and occur with decreasing frequency from twins on.

TWINS AND TWINNING

Twinning refers to the process that leads to the production of more than one offspring at one birth. In humans the most frequent type of twinning results in the birth of two babies (twins) at once, but repetition of twinning may lead to triplets, quadruplets, or other multiples of one.

The two major types of twins are identical and fraternal twins. Identical twins are two individuals that have developed from a single ovum fertilized by a single sperm. This fertilized ovum is called a zygote. At a relatively early stage in its growth, the zygote splits into two separate cell masses that go on to become embryos. These embryos are genetically identical to each other and are always of the same sex. Three-fourths of such embryo pairs share a common placenta. Because they both developed from a single zygote, such twins are called monozygotic (MZ) twins.

A zygote's atypical separation into two independent embryonic structures can occur at any of several growth stages. Its incomplete or late division into two cell masses results in conjoined twins. MZ twins usually show a striking physical resemblance to one another. It should be noted that even though hereditary characteristics such as eye colour and hair colour and texture are the same in MZ twins, these traits as well as most physical characteristics may be modified during embryonic development. Identical twins may therefore not truly be "identical." The correspondence between such twins is closer to what would be expected between the right and left sides of a single individual, which vary slightly from one another.

Fraternal twins develop from two separate eggs that have been fertilized by two separate sperm. Such ovum pairs stem from multiple ovulations in the same cycle. Each ovum develops singly, is fertilized singly, and forms its own individual placenta. Because fraternal twins develop from different zygotes, they are called dizygotic (DZ) twins. DZ twins may be of the same sex or of different sexes, and they are not genetically identical to one another. Fraternal twins bear the resemblance of ordinary siblings.

The occurrence of DZ twinning varies among racial groups: Multiple births are most common among people of African descent, less common among those of European descent, and least common among people of Asian descent. DZ twinning is most common in older mothers (up to about 40 years of age) and tends to recur in families having a history of multiple births, indicating that a hereditary factor may be involved. Conversely, MZ twinning occurs randomly in all races and follows no discernible genetic

Multiple order babies, such as twins, triplets, and quintuplets, are often born premature, putting them at greater risk for death and chronic health problems.
Nancy R. Cohen/Digital Vision/Getty Images

pattern, but it tends to occur more frequently in older mothers.

In the first decade of the 2000s in the United States, the twin birth rate was estimated to be approximately 32.1 in every 1,000 births. Although reported frequencies throughout the world vary from about 45 in 1,000 (such as in the Yoruba people of Nigeria) to 4 in 1,000 births, source records from many areas are unreliable. In North America DZ twins are more frequent than MZ twins, and this pattern is seen among other populations of European origin as well. Excluding the use of fertility drugs, approximate figures for the frequency of multiple births are 1 in 80 births for twins, 1 in 6,400 for triplets, 1 in 512,000 for quadruplets, 1 in 40,960,000 for quintuplets, and so on.

OTHER MULTIPLE BIRTHS

As with twins, the other types of multiple births may or may not be monozygotic. Any combination may occur. For example, triplets may be derived from a single zygote (MZ triplets), from two zygotes, one of which divided to produce MZ twins while the other developed as a singleton (the three constituting DZ triplets), or from three separate zygotes (trizygotic, or TZ, triplets). Similarly, quadruplets may originate from one up to four zygotes, and quintuplets may derive from one to five zygotes. After being carefully studied, the Canadian Dionne quintuplets (born in 1934) were shown to be a one-zygote set.

Since the 1960s a substantial increase in the number of births of quintuplets, sextuplets, and even septuplets has occurred. This unprecedented phenomenon stems from use by the female of fertility drugs, which cause the simultaneous ovulation of many eggs, and in vitro fertilization, a procedure in which several fertilized ova are implanted in a woman at one time. Because they are often born premature, multiple order babies are at greater risk of infant death and chronic health problems than those who are singletons. The first confirmed birth of octuplets was reported from Mexico City in March 1967, but none of the four boys and four girls born prematurely survived more than 14 hours. The first recorded set of nonuplets was born June 13, 1971, when an Australian woman gave birth to five boys and four girls (two boys were stillborn). The remaining seven infants died within a week.

CHAPTER 4

DISORDERS OF REPRODUCTIVE DEVELOPMENT AND FUNCTION

There are many different types of diseases and disorders that can affect the development and function of the human reproductive system. Major abnormalities in the structure of reproductive organs are apparent at birth and occur as a result of defects in embryonic or fetal development. In some cases, these defects are caused by anomalies in an individual's genetic code. Atypical development of the reproductive organs or of the function of the reproductive system also may be associated with abnormal hormone production, whether by the ovaries or testes or by other endocrine organs, such as the pituitary gland.

A number of other reproductive disorders become apparent after childhood. Indeed, disorders of sexual maturity and conditions affecting menstruation do not manifest physically until the time of puberty. The causes of conditions affecting reproductive maturity are diverse and may depend on factors such as nutrition and exposure to certain chemicals in the environment. In some cases, however, the exact cause of the condition may be unknown.

GENETIC AND CONGENITAL ABNORMALITIES

Genetic defects and congenital abnormalities cause various reproductive disorders in the male and female. Many of these conditions involve an abnormality of organ structure and, consequently, dysfunction of the human body. In congenital disorders, signs of such abnormalities arise during development and typically are apparent at birth. These conditions are sometimes associated with an underlying defect in chromosomal structure.

ABNORMALITIES IN MALES

Congenital anomalies of the prostate gland and seminal vesicles are rare. They consist of the absence of development or the underdevelopment (hypoplasia) of these organs or of the presence of fluid- or semisolid-filled sacs, called cysts, within the tissues. Cysts of the prostatic utricle (the uterine remnant found in the male) are often found in association with advanced stages of hypospadias (a defect in the urethra) and pseudohermaphroditism (a condition in which the secondary sexual characteristics are underdeveloped). Cysts may also cause urinary obstructive symptoms through local pressure on the bladder neck.

Severe anomalies of the penis are rare and are generally associated with urinary or other systemic defects that are incompatible with life. Anomalies are those of absence, transposition, torsion (twisting), and duplication of the penis. An abnormally large penis frequently is present in males with precocious puberty, dwarfism, an overactive pituitary, or adrenal tumours. A small penis is seen in infantilism and in underdevelopment of the genitals, or undersecretion of the pituitary or pineal gland, and failure of development of the corpora cavernosa (erectile tissue located on the dorsal side of the penis).

The only anomaly of the foreskin is congenital phimosis, characterized by a contracture of the foreskin, or prepuce, which prevents its retraction over the glans (the conical structure that forms the head of the penis).

The preputial opening may impede the flow of urine. The condition is treated by circumcision.

There is a considerable variety of urethral anomalies. Stenosis (contracture) of the external opening (meatus) is the most common, but congenital stricture of the urethra occasionally occurs at other points. Valves (or flaps) across the anterior or posterior part of the urethra may cause congenital urethral obstruction in males. Posterior urethral valves are more common than anterior valves and consist of deep folds of mucous membrane, often paper-thin and usually attached at one end to the verumontanum, a small prominence in the back wall of the part of the urethra that is surrounded by the prostate gland. If too tight, the valves may obstruct the urethra and damage the kidneys.

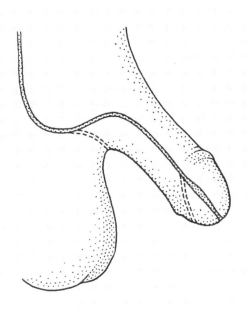

In hypospadias the underside of the urethral canal is open for a distance any-where from its outer end down to the base of the penis (indicated by dotted lines). Dorling Kindersley/Getty Images

Various defects are associated with incomplete closure of the urethra. One of the most common is hypospadias, in which the underside (ventral side) of the urethral canal is open for a distance at its outer end. Frequently the meatus is narrowed, and the penis has a downward curvature beyond the meatus. The posterior part of the urethra is never involved, and therefore the muscle that closes the urethra functions normally, enabling normal urinary control. Although the condition occurs in both sexes, it is seen predominantly in the male.

There is a high incidence of partial or complete failure of the testes to develop and of small external and internal genitalia. Epispadias, an opening in the upper (dorsal) side of the penis, is considerably less common than hypospadias. Dorsal curvature may also be present, but the disabling aspect is that the defect usually extends through the urinary sphincter and causes urinary incontinence. Other less common urethral anomalies include complete absence of the urethra, double urethra, urethra fistula (an opening in the urethra), urethrorectal fistula (an opening between the urethra and the rectum), and urethral diverticulum (a pouch in the wall of the urethra). Most of these conditions are correctable by surgery.

Anorchism (absence of one or both testes) is rare and may be associated with the absence of various other structures of the spermatic tract. Congenitally small testes may be a primary disorder or may occur because of underactivity of the pituitary. In both disorders there is a lack of development of secondary sexual characteristics and some deficiency in libido and potency. Supernumerary (extra) testicles are extremely rare. When present, one or more of the supernumerary testicles usually shows some disorder such as torsion of the spermatic cord. Synorchism, the fusion of the two testicles into one mass, may occur within the scrotum or in the abdomen.

The most common anomaly of the spermatic tract is cryptorchidism, also known as cryptorchism. This disorder occurs when one or both of the testes do not descend spontaneously to the usual position in the scrotum. (The testes normally descend around the time of the male infant's birth.) Usually, only one testis fails to descend into the scrotum. The other, descended testis suffices to ensure the individual's normal male sexuality. Cases in which both testes fail to descend are rare and are more serious because undescended testes are usually nonfunctional (i.e., produce few or no sperm), and the development of normal male sexuality is thus threatened. An undescended testis remains within the inguinal canal or in the abdominal cavity. Besides being nonfunctional, an undescended testis is more likely to be injured, and the blood supply to it is more likely to be cut off by twisting. Also, testicular cancer is 5 to 10 times more likely to develop in an undescended testis, even if the condition is corrected through surgery.

Gonadotropin and surgical therapy are the primary treatments for cryptorchidism. Human chorionic gonadotropin can help evoke maturation of the external genitals, and, in many cases of testes located in the inguinal canal, the testes move into the scrotum subsequent to this drug therapy. If medication fails, surgical treatment is used to move the undescended testis down into the scrotum manually. Both drug therapy and this procedure are best performed before the patient is two years of age. The sperm production of the now-descended testis after therapy may be lower than normal in some cases, but fertility is usually unimpaired.

ABNORMALITIES IN FEMALES

The female external genitalia are less complex than those of the male but have anomalies that can at times severely interfere with the functioning of the female urogenital tract. The clitoris, an erectile structure that corresponds to the penis, except that it does not contain the urethra, may be absent but in other cases may be enlarged on either a congenital or a hormonal basis. Fusion of the labia minora (small folds of skin covering the clitoris, the urethral opening, and the opening of the vagina) is a midline "sealing together." In this disorder, usually a minute unfused area is left just below the clitoris, through which urine and menstrual fluid can flow. The chief difficulty with this anomaly is concerned with obstruction to the flow of urine and associated urinary tract infection.

An imperforate hymen (the membrane closing off the opening of the vagina) causes distension of the uterus and vagina with fluid other than blood before puberty and with blood after puberty (the two conditions are called hydrometrocolpos and hematocolpometra, respectively). The distended vagina compresses the urethra enough to interfere with urination and commonly may even cause complete retention of urine in the bladder and distension of the entire upper urinary tract. Fusion of the urethra and the hymen is characterized by a dense hymenal ring and a stenosed urethral opening. The consequent urinary obstruction commonly results in persistent urinary infection. Most of the conditions are readily treated by surgery.

Anomalies of the vagina and uterus consist of complete absence, incomplete development, and duplication. The female urethra may have a congenitally narrow opening, or meatus; be distended; have an abnormal pouch, or diverticulum, in its wall; or may open abnormally into the vagina. Hypospadias may occur in the female but is far less common than in the male. Epispadias is also present in the female. Reconstructive surgery is the only method of treatment.

One of the rarest and most severe of the urogenital-tract anomalies, called urogenital cloaca, consists of congenital intercommunication between the rectum and the urinary bladder and vagina or between the rectum and the urethra and vagina.

INTERSEXUALITY

Intersexuality (having both male and female characteristics) may be noticeable at birth or may become apparent after puberty. Intersexuality noticeable at birth may be classified as female or male pseudohermaphroditism or true hermaphroditism. Intersexuality disorders that do not involve adrenal abnormalities are seen in infants whose mothers have been administered synthetic androgens or progestational compounds (substances that stimulate changes in the uterus that further the implantation and growth of the fertilized ovum) during pregnancy. Rarely, the condition is associated with the presence in the mother of a tumour of the ovary or adrenal gland. The newborn infant is a female with varying degrees of ambiguous genitalia, no treatment is necessary, and normal female development occurs at puberty.

True hermaphrodites have recognizable ovarian and testicular tissue. A uterus is always present, but the internal genitalia otherwise vary greatly, often including both male and female structures. Klinefelter syndrome, Turner syndrome, and testicular feminization are intersexuality syndromes that become apparent prior to or after puberty. Testicular feminization, or androgen insensitivity syndrome, is caused by genetic mutations on the X chromosome that cause a male to be resistant to the action of androgens. Affected persons seem to be normally developed females but have a chromosomal sex that is that of the normal male. The gonads are well-developed testes, and evidence indicates that there is a normal production of testosterone, but there is cellular resistance to the action of this hormone, and therefore the affected person becomes female in appearance. Because these gonads are apt to form malignant tumours, they are usually removed surgically. Female sexual characteristics are then maintained by the administration of estrogenic hormones.

Pseudohermaphroditism

Pseudohermaphroditism is a condition in which the individual has a single chromosomal and gonadal sex but combines features of both sexes in the external genitalia, causing doubt as to the true sex. Female pseudohermaphroditism refers to an individual with ovaries but with secondary sexual characteristics or external genitalia resembling those of a male. Male pseudohermaphroditism refers to individuals whose gonads are testes but whose secondary sexual characteristics or external genitalia resemble those of a female.

If during the first trimester of pregnancy a woman carrying a female fetus is given an androgen, an anabolic steroid, or a progestin (a substance with effects similar to those of progesterone), her fetus may be masculinized. Androgen-producing tumours of either adrenal or ovarian origin may also lead to masculinization of a female fetus.

Congenital adrenal hyperplasia, also known as adrenogenital syndrome, is a common cause of female pseudohermaphroditism. This disorder arises from an inherited defect in one of the enzymes needed for the production of cortisol, a hormone that plays a major role in the physiological response to stress. Excessive amounts of adrenal androgens must be produced to overcome the decrease in cortisol production. In female infants this results in masculinization with anomalous development of the genital organs, whereas in male infants it results in premature sexual development (precocious puberty).

Male pseudohermaphrodites are genetic males (45,XY) who develop female configurations and identities. These individuals have testes, but their genital ducts and external genitalia are female. Secondary sex characteristics may never appear in some, whereas others may achieve a fully feminized appearance. Male pseudohermaphroditism is rare and almost always results from autosomal recessive genetic defects (defects that must be inherited from both parents to be expressed). Several specific defects lead to feminization in genetic males. Each of these defects, by one mechanism or another, results in a loss of androgenic

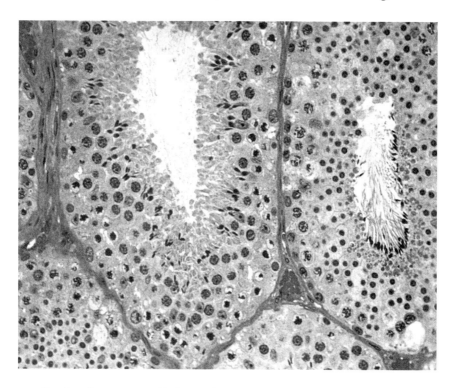

Leydig cells are responsible for producing and secreting testosterone. Dr. Fred Hossler/Visuals Unlimited/Getty Images

effects on body tissues. In rare instances, Leydig cells (the interstitial cells of the testes) are absent or greatly reduced in number, presumably because the receptors for luteinizing hormone (LH) are defective. Without Leydig cells, only small amounts of testosterone are produced. In other individuals there are enzyme deficiencies analogous to those that occur in female pseudohermaphrodites, but the enzyme deficiencies in males result in fetal androgen deficiency.

In some persons, tissue receptors for androgens are absent or reduced, forming a spectrum of syndromes of partial to complete resistance to androgens. The most striking example of resistance to androgens is complete testicular feminization. Affected individuals are born with female genitalia and a vagina that ends blindly (no cervix or uterus is present). Despite having testes located either in the labia or within the abdomen, these persons grow into well-proportioned females with normal breasts and scant or absent axillary and pubic hair. They have a strong female orientation, but they do not menstruate. Their hormonal aberrations are dramatic and predictable. With a loss of hypothalamic and pituitary androgen receptors, there is no inhibition of LH secretion. Serum LH concentrations are high, leading to stimulation of the Leydig cells and to high serum testosterone concentrations. The conversion of the increased amounts of testosterone to estrogen in peripheral tissues increases serum estrogen concentrations in males.

In another extraordinary variant, the lesion lies not in the loss of androgen receptors but rather in the loss of 5-alpha-reductase, an enzyme necessary for the conversion of testosterone to the more potent hormone dihydrotestosterone. In this syndrome, because of a lack of testosterone directing fetal development toward a normal male configuration, genetic males are born with what appears to be female genitalia with an enlarged clitoris. These persons are often raised as females, but at puberty an increase in testosterone secretion leads to masculinization. There then ensues a transition from the psychosocial behaviour of a prepubertal female to that of an adult male.

In some fetuses there occurs, for unknown reasons, regression and disappearance of the testes, known as the "vanishing testes syndrome." When this occurs early in pregnancy, before androgen-induced differentiation toward male genitalia, the child is born with female genitalia. If the testes disappear during the crucial period between 8 and 10 weeks of gestation, the child is born with ambiguous genitalia, whereas if the disappearance occurs after this key period the individual is born a male but without any testes (anorchia).

Treatment must be highly individualized. In many instances, gender identity has been established by the age of 18 to 24 months, and changes in sexual identity thereafter should be attempted only after careful consideration. Intra-abdominal testes should be removed because of an increased risk of tumour formation. The patient can be treated at the appropriate time with sex hormones.

Hermaphroditism

Hermaphroditism is the condition of having both male and female reproductive organs. Hermaphroditic plants (most flowering plants, or angiosperms) are called monoecious, or bisexual. Hermaphroditic animals—mostly invertebrates such as worms, bryozoans (moss animals), trematodes (flukes), snails, slugs, and barnacles—are usually parasitic, slow-moving, or permanently attached to another animal or plant.

In humans, hermaphroditism is an extremely rare sex anomaly. A true hermaphrodite is an individual who has both ovarian and testicular tissue. The ovarian and testicular tissue may be separate, or the two may be combined in what is called an ovotestis. Hermaphrodites have sex chromosomes showing male-female mosaicism (where one individual possesses both the male XY and female XX chromosome pairs). Most often, but not always, the chromosome complement is 46,XX, and in every such individual there also exists evidence of Y chromosomal material on one of the autosomes (any of the 22 pairs of chromosomes other than the sex chromosomes). Individuals with a 46,XX chromosome complement usually have ambiguous external genitalia with a sizable phallus and are therefore often reared as males. However, they develop breasts during puberty and menstruate and in only rare cases actually produce sperm. In contrast, individuals with the external appearance of one sex but the chromosomal constitution and reproductive organs of the opposite sex are pseudohermaphrodites.

Treatment of hermaphroditism depends on the age at which the diagnosis is made. If diagnosed at birth, choice of sex is usually made on the basis of the condition of the external genitalia (i.e., which sex organs predominate), after which surgery is performed to remove the gonads of the opposite sex. The remaining genitalia are then reconstructed to resemble those of the chosen sex. If it is decided that a male identity is deeply embedded and therefore a male role is preferable, all female tissues, including the oviducts and ovaries, are removed. In those persons to be reared as females, the male sexual tissues are removed. In older individuals the accepted gender is often reinforced by the appropriate surgical procedures and by hormonal therapy.

Klinefelter Syndrome

Klinefelter syndrome is a disorder of the human sex chromosomes that occurs in males. Klinefelter syndrome is one of the most frequent chromosomal disorders in males, occurring in approximately 1 in every 500 to 1,000 males. Men with Klinefelter syndrome have small, firm testes, and they often have breast enlargement (gynecomastia) and inordinately long legs and arms (eunuchoidism) and are infertile. Affected men have decreased serum testosterone concentrations, with urinary excretion of 17-ketosteroids (components of androgens) in the normal or low-normal range. They also have increased serum follicle-stimulating hormone (FSH) and luteinizing hormone (LH) concentrations. Diabetes mellitus, goitre (enlargement of the thyroid gland), and various cancers may be more prevalent among Klinefelter syndrome patients. Thyroidal trapping of radioactive iodine and the responses of the thyroid to injections of thyrotropin (thyroid-stimulating hormone; TSH) may be low. Although normal in intelligence, some affected men have difficulties making social adjustments.

Klinefelter syndrome is named for Harry Klinefelter, an American physician who in 1942 described a set of symptoms that characterized the condition. The syndrome was first identified with a specific chromosomal abnormality in 1959 by British researcher Patricia A. Jacobs and her colleagues. It results from an unequal sharing of sex chromosomes soon after fertilization, with one cell of a dividing pair receiving two X chromosomes and a Y chromosome and the other cell of the pair receiving only a Y chromosome and usually dying.

The normal male chromosome number and sex chromosome composition is 46,XY. However, because males with mosaic (tissues made up of genetically different cells) Klinefelter syndrome have an extra X chromosome, they typically have a chromosome composition of 47,XXY. Men with this form of the disorder usually have fewer symptoms than do men with the other chromosomal arrangements associated with Klinefelter syndrome. Other, rare chromosome complements that give rise to mosaic Klinefelter syndrome include 48,XXYY, 48,XXXY, 49,XXXYY, and 49,XXXXY. Men with these chromosome complements suffer from a variety of additional abnormalities, and, unlike men with 47,XXY Klinefelter syndrome, they often suffer from intellectual disability. One variant of the disorder in particular, the 49,XXXXY type, is characterized by fusion of the forearm bones and other skeletal anomalies, underdevelopment of the penis and scrotum, incomplete descent of the testes, and marked intellectual disability. Although about 40 percent of men affected by Klinefelter syndrome have a normal XY pattern, others possess a chromosome variant known as XX syndrome, in which Y chromosome material is transferred to an X chromosome or a nonsex chromosome (autosome). Men with XX syndrome have a male phenotype (physical appearance), but they have changes typical of Klinefelter syndrome.

Treatment with androgens reduces gynecomastia and evidence of male hypogonadism and increases strength and libido in patients with all variants of Klinefelter syndrome. In a few of these individuals, sperm obtained from the testes have successfully fertilized oocytes in vitro.

Turner Syndrome

Turner syndrome, also known as gonadal dysgenesis, is a relatively uncommon sex-chromosome disorder that causes aberrant sexual development in human females. Turner syndrome occurs when one sex chromosome is deleted, so that instead of the normal 46 chromosomes, of which two are sex chromosomes (XX in females and XY in males), the chromosomal complement is 45,X. In genetic terms, these patients are neither male nor female because the second, sex-determining chromosome is absent. However, phenotypically, affected individuals develop as females because there is no Y chromosome to direct the fetal gonads to the male configuration.

Clinically, patients with Turner syndrome are short, and they have a small chin, prominent folds of skin at the inner corners of the eyes (epicanthal folds), low-set ears, a webbed neck, and a shieldlike chest. Individuals with Turner syndrome also have an increased incidence of anomalies of the heart and large blood vessels. Both the internal and external genitalia are infantile, and the ovaries are only "streaks" of connective tissue. The diagnosis may be made during infancy or childhood on the basis of these anomalies or at puberty when the individual fails to develop secondary sex characteristics or has no menses. In genetic terms, Turner syndrome is common: One-tenth of all spontaneously aborted fetuses have a 45,X chromosome constitution, and only 3 percent of affected fetuses survive to term.

Patients with Turner syndrome can be treated with growth hormone during childhood to increase linear growth. Affected individuals should also be treated with estrogen and progestin (similar to progesterone) at the time of puberty to stimulate the appearance of secondary sexual characteristics and the monthly vaginal bleeding that simulates a menstrual cycle. Estrogen and progestin also prevent osteoporosis, which will occur if ovarian deficiency is not treated.

There are multiple variants of Turner syndrome. For example, there are mixtures of chromosomes (mosaics), such as a 45,X and 46,XX chromosomal complement or a 45,X and 47,XXX chromosomal complement, and chromosomal translocations, in which a portion of one chromosome is transferred to another chromosome. Another variant is the 45,X/46,XY mosaic, in which a person may be reared as either a male or a female because the genitalia are "ambiguous," meaning that it is difficult to determine whether the phallus is an enlarged clitoris or a small penis. Patients with this variant of Turner syndrome have streak gonads, and the presence of the Y chromosome is associated with an increased risk of development of a malignant tumour of the streak gonad.

DISORDERS OF SEXUAL MATURITY

Disorders of sexual maturity primarily include those conditions that affect the normal development and growth of reproductive organs during adolescence. The two primary types of sexual maturity disorders are precocious puberty and delayed puberty.

PRECOCIOUS PUBERTY

Precocious puberty is the abnormally early onset of human sexual development. In girls, precocious puberty is defined as the onset of menstruation before age 8, and in boys it is defined as sexual development before age 9. True precocious puberty is characterized by normal pubertal development at an abnormally early age, sometimes as early as age 2.

In girls, early onset of puberty is followed by adult cyclic hypothalamic-pituitary-ovarian function, including ovulation. Thus, a young girl affected by the disorder can become pregnant. The rise in estrogen production also stimulates skeletal growth, followed by premature closure of the epiphyses (expanded ends of the long bones), with eventual short stature. In most girls the cause of this disorder is unknown (idiopathic), and affected girls are otherwise normal. Occasionally, it is caused by a tumour or other abnormality of the hypothalamus that results in the secretion of gonadotropin-releasing hormone (GnRH). GnRH stimulates the release of female gonadotropins (i.e., LH and FSH) from the pituitary gland, and these hormones in turn stimulate the growth and development of the ovaries.

Treatment is important for proper psychological and social development and to prevent short stature. In the past, affected girls were often treated with a progestin, thereby inhibiting the secretion of gonadotropins from the pituitary, which resulted in some regression of breast development and cessation of menstruation but often did not prevent short stature. This form of treatment has been superseded by long-acting derivatives of GnRH that down-regulate GnRH receptors on the gonadotropin-secreting cells of the pituitary. Thus, gonadotropin secretion decreases, ovarian function ceases, and, in most girls, pubertal development gradually declines and growth rate slows.

Precocious pseudopuberty is partial pubertal development that results from autonomous (gonadotropin-independent) production of estrogen in prepubertal girls. Affected girls have premature development of their breasts and pubic hair, experience rapid growth, and may have irregular vaginal bleeding (caused by the stimulatory effects of estrogen alone on the endometrium). However, these girls do not have true menstrual cycles and are not fertile. Precocious pseudopuberty is usually caused by an ovarian tumour, a chorionic gonadotropin-secreting tumour (tumours that secrete a hormone normally produced by the placenta that stimulates the ovaries), or exogenous estrogen (e.g., certain environmental or industrial chemicals). Affected girls must be evaluated carefully to find the cause of the disorder, and they must be treated accordingly, such as by removal of the tumour.

Boys, similar to girls, can undergo true precocious puberty or various forms of precocious pseudopuberty. In true precocious puberty, there is premature activation of the hypothalamic-pituitary-testes axis, with spermatogenesis, virilization, and growth acceleration, which paradoxically causes premature closure of the epiphyseal disks and short stature. The causes of precocious puberty in boys include hypothalamic tumours and other brain tumours, traumatic brain injuries, and various brain disorders. However, in some boys no cause can be found (idiopathic precocious puberty). Because damage to the brain or disorders of the brain are the primary causes of true precocious puberty in boys, neurosurgical intervention may be needed. If neurosurgical intervention is unsuccessful or if no cause is found, affected boys can be treated with long-acting derivatives of GnRH that down-regulate GnRH receptors on the gonadotropin-secreting cells of the anterior pituitary. Thus, gonadotropin secretion decreases, testicular function ceases, and, in most boys, growth rate slows.

Precocious pseudopuberty is partial pubertal development that results from autonomous (gonadotropin-independent) production of testosterone in a prepubertal boy. Affected boys have premature virilization and rapid growth, but they do not produce sperm. Precocious pseudopuberty may be caused by a liver tumour or other tumour that secretes human chorionic gonadotropin (HCG; a hormone normally produced by the placenta), an adrenal or testicular tumour, congenital adrenal hyperplasia, a mutation that results in activation of the luteinizing hormone receptor (testotoxicosis), or exogenous androgen (e.g., caused by the intake of steroid drugs). Similar to girls, affected boys must be evaluated to find the cause of the condition, and they must be treated accordingly.

Delayed Puberty

Delayed puberty is the failure of physical development of the reproductive system by the normal stage or period of life when a child transforms into an adult capable of procreation. In girls, puberty is considered delayed if no pubertal development has occurred by age 13 or 14, and girls who have not menstruated by age 16 are considered to have primary amenorrhea. In boys, puberty is deemed delayed if no pubertal development has occurred by age 14.

In girls, delayed puberty and primary amenorrhea may be subdivided according to associated changes in stature. If the affected girl is short, the likely causes are gonadal dysgenesis (Turner syndrome) or hypopituitarism (with both gonadotropin and growth hormone deficiency). Gonadal dysgenesis results from the absence of a sex chromosome or other abnormality of a sex chromosome. In affected girls the gonads are streaks of fibrous tissue and contain no follicles, and these girls may have a variety of congenital anomalies, including a webbed neck, a shield-like chest, or a small jaw. If the affected girl's stature is normal, the likely causes are GnRH deficiency (sometimes with an absence of the sense of smell, called Kallman syndrome), gonadotropin deficiency, chronic illness, or excessive exercise. However, in many cases there is no cause to be found (idiopathic or constitutional delay in puberty). Rarely, the cause is decreased estrogen synthesis, which may result from the absence of the aromatase enzyme that converts androgens to estrogens or from the presence of defective estrogen receptors. In the latter disorder, estrogen is produced, but the receptors to which it must bind in order to act are missing or abnormal.

Some girls with normal stature have normal pubertal development but primary amenorrhea. Affected girls may have anomalous development of the uterus or vagina so that menstrual bleeding cannot occur. This may be caused by testicular feminization in genetic males. Testicular feminization is caused by a mutation in the gene for the androgen receptor that prevents testosterone from acting on its target tissues. Affected patients have female external genitalia, a short vagina (but no uterus), breast development, and other features of estrogen action.

Similar to girls, the causes of delayed puberty in boys are variable. If the boy's stature is short, the likely cause is hypopituitarism (with both gonadotropin and growth hormone deficiency). If the boy's stature is normal, the likely causes are deficiency of gonadotropin-releasing hormone (sometimes with Kallman syndrome), deficiency of gonadotropin, chronic illness, and primary gonadal disorders. However, in many cases no cause is found (idiopathic or constitutional delay in puberty). Primary gonadal disorders include absence of the testes, cryptorchidism, Klinefelter syndrome, enzymatic defects in testosterone biosynthesis, and testicular resistance to the action of LH.

The treatment of delayed puberty depends on the specific cause, and in some cases treatment is not necessary. When the cause is diagnosed and treated, most affected children will progress through puberty and do not experience adverse long-term effects. However, if diagnosis and treatment are delayed in patients with a severe disorder of delayed puberty that is not associated with malnutrition, the epiphyseal centres of the bones may remain open, allowing linear growth to continue. These individuals often become tall with unusually long legs and long arms, a body type referred to as eunuchoid habitus. Disorders of delayed puberty are treated with testosterone in boys and estrogen or progesterone in girls. These hormones stimulate the development of secondary sex characteristics.

DISORDERS AFFECTING MENSTRUATION

Abnormalities of menstrual function include painful menstruation, or dysmenorrhea; excessive blood loss during each menstrual cycle, known as menorrhagia; irregular bleeding, or metrorrhagia; absence of menstruation, called amenorrhea; and dysfunctional uterine bleeding. In addition, many women experience premenstrual syndrome, a group of physical and emotional symptoms that occur before the onset of each cycle. A few women have transient abdominal discomfort at the time of ovulation because of slight bleeding from the follicle into the peritoneal cavity; oral contraceptives remedy the condition by suppression of ovulation, or the discomfort can be treated with pain medications such as ibuprofen or naproxen.

DYSMENORRHEA

Dysmenorrhea is painful cramps felt before or during menstruation, sometimes so severe as to interfere with daily activities. Dysmenorrhea may be primary or secondary. Primary dysmenorrhea is caused by specific imbalances in the woman's endocrine system during the menstrual cycle. Secondary dysmenorrhea denotes menstrual cramps caused by some other distinct organic disorder. In most cases dysmenorrhea is primary.

Primary dysmenorrhea may occur a few days before the period, at the onset of bleeding, or during the total episode. The pain varies from a severe incapacitating distress to relatively minor and brief intense cramps. Other symptoms may include irritability, fatigue, backache, headache, leg pains, nausea, vomiting, and cramping. Primary dysmenorrhea is caused by the endocrine system's release of excessive amounts of prostaglandins. These are hormonelike substances that stimulate the uterus to contract, thus causing the familiar cramps of the disorder. Drugs that block prostaglandin formation can decrease the severity of uterine contractions and can eliminate pain for many women with dysmenorrhea.

Secondary dysmenorrhea is much less common. It can be caused by genital obstructions, pelvic inflammation or degeneration, abnormal uterine wall separation or development (i.e., endometriosis), chronic infection of the uterus, polyps or tumours, or weakness of the muscles that support the uterus. Often the pain is dull, aching, and persistent. Tumours produce sharper pains. Treatment is directed toward the underlying disorder.

MENORRHAGIA

Excessive menstrual bleeding, or menorrhagia, may result from an imbalance of the thyroid or adrenal hormones, but it may also be the result of local disease of the pelvic organs. This local disease may be inflammation due to infection; a benign tumour such as a fibroid; a polyp, or projecting mass of endometrium; or a cancer, especially after age 35. Some types of local pelvic disease may require removal of the uterus (hysterectomy) or treatment by chemotherapy or radiation, but polyps and some fibroids can be removed without loss of the uterus.

As menopause approaches, extremely heavy bleeding may occur, causing anemia, tiredness, and ill health. Menorrhagia in this instance is caused by overdevelopment of the endometrium as a result of excessive or unbalanced action of estrogens. Younger or childless women can be treated with progestogens, but for others removal of the uterus may be necessary.

METRORRHAGIA

Bleeding between menstrual periods, after intercourse, and at or after menopause is frequently caused by some abnormality of the cervix. The possibility of cancer must be borne in mind. Such bleeding may also come from a polyp on the cervix or a cervical erosion. The latter is an ulceration of the lining of the uterine cervix and is made evident by bright red or pink spots around the cervix opening.

In the earliest stage of cervical erosion, patches of mucous membrane are shed from the cervix. The following stages are usually associated with different degrees of healing. The primary lesion shows an ulcer. Its surface lacks mucous membrane, the tissue is granular, and there may be many white blood cells and bacteria associated with it. Soon after the ulcer erupts, the body starts repairs by covering the exposed area with a new epithelial (covering) layer. An erosion may heal completely or partially or may recur. The erosion does not totally heal until the infection and discharge that caused it originally are eradicated.

Erosions are most prevalent in women during their menstrual years, in those who have had children, and during cervical or vaginal infections. They are less common in virgins and in older women who have experienced menopause. The erosion itself is relatively insignificant, but occasionally, it may precede cervical cancer.

Extensive erosions can involve part of the surrounding vaginal wall. As the ulcer heals, it acquires patches of pinkish-tan epithelium (covering), which form small islands over the eroded area. The small islands eventually grow together, giving the lesion an uneven contour. There are mucous glands in the cervical tissue that lead to the surface of the epithelium. If these ducts are covered or blocked, the glands fill with retained fluids, causing small cysts.

Erosions that bleed on trauma or have an irregular, bumpy (papillate) surface are generally regarded as of the more hazardous variety. Most smooth, round erosions do not require treatment, because they heal by themselves when the cause is removed. Larger erosions are lightly cauterized in spots to stimulate epithelial growth. Erosions found to be cancerous are usually removed surgically. Removal of part or all of the cervix does not prevent fertilization and childbearing.

Treatment of other forms of metrorrhagia is often unnecessary, but polyps require removal. Irregular bleeding also may occur during pregnancy when there is danger of miscarriage. If any menstrual periods have been missed, this possibility must be considered.

AMENORRHEA

Amenorrhea, or absence of menstruation, is normal during pregnancy and for a variable time after delivery. If the mother is breast-feeding her baby, as much as six months may pass before return of menstruation. Earlier return of menstruation is not abnormal and is to be expected if the mother is not producing milk. Pregnancy is the most common cause of amenorrhea during the reproductive years.

Primary amenorrhea is the absence of menstruation in a woman who has never previously menstruated. In rare cases, primary amenorrhea results from gonadal dysgenesis, the failure of the ovaries to develop normally, and may be associated with chromosomal abnormalities. Instead of the normal female complement of 46 chromosomes in each cell, including two X chromosomes, a patient may have only one X chromosome (Turner syndrome) or even a male pattern of an X and a Y chromosome (Swyer syndrome). In such persons the uterus and fallopian tubes often are absent, but the general physique may be female.

Even with normal ovaries, absence of the uterus occasionally occurs. A less rare abnormality is vaginal atresia, or closure, an obstruction of the vagina by a membrane just above the level of the hymen; menstruation occurs, but the discharge cannot escape and distends the vagina. This condition, called false amenorrhea or cryptomenorrhea, is easily corrected by an incision in the membrane.

Cessation of periods after menstruation has been established but before the normal time for the menopause is usually the result of some general illness, emotional stress, or mental disorder. It may also be caused by disease of the endocrine system, not only of the pituitary gland but of other endocrine glands as well. Secondary amenorrhea results if the ovaries are removed or are irradiated but is unlikely to be caused by ovarian disease because both ovaries would have to be damaged to stop all function. Stein-Leventhal syndrome is a functional disorder of the ovaries in which production of estrogens is disturbed. Symptoms of this disorder include abnormal growth of facial hair because of abnormal androgenic—that is, masculinizing—activity. An ovarian tumour that secretes androgenic hormone, also called an arrhenoblastoma, is another extremely rare cause of amenorrhea and abnormal growth of hair. Most cases of secondary amenorrhea are temporary, and spontaneous improvement is to be expected, especially when the cause is some general illness or emotional stress. The feasibility of treatment with hormones is determined by a general medical examination and a complete pelvic examination.

OLIGOMENORRHEA

Oligomenorrhea is characterized by prolonged intervals between menstrual cycles. Menstruation is the normal cyclic bleeding from the female reproductive tract. Most women of reproductive age menstruate every 25 to 30 days if they are not pregnant, nursing a child, or experiencing other disorders such as tumours, anorexia nervosa, or Stein-Leventhal syndrome (polycystic ovary syndrome). In oligomenorrhea, menstruation occurs in intervals greater than 35 days. The cause of the disorder may be psychological, hormonal, or structural in nature.

Dysfunctional Uterine Bleeding

Dysfunctional, or anovulatory, uterine bleeding occurs most often in women during early adolescence and immediately before menopause begins. It is thought to be caused by imperfect ovarian functioning. Estrogens are produced in a cycle in amounts sufficient to cause endometrial proliferation, but ovulation does not occur. The endometrium breaks down and bleeds in each cycle as the estrogens are withdrawn. Cycles of this type occur in women who are using oral contraceptives. Dysfunctional bleeding can also be associated with obesity, excessive exercise, or emotional stress.

Premenstrual Syndrome

Premenstrual syndrome (PMS) is a medical condition in which a group of characteristic physical and emotional symptoms are felt by women before the onset of menstruation. The symptoms of PMS are cyclic in nature, generally beginning from 7 to 14 days before menstruation and ending within 24 hours after menstruation has begun. The medical condition was named by British physician Katharina Dalton in the 1950s.

Research suggests that as many as 75 percent of females have PMS, and the types of symptoms and the degree of their severity vary markedly. Physical symptoms may include headache, cramps, backache, bloating, constipation or diarrhea, and a number of related disorders. The emotional and psychiatric symptoms of premenstrual syndrome range from irritability, lethargy, and rapid mood swings to hostility, confusion, aggression, and depression. Women who have severe symptoms of depression that are associated with premenstrual syndrome may be diagnosed with premenstrual dysphoric disorder (PMDD). While premenstrual dysphoric disorder is closely related to major depressive disorder, the symptoms of severe depression are cyclical in nature, fluctuating with cycles of ovulation and menstruation. A distinguishing factor in the diagnosis of premenstrual dysphoric disorder is that

Symptoms of premenstrual syndrome can be physical (i.e., headache, cramps, backache, and bloating) or emotional and psychiatric (i.e., lethargy and hostility). ©www.istockphoto.com / Jon Horton

depression eventually becomes so severe that home, work, and daily life are disrupted.

Although they are the major subject of current research, the causes of PMS are not yet established. The most widely accepted theories centre on hormonal changes (the rapid fluctuation of levels of estrogen and progesterone in the bloodstream), nutritional deficiencies (particularly in regard to the vitamins—notably B vitamins—that affect nerve transmission in the brain), and stress (which has been shown to be a factor in the severity of symptoms). Many researchers suspect that fluctuations of chemical transmitters in the brain are largely responsible. Several genetic mutations have been identified that may increase a woman's predisposition toward developing premenstrual syndrome or toward developing the severe depression that is associated with premenstrual dysphoric disorder.

For purposes of treatment, a chart that records the nature and date of occurrence of a woman's symptoms can aid diagnosis. The major method of treatment for most cases of PMS involves some combination of regular physical exercise, avoidance of stress, nonsteroidal anti-inflammatory drugs (NSAIDs) such as ibuprofen or naproxen sodium, and hormone therapy. Restriction of sodium intake, avoidance of xanthines—found in coffee, tea, chocolate, and cola—and eating foods high in protein and complex carbohydrates are a few of the dietary measures that can be taken to reduce much of the physical discomfort. Women with premenstrual dysphoric disorder usually require antidepressant medications.

Stein-Leventhal Syndrome

Stein-Leventhal syndrome, also called polycystic ovary syndrome (PCOS), is a disorder in women that is characterized by an elevated level of male hormones (androgens) and infrequent or absent ovulation (anovulation). About 5 percent of women are affected by Stein-Leventhal syndrome, which is responsible for a substantial proportion of cases of female infertility. The syndrome was first described in 1935 when American gynecologists Irving F. Stein, Sr., and Michael L. Leventhal associated the presence of ovarian cysts with anovulation. For many years these factors were used as the diagnostic criteria of the syndrome. Later, it was realized that anovulation and an elevated level of androgens, not ovarian cysts, were the more correct diagnostic criteria because it is the combination of these factors that results from or is symptomatic of the other characteristics of the syndrome. Although the cause of the syndrome remains unknown, evidence suggests that the syndrome is complex, involving multiple physiological systems. For example, insulin resistance appears to play a central role in the development of the disease, with the ovaries being only one of several organs that may be affected.

Insulin resistance occurs when certain tissues, primarily skeletal muscles, do not respond to insulin. This results in a compensatory increase in the secretion of insulin by the pancreas, causing an increase in the serum concentrations of insulin (hyperinsulinemia). Hyperinsulinemia can lead to the excess production of androgens through a number of pathways, including stimulation of the hypothalamus, stimulation of the adrenal glands and the ovaries, and suppression of the circulating levels of sex-hormone-binding globulin, which allows androgens to readily leave the circulation and enter tissues (e.g., hair follicles) where they exert their actions. Insulin resistance and compensatory hyperinsulinemia are also risk factors for other metabolic diseases, including type II diabetes and atherosclerosis, which women with Stein-Leventhal syndrome may develop at an unusually young age. In addition, obesity is present in about 50 percent of affected women and is often associated with the presence of other metabolic problems. Hyperinsulinemia, obesity, and chronic anovulation may also lead to the development of endometrial cancer (uterine cancer).

The syndrome may become apparent at or prior to puberty, at which time symptoms may include premature development of pubic hair, hyperinsulinemia, and elevated levels of precursor molecules that can be converted to androgens. After puberty, symptoms may include infrequent or absent menstrual cycles, infertility, and signs of excess levels of androgens, including hirsutism (excessive midline body hair) and acne. As affected women grow older, menstrual irregularity and androgen excess become less of a problem, with these symptoms often improving after the age of 40. In fact, diagnosis of the syndrome is difficult to make after the onset of menopause. Because affected women exhibit a wide variety of signs and symptoms, some authorities believe that the syndrome is not one but several different syndromes. In addition, no genetic cause has been identified, although the syndrome sometimes appears in multiple women in one family.

The most basic form of treatment of women with Stein-Leventhal syndrome is the initiation of an exercise regimen combined with proper nutrition to encourage weight loss and to improve insulin sensitivity. If these measures are unsuccessful, or if the syndrome is severe, treatment is focused on suppressing excess androgen production. In women who do not wish to become pregnant, hirsutism and menstrual irregularities can be managed with oral contraceptives or anti-androgen drugs. In women who do wish to become pregnant, infertility is often treated with drugs that induce ovulation, such as clomiphene citrate or gonadotropins. Less commonly, laparoscopic surgery is used to destroy portions of the ovary and thus reduce the production of androgens. In addition, antidiabetic drugs have been used in some patients to increase ovulatory frequency and to decrease excess androgen levels.

DISORDERS OF THE TESTES AND PENIS

Disorders of the testes and penis are characterized by abnormalities such as fluid accumulation and atypical erection. These conditions can range from relatively mild, with little pain or no long-term effects, to severe, in which there is acute pain and the potential for permanent erectile dysfunction (impotence) or sterility. Two important conditions affecting the testes and penis include hydrocele and priapism. Both disorders are far more common in grown men than in adolescent boys.

HYDROCELE

Hydrocele is the excessive accumulation of fluids in the scrotal sac that surrounds the testes. There are many forms of hydrocele. The most common is chronic simple hydrocele, in which fluid accumulates gradually about the testes. It usually afflicts men older than age 40 and is of unknown cause. Hydroceles thought to be a result of other bodily disturbances are called symptomatic. Frequently, this type arises as a complication of testicular tumours. A direct blow or other physical injury to the testes may also cause a hydrocele.

Hydrocele typically causes the scrotal sac to swell up much like a bag filled with water. Hydroceles may be painless when small, but, when they reach a sufficient size, their weight pulls on the spermatic cords, which can cause a dull aching pain. Large hydroceles can obstruct urination. Treatment for mild hydroceles simply consists of bed rest and support for the scrotum, but more serious cases may require surgical drainage and repair and the administration of antibiotics.

Priapism

Priapism is a persistent, painful erection of the penis unaccompanied by sexual excitation or desire. When normal erection occurs, the sides and the bottom of the penis, the corpora cavernosa and the corpus spongiosum, respectively, become engorged with blood so that the penis enlarges, hardens, and assumes an erect position. The major symptom of priapism is pain and tenderness in the enlarged portions. There may be a short period during the onset when pleasurable sensations are felt, but this quickly gives way to constant pain. In only about 25 percent of the cases can the cause be identified. The causes are generally classified as nervous or mechanical disorders. The nervous disorders may be in the spinal nerves or in the peripheral nerves that lead to the reproductive tract. Syphilitic involvement of the nervous system can cause cases of priapism that may be prolonged for years, but most instances of the disorder last only a few hours, days, or weeks.

Not all cases involve the full penis. Sometimes only the corpora cavernosa are engorged. When the corpus spongiosum is also erect, serious urinary difficulties may result. The urethra, which is the duct for urine excretion, runs down the middle of the corpus spongiosum. Constant prolonged restriction of the tube can lead to retention of urine in the bladder. In some cases catheterization (mechanical drainage) can relieve the buildup. If urine retention is not relieved, urine can back up into the kidneys, with serious kidney disease as a result.

Among mechanical causes of priapism are obstructions such as large blood clots or tumours in the penis. In rare cases, chronic priapism may result from exceptionally prolonged and rough copulation. It is caused by a blood clot (thrombosis) in the vein that releases the blood from the penis. It is distressing, lasting for days or weeks, and it generally leaves the affected person permanently impotent. The penis is at first tensely erect and painfully tender. After several days, there is gradual lessening of tension and pain, and the organ may remain semierect for weeks before it gradually returns to a flaccid state. In this prolonged period, the erectile tissue of the penis is replaced by nonfunctioning fibrous scar tissue, so the sufferer is rendered impotent. This type of priapism may be helped by early treatment with anticoagulant drugs or by drainage with large needles inserted into the erectile tissue. Ordinarily, treatment is directed toward the cause. Usually, the penis is surgically opened only when abscesses or tumours are involved.

Children have been known to have brief episodes of priapism from full bladders, local irritation, or prolonged masturbation. Disorders such as inflammation of the urethra, calcium stones in the urethra, infections of the prostate gland, or rectal parasites can also cause the condition. More prolonged cases arise from congenital syphilis, leukemia, or sickle cell anemia. Male infants and toddlers are not exempt, but in most cases the sufferer is older.

CHAPTER 5

Infections and Cancers of the Reproductive System

Infections and cancers of the human reproductive system can inflict irreversible damage to organs, resulting in structural and functional changes within the tissues. Many such conditions can affect not only the reproductive system but also other body systems, including the nervous and cardiovascular systems, and can significantly shorten an individual's life span. For example, some sexually transmitted diseases, such as AIDS (acquired immuno-deficiency syndrome), are chronic, involving the gradual degeneration of various body systems over the course of years and finally culminating in premature death. Other infectious conditions of the reproductive tissues, such as chancroid and pubic lice, may be painful and distressing, but they are often temporary and are easily treated with therapeutic agents. In contrast, cancers of the reproductive organs are complex diseases that typically require treatment tailored to the type of cancer. In many cases, surgical intervention is necessary to prevent the spread of the disease to other tissues. Removal of malignant tissue can substantially increase the patient's chances for survival.

SEXUALLY TRANSMITTED DISEASES

Sexually transmitted diseases (STDs) include any disease (such as syphilis, gonorrhea, AIDS, or a genital form of herpes simplex) that is usually or often transmitted from person to person by direct sexual contact. It may also be transmitted from a mother to her child before or at birth or, less frequently, may be passed from person to person in nonsexual contact (such as in kissing, in tainted blood transfusions, or in the use of unsanitized hypodermic syringes). Sexually transmitted diseases usually affect initially the genitals, the reproductive tract, the urinary tract, the oral cavity, the anus, or the rectum but may mature in the body to attack various organs and systems. Tertiary syphilis, or paresis, for example, may affect skin, bones, the central nervous system, the heart, the liver, or other organs. Persons infected by HIV (human immunodeficiency virus), which causes AIDS, may remain outwardly healthy for years before the disease takes hold within the immune system. The term venereal disease (VD), denoting any disease transmitted by sexual intercourse, lost favour in the late 20th century and was largely supplanted by the more comprehensive term sexually transmitted disease.

SYPHILIS AND GONORRHEA

Sexually transmitted diseases have a long history. The best known of these diseases, syphilis, is caused by the bacterium *Treponema pallidum*. Syphilis was first widely reported by European writers in the 16th century, and some medical historians assume that it was imported into Europe by explorers returning from the New World. Other authorities believe that syphilis is of ancient origin and may at one time have been mistakenly identified as leprosy. At any rate, syphilis first became widely recognized and reported about the year 1500, when an epidemic swept Europe.

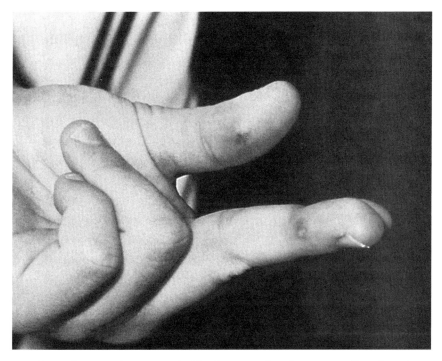

Gonorrhea sometimes enters the bloodstream, where it can cause disseminated gonococcal infection in almost any organ system. CDC/Dr. S. E. Thompson, VDCD/J. Pledger

Urethritis is the infection and inflammation of the urethra (the passage that transmits urine from the bladder to the exterior of the body). Most cases are sexually transmitted. Urethritis that is caused by the gonococcus bacterium (*Neisseria gonorrhoeae*) is called gonorrhea and is one of the best-known sexually transmitted diseases. Gonorrhea was named by the Greek physician Galen and is thought to have been known to the ancient Chinese and Egyptians.

Syphilis and gonorrhea were long thought to be one disease. Real progress in characterizing them did not occur until the early 20th century, when their different causative microorganisms were identified and reliable diagnostic tests were developed. Effective treatment in the form of sulfa drugs and penicillin was introduced in the 1930s and '40s, and the eradication of such diseases seemed imminent. By the end of the 1950s, however, the frequency index had begun to rise again. Among the many reasons cited were the tapering off of active "anti-VD" campaigns, the causative microorganisms' growing immunity to the antibiotics used in treatment, and a variety of sociological factors influencing sexual behaviour. The widespread acceptance of oral contraceptives and their supplantation of other methods of birth control were possibly linked, for a variety of reasons, to the spread of sexually transmitted diseases. Not only had the lack of oral contraceptives tended to discourage sexual promiscuity but also the older methods of condom and diaphragm had provided some protection against disease. Only with the outbreak of the AIDS epidemic did a return to the condom and "safe sex" receive new encouragement.

GENITAL HERPES

A disease that became especially widespread beginning in the 1960s and '70s was genital herpes. This condition is caused by an infectious agent known as HSV-2, or herpes simplex virus type 2. Following initial infection with HSV-2, which often produces symptoms such as genital pain and itching and the formation of blisters on the penis or vagina, the virus enters a state of dormancy within cells, and symptoms of infection subside. In many persons, periodic activation of the latent (dormant) virus occurs, giving rise to recurrent outbreaks that produce symptoms. In some individuals, recurrence is frequent and severe. The virus is highly contagious and can be transmitted by individuals who are lifelong carriers but who remain asymptomatic (and may not even know they are infected).

HSV-2 infections are most often acquired through direct genital contact. Sexual practices involving genital-oral contact may be responsible for HSV-2 infections of the mouth and lips. Similar infections may be the result of self-infection through hand-genital-mouth contact. Genital herpes infections are significant not only in terms of the discomfort they cause but also for the potentially serious illness that might occur in infants born to mothers with genital herpes infections. In addition, HSV-2 infections have been associated with the later development of cervical cancer in women. A variety of treatments have been used for genital herpes, but none have been entirely satisfactory. Thus, for many persons, genital herpes is a disease that remains with them throughout their lives.

AIDS

The sexually transmitted disease that caused perhaps the greatest alarm in the late 20th century was acquired immunodeficiency syndrome, or AIDS. From the time of its first clear identification in 1981, AIDS spread rapidly, with reported cases rising at a high rate, especially among homosexuals and intravenous drug users in the United States and western Europe and among heterosexuals in tropical Africa. The high mortality rate from AIDS and the absence of a cure or vaccine against the disease had a sobering effect on sexually permissive societies. Promiscuity tended to be more widely discouraged, and the adoption of practices presumed to constitute "safe sex" (or, rather, safer sex)—such as the use of condoms or avoiding anal intercourse—tended to be encouraged.

Prior to the development of screening procedures and heat-treating techniques that destroy HIV in blood products, transmission also occurred through contaminated blood products. Today, however, the risk of contracting

The rapid spread of AIDS in the 20th century caused great alarm, inspiring creative ad campaigns to encourage safe sex. Chung Sung-Jun/Getty Images

HIV from a blood transfusion is extremely small. The virus also can be transmitted across the placenta or through the breast milk from mother to infant. The administration of antiretroviral medications to both the mother and infant around the time of birth reduces the chance that the child will be infected with HIV. HIV is not spread by coughing, sneezing, or casual contact (e.g., shaking hands) because it is fragile and cannot survive long outside of the body.

The course of HIV infection involves three stages: primary HIV infection, the asymptomatic phase, and AIDS. During the first stage the transmitted HIV replicates rapidly, and some persons may experience an acute flulike illness that usually persists for one to two weeks. The second phase of HIV infection, the asymptomatic period, lasts an average of 10 years. During this period the virus continues to replicate, and there is a slow decrease in the number of immune cells capable of defending the body against the virus. Eventually, as levels of immune cells become very low, patients begin to experience opportunistic infections (infections that arise only in individuals with a defective immune system). This stage, the final stage in HIV infection, is known as AIDS.

There is no cure for AIDS, and thus prevention, such as through abstinence, using condoms, reducing intravenous drug use, and discouraging needle sharing, is imperative. HIV infection is treated using antiretroviral agents. However, because HIV rapidly becomes resistant to any single antiretroviral drug, combination treatment is necessary for effective suppression of the virus. Although patients successfully treated with combination therapies no longer suffer from AIDS-associated conditions, the virus is still capable of causing deterioration of the immune system.

CHLAMYDIA

Nearly a score of other sexually transmitted diseases are known. All have reasonably effective drug cures. About half of all cases of urethritis that are not gonorrhea are chlamydia, which is caused by an infection with *Chlamydia trachomatis*. The latter bacterium is also the infecting agent in pelvic inflammatory disease and in still another sexually transmitted disease, lymphogranuloma venereum. The cause for the remaining 50 percent of nongonococcal urethral infections is unknown. No organism has been definitely related.

TRICHOMONIASIS AND CANDIDIASIS

Trichomoniasis is an infection of the urogenital tract caused by a protozoan, *Trichomonas vaginalis*. Males usually have no symptoms with this infection, and only a portion of infected females have a vaginal discharge.

Candidiasis (yeast infection) is caused by *Candida albicans* (sometimes called *Monilia albicans*), which produces in women a thick, whitish vaginal discharge and causes irritation and itching in the genital area. Males may have irritation of the glans or skin of the penis. Because this yeast is ubiquitous in the environment, these infections are not always sexually acquired.

GENITAL WARTS

Warts occurring in the genital areas are caused by certain types of papilloma viruses, and these types of warts can be transmitted to other people by sexual contact. Most often, genital warts are nothing more than a nuisance, but occasionally they can become so numerous or so large as to interfere with urination, bowel movements, or vaginal delivery. There is also mounting evidence that papilloma viral infections of the genital tract are a factor in the development of cancer of the cervix and possibly of the genitals themselves.

CHANCROID AND GRANULOMA

Chancroid, granuloma inguinale, and lymphogranuloma venereum are three diseases that have their highest incidence in the tropics. Chancroid, also called soft chancre, is caused by the bacterium *Haemophilus ducreyi* and resembles in appearance the primary chancre of syphilis. Granuloma inguinale is thought to be caused by a bacterium, *Calymmatobacterium* (*Donovania*) *granulomatis*. The lesion begins as a small sore but may spread to involve large areas, usually in the genital region, in a destructive, ulcerating lesion. Lymphogranuloma venereum is caused by *Chlamydia trachomatis* and begins with a frequently unnoticed bump on the genitals. Later, lymph glands in the groin enlarge and may proceed to rupture and drain purulent material. Swelling of the genitals may develop much later.

CYTOMEGALOVIRUS AND HEPATITIS B

All the aforementioned diseases are spread primarily by sexual contact, but there are other diseases that are transmitted sexually only in a minority of cases. Chief among such diseases are cytomegalovirus, a viral infection that is ubiquitous in humans and is spread by various means, including sex, and the hepatitis B virus, which is spread primarily through intravenous injections and blood transfusions but can also be transmitted sexually.

Pubic Lice

Finally, a common infestation is pediculosis pubis. The crab louse, *Phthirus pubis,* infests the hair of the pubic region, where louse eggs, or nits, are attached to the hairs. After about one week the larvae hatch, and in about two weeks they develop into mature crab lice. The lice attach themselves to the base of the hair and feed on the blood of the host. Persons become aware of the infection because they see the lice or the eggs or because intense itching develops after two or three weeks.

OTHER INFECTIONS OF THE REPRODUCTIVE SYSTEM

There are a variety of other infections that affect the function of the reproductive system. The causes of these conditions are diverse, and thus they are not necessarily associated with the introduction of an infectious agent transmitted via sexual contact. Indeed, a host of reproductive infections can arise from poor hygiene, and in some cases the reproductive organs are affected by systemic diseases such as tuberculosis.

Puerperal Fever

Puerperal fever, also known as childbed fever, is an infection of some part of the female reproductive organs following childbirth or abortion. Cases of fever of 100.4 °F (38 °C) and higher during the first 10 days following delivery or miscarriage are notifiable to the civil authority in most developed countries, and the notifying physician clarifies the diagnosis later, if possible. Puerperal infection is most commonly of the raw surface of the interior of the uterus after separation of the placenta (afterbirth), but pathogenic organisms may also affect lacerations of any part of the genital tract. By whatever portal, they can invade the bloodstream and lymph system to cause septicemia (blood poisoning), cellulitis (inflammation of cellular tissue), and pelvic or generalized peritonitis (inflammation of the abdominal lining). The severity of the illness depends on the virulence of the infecting organism, the resistance of the invaded tissues, and the general health of the patient. Abortions performed in unhygienic surroundings commonly result in puerperal fever.

Organisms commonly producing this infection are *Streptococcus pyogenes*; staphylococci (inhabitants of the skin and of pimples, carbuncles, and many other pustular eruptions); the anaerobic streptococci, which flourish in devitalized tissues such as may be present after long and injurious labour and unskilled instrumental delivery; *Escherichia coli* and *Clostridium welchii* (inhabitants of the lower bowel); and, rarely and fatally, the bacillus of tetanus.

In the second half of the 20th century, puerperal fever became scarce in developed countries. The decline of the disease was partly attributed to improved environmental conditions, better obstetrical care, and the use of sulfonamides and antibiotics. Another reason appears to be a lessening of the virulence or invasiveness of *Streptococcus pyogenes*. This organism is also the cause of scarlet fever, which over the same period has also declined markedly in severity and incidence.

TUBERCULOSIS

Primary tuberculosis of the reproductive system is rare and is usually brought from elsewhere in the body through the bloodstream. Nodular or pustular lesions on the penis or scrotum of men or the vulva of women, resembling the gumma (nodules) of tertiary syphilis, may appear one week after tubercular infection. The nodules can become ulcerated, resembling the primary chancre of syphilis. Tubercular abscesses can also develop in most of the internal reproductive organs. Treatment consists of administration of antibiotics.

BALANITIS, POSTHITIS, AND EPIDIDYMITIS

Balanitis, or inflammation of the glans penis, and posthitis, or infection of the foreskin, result from the retention of secretions and bacteria beneath the foreskin and can be prevented with proper hygiene. Balanitis can also develop as a complication of certain sexually transmitted diseases. Acute prostatitis, inflammation of the prostate gland, may be caused by any of a variety of microorganisms, including those cause sexually transmitted diseases. Chronic prostatitis, the most common reproductive system infection in men older than age 50, often follows the acute infection. Epididymitis, inflammation of the epididymis, can result in sterility. All these are nonspecific infections that must be treated with antibiotics appropriate for the causative organisms.

ORCHITIS

Orchitis is inflammation and swelling of the testes as a result of infection or physical injury. The rich blood supply and lymphatic supply in the testes prevent most infections from obtaining a strong foothold in these organs. Infections can spread from elsewhere in the body by way of the bloodstream, lymphatic channels, or the spermatic cords to the epididymides and testes. Organisms causing inflammation can be bacterial, viral, fungal, or parasitic, and inflammation can come from chemical or physical

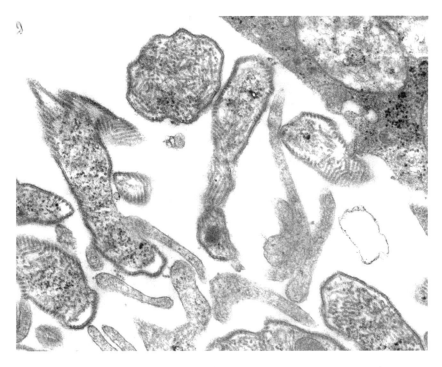

Transmission electron micrograph of mumps virions. A. Harrison and F. A. Murphy/Centers for Disease Control and Prevention (CDC) (Image Number: 8757)

injury. The usual symptoms of orchitis are high fever, sudden pain in the testicle, nausea, vomiting, swelling, tightness, and tenderness of the gland upon touching. Fluids that may accumulate around the testes may contain pus or blood. The scrotum is generally red and thickened.

Orchitis may result from infections and other diseases elsewhere in the body. Mumps is probably the systemic disease most likely to affect the testes because it is caused by a virus. The orchitis generally subsides spontaneously in 10 days or less and permanent damage is rare. Usually, only one testis is influenced, with sometimes the epididymis, but in the rare cases where both testes are involved, impotence and sterility may ensue.

Physical injuries, such as those caused by blows, are generally followed by infections when severe because the injury lowers the resistance to bacteria. Chemicals such as iodine, lead, and alcohol have on occasion caused testicular injury. Treatment for most orchitis is administration of antibiotics, bed rest, support of the testes, use of compresses, and surgical relief or drainage when required.

VESICULITIS

Vesiculitis is inflammation and infection of the seminal vesicles in the male reproductive tract. The seminal vesicles are ductlike glands that add fluid secretions to the seminal fluid as it passes from the body during intercourse. Infections present in the prostate or related organs usually also involve the seminal vesicles. Infections can reach the glands through the urethra or by way of the bloodstream.

The symptoms of vesiculitis are similar to those in cases of prostate infection. They may include a dull aching pain in the abdomen, discomfort in the urethra, pain after sexual intercourse, the presence of blood in the seminal fluid, premature or painful ejaculation, and impotence. Treatment is usually administration of antibiotics.

LEUKORRHEA

Leukorrhea is the flow of a whitish, yellowish, or greenish discharge from the vagina of the female. Such discharges may originate from the vagina, ovaries, fallopian tubes, or, most commonly, the cervix. Leukorrhea may occur during pregnancy and is considered normal when the discharge is thin, white, and relatively odourless. Physiologic leukorrhea is a normal condition occurring within several months to a year of the onset of menses in adolescent girls and is sometimes present in newborn girls, usually lasting one to two months. However, in many cases, leukorrhea is a sign of infection, especially when the discharge is yellow or green, has an offensive odour, and is accompanied by irritation, itching, pain, or tissue inflammation.

Abnormal leukorrhea may be caused by infections with bacteria, yeast, or other microorganisms. For example, many sexually transmitted diseases are major causes of leukorrhea. These diseases lead to infection of the cervix, which is indeed one of the most common gynecological disorders. The infection has a tendency to irritate the mucus glands of the cervix, causing them to secrete an excess of mucous mixed with pus. Leukorrhea is also a sign of vaginitis (inflammation of the vagina), which may give rise to an irritating discharge that is often quite resistant to treatment. A tampon, diaphragm, or other foreign object left too long in the vagina can also cause leukorrhea. Douching (washing the vagina with a stream of liquid) is not recommended because this practice often disturbs the balance of normal vaginal flora, thereby exacerbating infection. A clinical examination to determine the cause of the discharge is necessary. Treatment is aimed at eliminating the underlying cause and typically involves administration of an antimicrobial agent.

VAGINITIS

Vaginitis is inflammation of the vagina, usually caused by infection. The chief symptom is the abnormal flow of a whitish or yellowish discharge from the vagina (leukorrhea). The treatment of vaginitis depends on the cause of the inflammation. Several different microorganisms can produce vaginitis in women of reproductive age. Atrophic vaginitis, caused by reduced estrogen levels, can occur in women after menopause; and certain chemicals can cause an irritant or allergic vaginitis.

Among the microorganisms that commonly cause vaginitis are *Candida albicans*, a common yeast that is the cause of candidiasis; *Gardnerella* bacteria; and *Trichomonas vaginalis*, a protozoan. The last two types of vaginal infections are usually transmitted through sexual contact. Candidiasis can also occur during pregnancy and can cause infant thrush in children born to infected mothers. Treatment of these infectious forms of vaginitis is by appropriate antimicrobial drugs.

Atrophic vaginitis occurs in postmenopausal women because the lack of estrogen stimulation causes the surface membrane of the vagina to become thin, dry, and fragile, increasing the likelihood of infection. Hormone replacement therapy restores the protective surface and eliminates vaginitis.

Vulvitis

Vulvitis is inflammation and infection of the vulva—the external genitalia of the female. The external organs of the vulva include the labia majora and minora (folds of skin), the clitoris, and the vestibular glands. The basic symptoms of vulvitis are superficial red, swollen, and moisture-laden lesions on the skin of the vulva. Itching sensations are a particularly prominent and consistent symptom. The areas of affected vulvar skin may turn white, crack, or develop fluid-filled blisters that break open, ooze, and crust over.

The skin of the vulva is subject to all the irritations, infections, and other conditions that affect skin elsewhere on the body. Moreover, the skin of the vulva is unusually susceptible to irritation because it is moist and warm.

Besides sometimes providing a breeding ground for bacteria, these conditions can render the vulva susceptible to allergic or inflammatory reactions from direct contact with underwear or commercial hygiene products. The vulva can become the site of infections by bacteria, fungi, or viruses, and vulvitis may also accompany similar infections of the vagina (vaginitis). Depletion of estrogen, as occurs in postmenopausal women, can lead to drying and thinning of the vulvar tissues, rendering them more susceptible to irritation and infection. The vulva can be contaminated by urine, feces, vaginal discharges, and menstrual flow.

Among the most common causes of vulvitis are inflammations arising from vulvar skin's allergic reaction to soaps, vaginal sprays and deodorants, sanitary napkins, panty hose, synthetic underwear, or the detergents used to wash underwear. Allergic reactions usually take a few days to manifest themselves and produce such symptoms as itching, mild redness, and swelling.

Vulvitis may also be caused by fungi, bacteria, or herpes or other viral infections. Fungal diseases of the vulva are common, and usually the agent of infection is *Candida albicans,* a yeastlike fungus. Women with diabetes are especially susceptible to these infections, as are women who eat large amounts of carbohydrates (starches). *Gardnerella vaginalis* is the most common bacterial cause of vulvitis. *Mycoplasma, Escherichia coli*, and staphylococci and streptococci may also cause infections. Tight, nonporous, nonabsorbent underwear in combination with poor hygiene may foster the growth of bacterial or fungal infections on the vulvar skin.

A cortisone cream is sometimes used to relieve the itching of vulvitis until a specific therapy can be decided upon. The particular causative agent of the condition must be isolated if treatment is to be effective. Wearing loose, absorbent underwear that allows the circulation of air is often the only necessary treatment for contact vulvitis. The substitution of cotton for synthetic garments may also help to alleviate the problem. Vulvitis arising from fungal and bacterial infections is usually treated by the topical application of creams that kill the causative microorganisms. *Candida* vulvitis is treated with clotrimazole, nystatin, or miconazole creams; *Gardnerella* and other bacterial infections with metronidazole; and *Chlamydia* infections with the antibiotics doxycycline or erythromycin.

CERVICITIS

Cervicitis is inflammation of the uterine cervix. The narrow central canal of the cervix is lined with a moist mucous membrane, and it contains mucous glands. The cervix secretes most of the mucus and other fluids found in the reproductive tract. In normal circumstances, the secretions help to preserve and transport sperm from the male, and they keep the vagina bathed in fluids. However, these properties of the cervix also make it an excellent warm, secluded spot for bacterial invasion and growth. Vaginal infections can easily spread to the cervix. Poor drainage or blockage of the cervix causes a chronic infection. Irritation can be caused by trauma incurred during abortions or delivery, medical instruments, cauterization, radiation therapy, or intrauterine contraceptive devices. Cervicitis is most common during the years of active menstruation. It seldom affects young girls and is only occasionally found in older women.

Infections can be localized in one part of the cervix, or they may affect the whole structure. When the whole cervix is involved in an acute infection, there is inflammation and swelling of the mucous membrane. The cervix is enlarged, firm, congested with blood, and filled with tissue fluids. The vagina is also reddened and glazed from irritation caused by the discharge. In the chronic condition, the discharge is thicker but less abundant and irritating. Usually, there is no pain. The chronic infection can spread to surrounding tissue. Common causes of a chronic condition are radiation therapy, surgical operations, deep lacerations, or deep cauterization. Overgrowth of the mucous membrane causes cervical polyps (projecting lumps of tissue). The major symptom of all cervicitis is a profuse creamy-yellow or grayish-green discharge that may have an unpleasant odour and may be irritating. The excessive discharge can inhibit fertilization.

Cervicitis may worsen during pregnancy. The eroded surface enlarges, polyps increase in size, and discharges are more prevalent. Infections can cause constrictions of the cervix, which may lead to difficult labour. Treatment of cervicitis may be cauterization, prophylactic (protective) measures, or, sometimes, surgery. Surgical procedures include cervix repair or removal. The latter does not prohibit further pregnancies.

Mastitis

Mastitis is inflammation of the breast in women. Acute mastitis is a sudden infectious inflammation caused usually by the bacterium *Staphylococcus aureus,* or sometimes by streptococcus organisms. It begins almost exclusively during the first three weeks of nursing and is limited to the period of lactation (milk production). The bacterial organisms invade the breast through cracks in the nipples, the exposed lymphatic ducts, or the milk ducts. Irregular nursing, which leads to overfilling of the

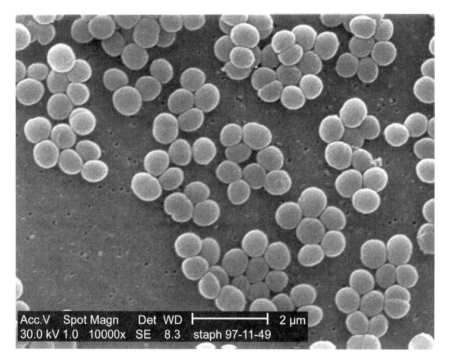

Microscopic image of Staphylococcus aureus, *the causative agent of mastitis; magnified 10,000x.* Matthew J. Arduino, DRPH; Janice Carr/Centers for Disease Control and Prevention (CDC)(Image Number: 6486)

breasts, increases the effects of infections. The breasts become swollen, painful, reddened, hardened, and tender. The infection may be in one or both breasts and can be localized or spread over an area. Purulent discharges may occur, frequently indicating abscess formation. Abscesses may remain internal or they may involve the skin. The lymphatic system's nodes and vessels are commonly enlarged and tender. Acute mastitis accompanied by abscesses is often mistaken for acute inflammatory carcinoma (cancer) of the breasts. In a female child, after birth and during puberty, there may be brief episodes of breast inflammation, which are usually hormone induced and are not caused by bacterial infection.

Chronic mastitis is usually a secondary effect of systemic diseases such as tuberculosis, fungal infections, yeast infections, or syphilis. A relatively uncommon type of mastitis, called plasma cell mastitis, occurs most frequently in older women who have had a number of children and have a history of difficulty in nursing. It is sometimes hard to distinguish from cancer of the breast. In this disease lymphatic fluids stagnate in the breast, and the stagnated fluids are treated by the body as foreign objects. Plasma cells, white blood cells, and fatty acid crystals accumulate, and fatty tissue suffers degeneration. A hard lump forms under part of the nipple, and there may be distortion of the nipple because of the lesion. The nipple area is painful, tender, and inflamed and may exude a cloudy discharge. The milk ducts and lymph nodes are commonly thickened and enlarged. As the condition progresses, small areas of the breast become hardened as the original tissue is destroyed and replaced by fibrous or granular tissue.

Injury to the breast tissue is sometimes followed by inflammation and necrosis (death) of the fatty tissue resulting in a hard fixed lump with no skin discoloration. The symptoms of mastitis may be present for many years or may arise after a disease of the breast that involves purulent discharges and abscesses.

Pelvic Inflammatory Disease

Pelvic inflammatory disease (PID) is a general acute inflammation of the pelvic cavity in women, caused by bacterial infection of the cervix, uterus, ovaries, or fallopian tubes. The disease is most often transmitted by sexual intercourse and is usually the result of infection with gonorrhea or chlamydia. Women who use intrauterine devices (IUDs) are somewhat more likely to contract PID because some types of these devices enable infective bacteria to gain entry to the upper reproductive tract (via the cervix) more easily. PID occurs mainly in sexually active women who are younger than age 25.

The symptoms of PID are similar to and may be mistaken for those of gonorrhea. They include pain in the abdomen and lower pelvis, chills, nausea, fever, and a thick and peculiarly odorous vaginal discharge. The major complication of PID is scarring of the fallopian tubes, often resulting in infertility. Indeed, PID is a major cause of female infertility. The incidence of ectopic pregnancies (i.e., those in which the fertilized ovum becomes embedded outside the uterus) is much higher in women with a history of PID.

The treatment of PID consists of antibiotic therapy to fight the infection. The diagnosis and treatment of male sexual partners of women with PID is also called for because failure to do so exposes the women to further infections.

HYPERPLASIA AND MAJOR CANCERS OF THE REPRODUCTIVE ORGANS

The organs of the reproductive tract can be affected by hyperplasia, an abnormal increase in the number of cells in a tissue, and by cancer, the malignant, uncontrolled growth of cells within a tissue. Hyperplasia frequently results in the formation of a tumour, which may be benign (or relatively harmless). However, in some instances, tumours become malignant, giving rise to cancer, which can spread from the affected tissue and cause disease within other organs of the body. Examples of major cancers of the reproductive organs include testicular cancer, prostate cancer, and cervical cancer.

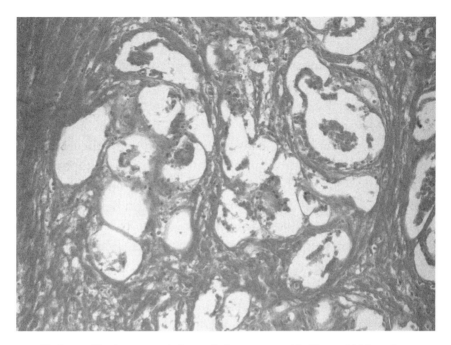

Undetected benign prostatic hyperplasia may cause bladder and kidney damage, but the prognosis is good with early detection and treatment. CMSP/J. L. Carson/Getty Images

BENIGN PROSTATIC HYPERPLASIA

Benign prostatic hyperplasia, an overgrowth of normal glandular and muscular elements of the prostate gland, arises in the immediate vicinity of the urethra and is the most frequent cause of urinary obstruction. The enlarged prostate usually causes symptoms after age 40. If undetected, the obstruction may cause bladder and kidney damage. The diagnosis is made by rectal examination or ultrasound, intravenous pyelogram (an X-ray of the urinary tract), and cystoscopy (direct viewing of the bladder and urethra). Treatment is by surgical removal of the excess tissue. The prognosis is good if detection is early and treatment occurs before the kidneys are damaged.

TESTICULAR CANCER

Testicular tumours are usually malignant and most often occur between ages 15 and 35. This type of cancer accounts for about 1 percent of all malignant growths in men. Most testicular tumours (greater than 90 percent) are of types that do not reproduce cells resembling those of the tissue of origin. The major route of metastases for these types of tumours is via the lymphatic system. The lymph nodes in the groin and the mediastinum—the region between the lungs—are most commonly involved, but the lungs and liver are also frequent sites of tumour spread. The remaining 10 percent of the testicular tumours, which usually resemble the cells from which they arise, include the hormone-secreting tumours. In general, these tumours have been described in all age groups, are usually benign, and frequently arise in individuals with poorly developed or undescended testes.

The most common symptom first observed in all groups is painless enlargement of the testis. If, after careful examination, biopsy, or ultrasound, a tumour cannot be ruled out, the testicle may be removed for microscopic examination. Further treatment may consist of radiation or chemotherapy.

PROSTATE CANCER

Prostate cancer is rare before age 50 but increases in frequency every decade thereafter. It is the third most common cancer in males, second only to lung and stomach cancer. Like most tumours, prostate cancer has various causes, but it is thought to be influenced largely by androgens. The progress of the cancer is so slow that, by the time it produces symptoms of urinary obstruction or sexual dysfunction, metastasis has occurred in many cases, most frequently to the spine, the pelvic bones, or the upper portions of the thighbones.

The diagnosis of prostate cancer is made by rectal examination or transrectal ultrasound (TRUS). Tests that detect elevated levels of prostate-specific antigen (PSA) in the blood are also used to detect tumours of the prostate. If preliminary tests suggest prostate cancer, a biopsy is performed to confirm the diagnosis. If the tumour is discovered before it has extended beyond the prostate, the gland may be surgically removed. If spread has occurred, treatment may include radiation, hormone therapy, chemotherapy, or a combination of these approaches.

VULVAR CANCER

Primary carcinoma of the vulva usually occurs in women older than age 50 and usually arises from the labia majora or labia minora. Most patients first notice a lump on the vulva or perineum. The diagnosis is made by examination of a specimen of tissues, and treatment consists of radiation, chemotherapy, or surgery.

CERVICAL CANCER

The causes of cervical cancer vary, but most cases are caused by complications associated with human papillomavirus (HPV) infection. The average age of occurrence for cancer of the cervix is 45. Symptoms include vaginal bleeding or other discharge, pelvic pain, or pain during intercourse. The initial diagnosis is made by a Pap smear, a test in which cells obtained from the cervix are examined for cancer cells. The final diagnosis rests on examining specimens of tissue from the cervix, obtained from a

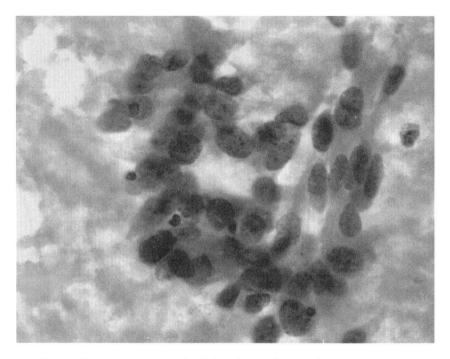

Routine Pap smears can reveal cellular abnormalities, such as cervical cancer, as shown in these cells. Spike Walker/Stone/Getty Images

biopsy or colposcopy. Treatment is usually radiation, chemotherapy, or surgery, depending on the size of the lesion. The prospect of five-year survival is quite high if the cancer has not spread beyond the cervix.

UTERINE AND OVARIAN CANCER

Cancer of the lining of the uterus (endometrium) is the most common cancer of the female genital tract. The risk factors of uterine cancer stem from an imbalance in which the levels of the hormone estrogen in the uterus are regularly higher than the levels of progesterone. The peak incidence is in the mid-50s, and there is also a strikingly high incidence in women who have not borne children.

The chief symptom of the cancer is postmenopausal uterine bleeding or discharge. An examination of a specimen of endometrial tissue must be performed in order to diagnose uterine cancer. The treatment is primarily surgical but is often supplemented with chemotherapy, radiation, or hormone therapy. The survival rate from this disease is relatively good if the tumour is confined to the uterine body.

The treatment of ovarian cancer consists of surgery, radiation, chemotherapy, or a combination of these approaches. The prognosis is variable and depends on the type of tumour as well as the extent of metastasis.

CHAPTER 6

INFERTILITY AND DISORDERS OF PREGNANCY

I nfertility is the inability of a couple to conceive and reproduce. Infertility can affect the female as well as the male. There are many different causes of infertility, ranging from genetic conditions to physical trauma that damages reproductive tissues. Human behaviours, including smoking and excessive alcohol consumption, also can decrease fertility. Fortunately, advances in assistive reproductive technologies have enabled many infertile couples to conceive.

Women are also susceptible to various disorders that may arise during pregnancy. These conditions can result from any of a number of abnormal processes, from aberrant blastocyst implantation to abnormalities in the development of the placenta or in the formation of the umbilical cord. In some cases, disorders affecting the conceptus are severe and prompt the natural termination of pregnancy through miscarriage (spontaneous expulsion of the embryo or fetus from the uterus). In other cases, the condition of being pregnant causes abnormal physiological changes in the mother. Among the most common of these maternal conditions is gestational diabetes mellitus, a temporary disorder of carbohydrate metabolism.

INFERTILITY

Infertility is defined as the failure to conceive after one year of regular intercourse without contraception or the inability of a woman to carry a pregnancy to a live birth.

Infertility can affect either the male or the female and can result from a number of causes. About 1 in every 10 couples is infertile, or somewhere between 10 and 15 percent of the population.

Normal fertility depends on the production of a sufficient number of healthy, motile sperm by the male, delivery of those cells into the vagina, successful passage of the sperm through the uterus and into the fallopian tubes, and penetration of a normal ovum (egg) by one of the sperm. A successful pregnancy also requires that the fertilized ovum subsequently become implanted in the lining of the female uterus. A problem at any one of these stages can result in a couple's infertility.

Factors that can have deleterious effects on reproductive capacity in both men and women include previous and current alcohol consumption and drug use, a history of sexually transmitted diseases (STDs), and a number of general medical problems. The effect of smoking on reproduction is considerable. Cigarette smoke is known to contain hundreds of toxic substances, the negative health effects of which have been well documented. By interfering with the production of sperm, smoking can adversely affect male fertility. In women, smoking can affect different stages in the reproductive process, from the pickup of the ovum by the fallopian tube to the growth and development of the fetus.

The inability to conceive when desired has been a problem throughout recorded history. The development of modern infertility treatments has enabled many infertile men and women to produce children. However, these treatments have raised many concerns because they significantly increase the chances for multiple births (multiple fetuses carried to term in a single pregnancy). Multiple births are extremely risky. The babies who survive gestation are often born prematurely and at very low birth weights. These babies are further predisposed to physical, mental, and developmental health problems, as well as neurological disorders such as cerebral palsy.

FEMALE INFERTILITY

Female infertility may be caused by ovulatory, cervical, and uterine factors, as well as by advanced age. Repeated abortions followed by dilatation and curettage (dilation of the cervix and scraping of the endometrial lining) can cause intrauterine scar formation and thereby interfere with implantation of the fertilized ovum. The presence of adhesions (rubbery or filmy bands of scar tissue) in and around the fallopian tubes interferes with the ability of the tube to take up the ovum after it has been released from an ovary and can affect movement of the sperm through the tube. Congenital anatomic deformities of the uterus may contribute to infertility by causing recurrent miscarriages. Another cause of infertility is gonadal dysgenesis, a condition in which the ovaries form but contain no eggs.

Aging

Female fertility begins declining when a woman is in her mid-30s, about 10 years before the onset of menopause. Age-related decline in fertility is a consequence of both a decrease in the woman's ovarian function and a reduction in her ovaries' reserve of eggs. An important marker of this process is follicle-stimulating hormone (FSH), which controls the development of eggs in the ovaries and occurs in elevated levels in the blood during menopause. In addition, with increasing age in women there is increased risk for chromosomal abnormalities in the fetus—most notably, Down syndrome. An increase in the incidence of miscarriages is also seen in older women. This means that even if normal fertilization takes place, the resulting embryo has a decreased chance of implanting normally. The reason for this reduced implantation rate is unclear but probably has more to do with the poor quality of the ovum than it does with any abnormality in the woman's uterine environment. Successful pregnancies have been achieved in older women who have undergone in vitro fertilization (IVF) with a donor egg from a young woman.

Disorders of Ovulation

Ovulation disorders are responsible for approximately 25 percent of female infertility problems. Anovulation (failure to ovulate) and oligoovulation (irregular ovulatory cycles) are among the most common disorders, and there are several tests that can be used to determine whether ovulation is occurring on a regular basis. For example, daily measurements of basal body temperature can be charted and used to track progesterone production by the corpus luteum. Progesterone increases a woman's body temperature by about 0.5 °C (1 °F) around mid-cycle, indicating that ovulation has occurred. Ovulatory status can also be confirmed by testing the urine for preovulatory elevation of luteinizing hormone (LH), which controls the development of ova in the ovaries. Sensitive LH test kits, which a woman can use at home, detect increases of this hormone. Examination of the ovaries by pelvic ultrasound can also determine whether ovulation is occurring. In addition, when progesterone levels in the blood are measured, an elevated level of the hormone indicates that ovulation has occurred.

Several drugs, notably clomiphene citrate, bromocriptine, and human menopausal gonadotropin, have successfully corrected hormonal imbalances that cause erratic or absent ovulation. However, these "fertility drugs" also increase a woman's chances of having multiple births, owing to the release of more than one ovum at ovulation under the influence of the drug.

Damage of the Fallopian Tubes

Blockage and scarring of the fallopian tubes—the passageways for the sperm and ova—are other common causes of infertility. A number of conditions can result in tubal scarring or obstruction, including untreated pelvic inflammatory disease (PID), an infection of the upper reproductive tract. PID often follows infection with an STD, such as gonorrhea or chlamydia.

The traditional test for evaluating the patency (openness) of the fallopian tubes is a radiological exam called hysterosalpingography. Dye injected through the cervix flows into the uterus and through the fallopian tubes. X-rays can then precisely define abnormalities in the fallopian tubes. Spillage of the dye into the abdominal cavity is an indication of tubal patency. A more direct procedure for evaluating the fallopian tubes is salpingoscopy. A flexible fibre-optic instrument with camera attachments is introduced into the abdominal cavity. This procedure allows detection of subtle abnormalities in the lining of the fallopian tube that can contribute to infertility. Salpingoscopy "scores" are assigned on the basis of the extent of abnormalities found in the tube. The scores have been shown to be highly predictive of the ability to achieve pregnancy. The falloposcope is another device that permits visualization of the interior of the entire fallopian tube. A flexible guidewire is introduced through a catheter into the fallopian tube to the point of obstruction. The wire is then removed, and a tiny camera with an outer diameter of no more than 0.5 mm (0.02 inch), attached to another wire, photographs the area of obstruction and allows the overall quality of the tubal lining to be assessed.

Microsurgical reconstruction of the fallopian tube can be used to remove an obstruction and, as a result, correct the underlying fertility problem. Less invasive techniques also may be used to unblock obstructed fallopian tubes. For example, balloon tuboplasty involves the insertion of a catheter through the cervix into the fallopian tube to the point of obstruction. A small deflated balloon is then inserted through the catheter and inflated to dilate the tube. Aqueous dissection (flushing with water) is another method for eliminating blockages, which is often done during falloposcopy to flush out tube-obstructing mucus plugs. When these procedures are successful, other fertility treatments may not be needed.

Uterine Fibroids

Uterine fibroids (also called uterine leiomyomata), which occur in one in every four or five American women, are benign tumours that originate from the smooth muscle cells within the muscular wall of the uterus. Fibroids can cause excessive uterine bleeding and pain, as well as a sensation of pressure in the uterus, and may contribute to infertility by interfering with ovum implantation or by compressing the opening of the fallopian tubes so that the sperm are prevented from reaching the ovum. Occasionally, excision of fibroids that are protruding into the endometrial cavity is necessary.

Endometriosis

Endometriosis is a condition in which the lining of the uterus, which is normally shed during menstruation, grows outside the uterine cavity. It is estimated to affect 1 in 10 women of reproductive age. Common symptoms are pain before, during, and after the menstrual period, pain during sexual intercourse, and spotting (bleeding between periods). In some cases, however, a woman does not experience symptoms.

The condition is diagnosed and assessed by laparoscopy, an outpatient procedure performed under general anesthesia. In most cases a 5- to 10-mm (0.2- to 0.4-inch) incision is made just below the navel, after which the abdominal cavity is distended with carbon dioxide gas. The physician then inserts a narrow lighted tube that allows visualization of the entire reproductive anatomy. Depending on the nature and extent of the endometrial growths, laparoscopic surgical procedures may be undertaken at the same time, using instruments that are guided into the abdominal cavity through additional small incisions in the abdomen. The goal of surgical therapy is to excise or destroy all endometrial growths without damaging adjacent tissues.

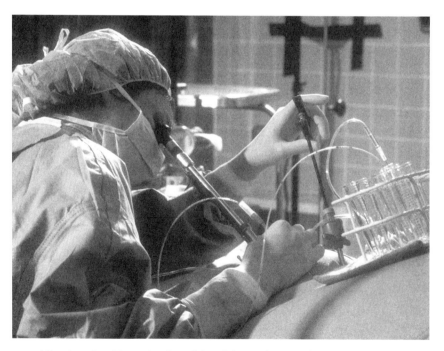

Allowing visual investigation of the abdominal cavity, laparoscopy was initially used to diagnose pain, but it now helps prepare for in vitro fertilization and other surgeries. Yvonne Hemsey/Getty Images

The use of various medications is an alternative to surgery. Agents used in the treatment of endometriosis include GnRH (gonadotropin-releasing hormone) agonists, which act on the pituitary gland; various progesterone preparations; danazol, a testosterone derivative; and nonsteroidal anti-inflammatory medications, such as ibuprofen or naprosyn (naproxen). Medication offers the advantage of treating lesions that may not have been detected visually, and it avoids complications associated with postoperative scarring. Treatment of endometriosis—whether by drugs, surgery, or a combination of both—often alleviates infertility. However, some women, even after treatment, may still be unable to conceive.

MALE INFERTILITY

The causes of male infertility include problems with sperm production, blockage of the sperm-delivery system, the presence of antibodies against sperm, testicular injury, anatomic abnormalities, and the presence of a varicose vein around the testicle (varicocele). All these causes can affect sperm quality or quantity.

Sperm number, concentration, motility, and morphology (shape) are usually assessed by means of a microscopic examination of the semen. Sperm count is the total number of sperm in the ejaculate. Counts vary widely, but values less than 20 million are usually considered low. Low sperm count is generally referred to as oligospermia. In some cases, male infertility is caused by complete absence of sperm in the ejaculate, a condition known as azoospermia. This condition can be caused by an obstruction of the genital tract, testicular dysfunction associated with congenital disorders such as sickle cell disease, or various illnesses.

Sperm concentration is the number of sperm per cubic centimetre of semen. Sperm concentrations of 20 million to 250 million per cubic centimetre are usually considered normal, but fertilization of an ovum can be achieved by men with values well below this range. Older men produce fewer and less-motile sperm, and advancing age is associated with a drop in circulating testosterone levels, as well as a decrease in the overall functioning of the testicles.

ASSISTIVE REPRODUCTIVE TECHNOLOGIES AND ARTIFICIAL INSEMINATION

Assistive reproductive technologies are infertility treatments in which both eggs and sperm are handled in a laboratory. There are several assistive approaches that effectively help infertile couples to conceive, including in vitro fertilization and intracytoplasmic sperm injection. Although artificial insemination is not considered an assistive technology because only sperm are handled, this approach has proven successful in enabling some infertile couples to conceive.

In Vitro Fertilization

In vitro fertilization (IVF), also called test-tube conception, is a medical procedure in which mature egg cells are removed from a woman, fertilized with male sperm outside the body, and inserted into the uterus of the same or another woman for normal gestation. Although IVF with reimplantation of fertilized eggs (ova) has long been widely used in animal breeding, the first successful birth of a human child from IVF, carried out by British gynecologist Patrick Steptoe and British medical researcher Robert Edwards, did not take place until 1978. A controversial aspect of IVF is the exceptionally high risk of multiple births associated with the procedure. Indeed, more than

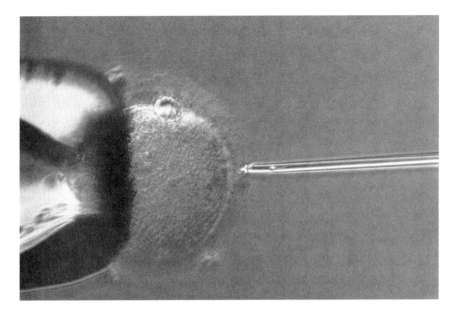

With in vitro fertilization, a woman's mature egg cells are fertilized with male sperm outside the body and then inserted into the uterus of the same or another woman for gestation. Mark Harmel/Stone/Getty Images

one-third of IVF pregnancies result in twins or triplets, and 1 percent result in even higher order multiples.

Evaluation and Technique

In vitro fertilization is generally undertaken only after an exhaustive evaluation of infertility has been made. Many IVF candidates are women who suffer from blocked or absent fallopian tubes, whereas others are couples in which the male partner has a low sperm count or couples whose infertility is unexplained. The IVF procedure includes the recovery (by needle aspiration) of mature ova and the incubation of the ova in a culture medium, as well as the collection and preparation of sperm and its addition to the medium. In certain cases (e.g., low sperm count) intracytoplasmic sperm injection (ICSI) may be necessary. This approach is often taken when a man has very low sperm counts or has sperm that for some other reason are unable to fertilize an ovum. In this technique DNA (deoxyribonucleic acid) from sperm is injected via a needle into an ovum. Fertilization generally occurs within 12 to 48 hours. The potential embryo is then placed in a growth medium, where it is observed periodically for division into two-, four-, and eight-cell stages. During this period the mother receives progesterone to prepare her uterine lining for implantation of the embryo. The embryo, which at this point is known as a blastocyst, is introduced through the cervix into the uterus, in which the blastocyst seems to float free for about three-and-a-half days. If the procedure is successful, the embryo implants itself in the uterine wall, and pregnancy begins. The first child conceived by this method was born in 1992.

If a man has an obstruction in the genital tract that prevents sperm from moving through the genital ducts, sperm needed for ICSI can be taken directly from the epididymis, the coiled channels that provide nourishment to the sperm. This is done by using a needle in a procedure known as microsurgical epididymal sperm aspiration (MESA).

Failure of IVF is typically the result of unsuccessful implantation or miscarriage. Possible explanations for failed implantation are immune rejection by the woman; an embryo with an abnormally thick outer membrane (zona pellucida) that prevents embryo hatching once inside the uterine cavity; lack of synchronization between embryonic stage and endometrial development at the time of embryo introduction into the uterus; and embryonic aneuploidy (abnormal chromosome number). Aneuploidy is a central cause of miscarriage in IVF.

Preimplantation Genetic Diagnosis

In women who have had repeated IVF failures or who are older than 38 years old, the success of IVF may be improved by preimplantation genetic diagnosis (PGD). PGD is used to detect the presence of embryonic genetic abnormalities that have a high likelihood of causing implantation failure or miscarriage. In PGD a single cell is extracted from the embryo once the embryo has divided to produce more than five cells. (This step—the extraction of a cell—is an inherent risk of PGD because it sometimes damages the embryo.) The cell is then analyzed by fluorescence in situ hybridization (FISH), a technique capable of detecting structural abnormalities in chromosomes that standard tests such as karyotyping cannot detect. In some cases DNA is isolated from the cell and analyzed by polymerase chain reaction (PCR) for the detection of gene mutations that can give rise to certain disorders such as Tay-Sachs disease or cystic fibrosis.

Another technique, known as comparative genomic hybridization (CGH), may be used in conjunction with PGD to identify chromosomal abnormalities. CGH is more sensitive than FISH and is capable of detecting a variety of small chromosomal rearrangements, deletions, and duplications. CGH is particularly useful in reducing the chance of multiple births (multiple embryos implanted and carried to term simultaneously) by identifying a single healthy embryo with the best chance for successful implantation. The success of IVF can also be improved through assisted hatching, a technique used to thin the outer membrane of an embryo in order to facilitate implantation.

Variations of IVF

A procedure called gamete intrafallopian transfer, or GIFT, is a variation of IVF. After the ovaries have been stimulated and mature oocytes collected, the latter are mixed with sperm and, under laparoscopic guidance, placed in the unobstructed fallopian tube. Fertilization then occurs naturally—inside the body (in vivo)—rather than in the laboratory. Although this procedure is usually used when a woman has at least one normal fallopian tube, unlike standard IVF, GIFT requires anesthesia.

Zygote intrafallopian transfer, or ZIFT, is another IVF variation, one that is generally reserved for women who have cervical damage but at least one unblocked fallopian tube. As in IVF, oocytes are removed and fertilized in the laboratory. Before it divides (i.e., at the zygote, or pronuclear, stage), the fertilized ovum is transferred to the unblocked fallopian tube. ZIFT and IVF have an advantage over GIFT in that fertilization has already occurred. Similar to IVF, a controversial risk associated with these procedures is multiple births.

Ethical Issues

IVF has been a source of moral, ethical, and religious controversy since its development. Although members of all religious groups can be found on both sides of the issues the major opposition has come from the Roman Catholic church, which in 1987 issued a doctrinal statement opposing IVF on three grounds: (1) the destruction of human embryos not used for implantation; (2) the possibility of in vitro fertilization by a donor other than the husband, thus removing reproduction from the marital context; and (3) the severing of an essential connection between the conjugal act and procreation.

Other ethical questions raised have involved the unusually high rate of multiple births (twins, triplets, etc.) associated with IVF. This issue is addressed primarily through the development of better techniques aimed at using fewer fertilized embryos to achieve pregnancy. For example, in the 1980s and 1990s an average of four fertilized embryos were transferred into a woman's uterus to increase the chance of implantation and pregnancy. However, in the early 2000s, following the implementation of improved methods, just two embryos were transferred, maintaining the same rate of success as with four embryos.

The technique of single embryo transfer (SET) is available, but less than 10 percent of women opt for it because it has a lower rate of success relative to multiple embryo transfer. In many cases at least two cycles of SET are necessary for success. Furthermore, many women are unable to afford additional cycles of IVF using SET and therefore are more likely to choose multiple embryo transfer, even though a multiple birth may be less desirous than a single birth. Thus, the incidence of twins has continued to rise, especially in the United States, where the rate of twin births has increased 70 percent since the 1980s. IVF has also raised a number of unresolved moral issues concerning the freezing (cryopreservation) of ovaries, ova, sperm, or embryos for future pregnancies.

Artificial Insemination

Artificial insemination is an alternative method of treating infertility. This process is defined as the introduction of semen into the vagina or cervix of a female by any method other than sexual intercourse. Artificial insemination has become a useful, if somewhat controversial, technique to impregnate women. Fresh semen is obtained from the husband (if he is impotent) or from some other male donor (if the husband is sterile) and is introduced by a syringe into the woman's vagina or cervix during the middle of her menstrual cycle. The semen can also have been previously frozen and stored in a sperm bank. The technique is reasonably successful in achieving conception and pregnancy, but the delicate moral issues surrounding it have yet to be fully resolved.

ABNORMAL CHANGES IN PREGNANCY

Abnormal changes in pregnancy can place the lives of the conceptus and the mother at risk. Examples of these conditions include ectopic pregnancy, in which the conceptus, or blastocyst, implants in a site other than the normal location in the uterine wall; defects in the implantation and development of the placenta; and abnormally high blood pressure induced by pregnancy. Disorders of pregnancy tend to be psychologically distressing for the couple and particularly for the mother.

ECTOPIC PREGNANCY

An ectopic pregnancy is one in which the conceptus (the products of conception—i.e., the placenta, the membranes, and the embryo) implants or attaches itself in a place other than the normal location in the lining of the upper uterine cavity. The site of implantation may be either at an abnormal location within the uterus itself or in an area outside the uterus. Ectopic pregnancies outside the uterine cavity occur about once in every 300 pregnancies. They are one of the major causes of maternal deaths.

Normally an ovum, or egg, passes from the ovary into the tube, is fertilized in the tube, and moves downward into the uterus. It buries itself in the lining of the upper part of the uterine cavity. It may pass farther down and attach itself to the lining of the mouth of the uterus (the cervix), creating a cervical pregnancy. These are rare and cause severe vaginal bleeding; the conceptus is expelled or discovered within a few months after implantation.

If a conceptus attaches itself to the lower part of the uterine cavity, it is a low implantation. When a low

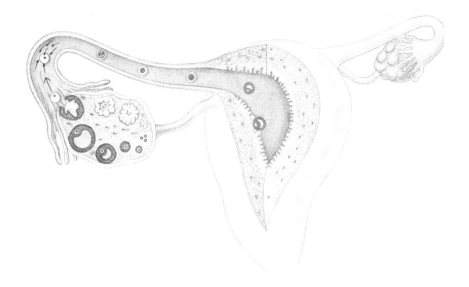

In a normal pregnancy, the fertilized egg passes through the fallopian tube and implants in the uterus, but scars, pockets, kinks, or adhesions in the tubal lining resulting from infections likely cause most tubal pregnancies. Annabel Milne/Getty Images

implantation occurs, the placenta grows over the cervical opening, in a formation called a placenta praevia. This causes the woman to bleed, often profusely, through the vagina because the placenta tears as the cervix begins to open during the latter part of pregnancy.

When the fertilized ovum implants in the narrow space or angle of the uterine cavity near the connection of the uterus with the fallopian tube, it is called an angular pregnancy. Many angular pregnancies terminate in abortions. Others go to term but are complicated because the placenta does not separate properly from the uterine wall after the birth of the baby. An angular pregnancy differs from a cornual pregnancy, which develops in the side of a bilobed or bicornate uterus.

Implantation in the narrow part of the fallopian, or uterine, tube, which lies within the uterine wall, produces what is called an interstitial pregnancy. This occurs in approximately 4 percent of ectopic pregnancies. An interstitial pregnancy gradually stretches the wall of the uterus until—usually between the 8th and 16th week of gestation—the wall ruptures in an explosive manner and there is profuse bleeding into the abdomen.

Most persons associate ectopic pregnancies with tubal pregnancies because most ectopic pregnancies occur in the uterine tubes. The tube beyond the uterus has three parts: (1) the isthmus, a narrow section near the uterus; (2) the ampulla, which is wider and more dilatable; and (3) the infundibulum, the flaring, trumpetlike portion of the tube nearest the ovary. A tubal ectopic pregnancy is designated by the area of the tube in which it is implanted. An isthmic pregnancy differs from one in the ampulla or infundibulum because the narrow tube cannot expand. Rupture of the affected tube with profuse intra-abdominal hemorrhage occurs early, usually within eight weeks after conception.

Ampullar pregnancies, which are by far the most common, usually terminate either in a tubal abortion, in which the embryo and the developing afterbirth are expelled through the open end of the tube into the abdomen; by a tubal rupture; or, less commonly, by absorption of the conceptus. Sometimes the tube ruptures into the tissues attaching it to the wall of the pelvis, producing an intra-ligamentous pregnancy. Rarely, the embryo is expelled into the abdomen and the afterbirth remains attached to the tube; the embryo lives and grows. Such a condition is referred to as a secondary abdominal pregnancy. Primary abdominal pregnancies, in which the fertilized ovum attaches to an abdominal organ, and ovarian pregnancies are rarer still.

It is generally believed, but not proved, that most tubal pregnancies are caused by scars, pockets, kinks, or adhesions in the tubal lining resulting from tubal infections. The infection may have been gonorrhea; it may have occurred after an abortion, after the delivery of a baby, or after a pelvic surgical operation; or it may have been caused by appendicitis. Kinking, scarring, and partial adhesions of the outside of the tube may be the result of inflammation following a pelvic operation or of an abdominal inflammation. Tubes, defective from birth, may be too small for the passage of the conceptus or may be pocketed or doubled with one tubal half forming a blind pocket. There may be areas in the tubal lining that behave like the lining of the uterus (they show a decidual reaction that is conducive to implantation) so that they offer a favourable spot for the fertilized ovum to implant. Pelvic tumours may distort the tube and obstruct it so that the conceptus cannot move downward. Theoretically, endocrine disturbances may delay tubal motility.

Whatever the cause, when a tubal implantation occurs, it may be assumed that either migration of the fertilized ovum within the tube was delayed by an extrinsic factor so that the ovum grew to the point where it should implant or that the mechanism for implantation within the ovum itself was prematurely activated in the tube. One or the other of these causative factors can sometimes be seen when a woman is operated on for an ectopic pregnancy. In a great number of cases, however, no tube abnormality can be found. Although there is no satisfactory explanation for most abnormal implantations in the uterus, defective uterine structure has been noted in some cases.

Primary abdominal and ovarian pregnancies can best be explained by a mechanism in which the fertilized ovum is swept out of the tube by a reverse peristalsis of the tube. In rare instances, however, it is quite possible that the ovum and sperm meet and fertilization and implantation take place within the abdomen.

Ectopic pregnancy is frequently mistaken for other disorders. Typically, but not invariably, the woman who has an ectopic pregnancy in the ampullar part of the tube will have missed one or two menstrual periods but need not have other symptoms of pregnancy. She has felt enough discomfort in the lower part of her abdomen to lead her to consult a physician and has had recurrent episodes of rather light, irregular bleeding from the vagina. She has felt weak or faint at times. The signs of pregnancy are unlikely to be present, and results of a pregnancy test are more often negative than positive. The physician, on pelvic examination, feels a tender, soft mass in one side of the pelvis. At this stage the differentiation must be made between an ectopic pregnancy and an intrauterine pregnancy with abortion, acute appendicitis, intestinal colic, inflammation of a fallopian tube, and a twisted ovarian tumour. Unless the diagnosis can be made, the patient continues to complain for several more days and then has a sudden severe pain and collapses from brisk bleeding within the abdomen.

Sudden and acute abdominal pain and collapse because of severe hemorrhage are only rarely the first signs that something is amiss. If this does happen, it is usually because implantation has occurred in the isthmic portion of the tube and hemorrhage and tubal rupture simultaneously occur. More frequently, a woman has missed one menstrual period, has a sensation of pelvic pressure, feels that she must urinate, and collapses in the bathroom. She may be unconscious and pulseless from loss of blood when she arrives at the hospital.

Interstitial pregnancies are often mistaken for intra-uterine ones, but the patient has pain and may have intermittent vaginal bleeding. After several months she has sudden, severe pain, collapses from a massive intra-abdominal hemorrhage, and may die before surgical help can reach her. Most of the women who die from ectopic pregnancies do so from interstitial ones.

Combined pregnancies, in which there is an ectopic pregnancy and a normal one in the uterus, or a fetus in each tube, have occurred and have compounded the difficulty in making a diagnosis. In a number of instances, the ectopic conceptus has been removed without complications, and the uterine fetus has progressed to term.

Not all ectopic pregnancies end with a catastrophic hemorrhage and collapse. In a few instances tubal, abdominal, and broad ligament pregnancies have gone on until a living baby was obtained at the time of operation. In other cases the fetus died and, if very young, was resorbed. Still other cases involved a larger fetus: Death was followed by absorption of the fluid in the sac, and the fetus was gradually converted into a more or less mummified mass. Some ectopic pregnancies of this type have caused no symptoms and have been carried by women for years. Undoubtedly, many ectopic pregnancies that are in an early stage when they are expelled emerge through the open end of the uterine tube, are resorbed, and are never recognized. Once diagnosed, the treatment of ectopic pregnancies outside the uterine cavity is almost always a matter of prompt surgical intervention with proper attention to replacement of blood and fluid.

MISCARRIAGE

Miscarriage is the spontaneous expulsion of the embryo or fetus from the uterus before the 20th week of pregnancy, prior to the conceptus having sufficiently developed to live without maternal support. An estimated 10 to 25 percent of recognized pregnancies are lost as a result of miscarriage, with the risk of loss being highest in the first six weeks of pregnancy. Because many miscarriages occur prior to a woman knowing she is pregnant, the actual prevalence of miscarriage is suspected to be higher than that reflected in the data for clinically recognized cases.

The loss of pregnancy in the first weeks following implantation typically results in bleeding at about the time of the next expected menstruation. This form of early miscarriage, which accounts for most miscarriages, is described as chemical pregnancy. The consecutive loss of pregnancies, which occurs in about 1 to 2 percent of cases, is known as recurrent miscarriage.

The most common cause, accounting for more than 60 percent of miscarriages, is an inherited defect in the fetus, which might result in a deformed or otherwise abnormal child. An acute infectious disease may play a role in causing some miscarriages, particularly if it reduces the oxygen supply to the fetus. Certain uterine tumours or other uterine abnormalities also may induce a miscarriage. Death of the fetus stemming from external trauma or from knotting of the umbilical cord is another cause of miscarriage. Physical traumas (such as blows to or falls of the mother) and psychological traumas are rarely implicated in miscarriage. Endocrine disorders such as the deficient secretion of the hormone progesterone may cause poor development of the decidua (the mucal lining of the uterus) or an abnormally irritable uterus and may thus sometimes result in miscarriage.

Women older than age 35 tend to be at increased risk of miscarriage relative to younger women. Other risk factors include the presence of a preexisting medical condition such as thyroid disease, a history of miscarriage, and prenatal testing such as amniocentesis. Smoking, drinking alcohol, or taking certain drugs during pregnancy are also recognized risk factors.

The principal sign of an impending or threatened miscarriage is vaginal bleeding. Other symptoms may include pain in the abdomen and lower back.

DISORDERS OF THE PLACENTA

Major disorders of the placenta include placenta praevia, placentae abruptio, and placenta accreta. These conditions are characterized by the abnormal implantation, formation, and function of the placenta. Other disorders include the replacement of placental tissue with scar tissue (placental infarction), the development of placental cysts, and general inflammation of placental tissue.

PLACENTA PRAEVIA

Placenta praevia is the implantation of the placenta at a point so low in the uterus that the placenta is close to the opening into the cervix or covers the opening, either partially or completely. The placenta is the temporary organ that develops during pregnancy to nourish the fetus and to carry away its wastes, and the cervix is the narrow lower portion of the uterus that projects into the vagina.

Placenta praevia is suspected if there is painless bleeding during the last three months of pregnancy. The likelihood of the abnormality increases with the number of pregnancies of the individual woman and with the rapidity with which one pregnancy follows another. Untreated, the condition may result in early labour, delivery of a premature or stillborn child, and danger of death to the mother from bleeding. Treatment includes hospitalization, control of the bleeding and replacement of lost blood by transfusion, and delivery of the infant by cesarean section if the mother or the child would be endangered by delivery through the vagina.

PLACENTAE ABRUPTIO

Placentae abruptio is the premature separation of the placenta from its normal implantation site in the uterus. The placenta is the temporary organ that develops during pregnancy to nourish the fetus and carry away its wastes. Placentae abruptio occurs in the latter half of pregnancy and may be partial or complete. The separation causes bleeding, so extensive in cases of complete separation that replacement of the lost blood by transfusion is necessary. In instances of complete placentae abruptio, the infant dies unless delivered immediately. In partial separation the mother is given oxygen, and the infant is delivered as soon as it is safe to do so. The cause of placentae abruptio is unknown. It is more common in women who have borne several children and in women suffering from high blood pressure.

PLACENTA ACCRETA

Placenta accreta is the abnormal adherence of the placenta to the wall of the uterus, so that it remains in the uterus after the baby has been delivered. Although uncommon, placenta accreta poses serious dangers to the mother. If complicated by coexisting placenta praevia (development of the placenta in an abnormally low position near the cervix), severe bleeding before labour is common. If placenta accreta arises on the site of a scar from a former cesarean section, the uterus may rupture during labour.

Otherwise, depending on the firmness with which the placenta is anchored, it may be removed manually after the baby is delivered. If such removal is unsuccessful, an immediate total hysterectomy is usually indicated.

OTHER ABNORMALITIES OF PLACENTA

Placental infarction is the degeneration and death of placental tissue and its replacement with scar tissue. Small yellowish-white deposits of fibrin (a fibrous protein), caused by interference with the maternal circulation, occur normally in the placenta as pregnancy progresses. Usually, the fetus is unaffected by infarction of the placenta unless the process is extensive.

Placental cysts and benign tumours are relatively rare. Chorionic cysts of small size are disk-shaped, grayish-white structures filled with a yellowish fluid and located on the fetal side of the placenta. Decidual cysts are smoothly lined small cavities in the centre of the placenta. They are the result of decidual degeneration and are not true tumours. Angiomas, hemangiomas, fibromas, myxofibromas, and the like are benign growths arising from the placental blood vessels and connective tissue. Solid or semisolid tumours, usually creating small nodular elevations on the fetal side of the placenta, are rarely of clinical significance.

Inflammation of the placenta is usually secondary to infection of the membranes. Most often such infections follow the introduction of pus-forming bacteria into the uterus by instrumentation through the vagina. They are the aftermath of prolonged labour or of prolonged rupture of the membranes. If labour is prolonged, bacteria penetrate the fetal side of the placenta, enter the fetal circulation, and often cause death of the infant after delivery.

The placenta also may become infected from organisms in the maternal blood. Maternal syphilis, toxoplasmosis, tuberculosis, and malaria may affect the placenta. The viruses of chickenpox and smallpox may cause placental lesions. Many pathogenic bacteria and viruses cross the placenta and sometimes kill the fetus without causing any specific changes that have been noted in the placenta.

Abnormalities in the structure of the placenta are relatively common. It may be partially divided into two or more lobes, there may be extra lobes, or the placenta may be divided into two or more separate structures. Abnormal placentas result from shallow as well as deep implantation. The former type, called placenta circumvallata, is associated with several maternal and fetal complications; the latter type, called placenta membranacea, may cause problems at delivery (e.g., bleeding, failure of the membrane to separate).

OTHER DISORDERS OF PREGNANCY

Other disorders of pregnancy include defects in the development of the umbilical cord, excessive or deficient amounts of amniotic fluid, tumour growth, and abnormally high blood pressure. In addition, the increased production of various substances by the mother and by the fetus can lead to pregnancy-associated metabolic disorders, including gestational diabetes mellitus.

ANOMALIES OF THE UMBILICAL CORD

"False knots," which are simply enlarged blood vessels in the cord, are not significant. Actual knots in the cord , however, may become tightened and kill the fetus by cutting off the blood to it. Twisting of the cord also may kill the fetus in the same manner. Spontaneous rupture of the cord interferes with the fetal blood supply and causes fetal death. Extreme shortness of the umbilical cord may interfere with delivery, cause premature separation of the placenta, or tear and cause fetal death from hemorrhage. Another abnormality, called velamentous insertion of the cord, in which multiple blood vessels spread out over the membranes and cervix rather than forming one single cord, is dangerous for the baby because the vessels may tear or be compressed during labour and delivery.

HYDRAMNIOS

Hydramnios, sometimes called polyhydramnios, is the presence of an excessive amount of amniotic fluid. Normally, the uterus contains approximately 1,000 ml (slightly more than one quart) of amniotic fluid, so anything greater than 2,000 ml is abnormal. Accumulations of more than 3,000 ml occur in approximately one pregnancy in a thousand. Lesser degrees of hydramnios probably occur in about 1 in 150 deliveries. The appearance of large amounts of fluid within the space of a few days is rare, and such a condition is met with in fewer than 1 in 4,000.

Hydramnios occurs most often in association with fetal abnormalities, particularly those of the nervous, digestive, and renal systems; when the fetus has erythroblastosis, a disease resulting from incompatibility between the infant's and the mother's blood; when there is more than one fetus; or when the mother has diabetes or pre-eclampsia. Almost all pregnancies in which the fetus suffers from obstruction of the esophagus and half of those in which there are severe brain anomalies are accompanied by excessive amniotic fluid.

Acute hydramnios causes rapid overdistention and enlargement of the uterus. The woman experiences abdominal pain, nausea and vomiting, and difficulty breathing. Her heart and blood vessels are put under such severe stress that she may show signs of heart failure. Swelling of the feet and legs develops. These manifestations are all caused by the pressure of the rapidly enlarging uterus upon the other viscera. Chronic hydramnios usually causes enough pressure from the abnormally enlarged uterus to make the affected person uncomfortable.

The cause of hydramnios is unknown. The most tenable theory is that there is a reduction in the amount of fluid that passes from the fetus to the mother and an increase in the amount that passes from the fetus to the amniotic sac. This appears to explain the relationship between fetal anomalies and hydramnios.

Many pregnancies complicated by an abnormal amount of amniotic fluid prematurely terminate. The fetus has a greatly increased chance of suffering from congenital anomalies. Roughly half of the babies in this group have been lost in the series of cases that have been reported. The greater the amount of fluid, the higher the fetal mortality. Women with hydramnios also are faced with a somewhat higher risk. Premature separation of the placenta and postpartum hemorrhage are the two most significant maternal complications associated with it.

Minor degrees of hydramnios require no treatment. Removal of the excess fluid is the only effective management if symptoms from uterine distention become too distressing. This may be done either by perforating the membranes through the cervix or, preferably, by inserting a needle through the abdominal wall and the wall of the uterus. Care is taken to avoid injury to the woman's bowel or the placenta. Either procedure is likely to start labour.

OLIGOHYDRAMNIOS

True oligohydramnios, a deficiency in amniotic fluid, is a rare condition of unknown cause. It is seen more often in pregnancies that have extended beyond the projected time of delivery. If it occurs early in pregnancy, there are usually firm adhesions between the membranes and the embryo, with distortion of the fetus. A decrease in the amount of fluid later in pregnancy allows the membranes and uterine wall to press on the baby. The baby's position is distorted, and as a result it may be born with a clubfoot or wryneck. Its skin is dry and thickened. Defective development of the kidneys is common with oligohydramnios. As a rule, the condition causes the mother no distress, but the infant has a greatly increased chance of being born with major anomalies.

HYDATIDIFORM MOLE

A hydatidiform mole is an abnormal growth of the chorion, the outermost vascular membrane that in a normal pregnancy would enclose the embryo and ultimately give rise to the placenta. In the situation in which the hydatidiform mole develops, the embryo is usually either absent or dead. The mole, a collection of sacs (cysts) containing a jellylike substance, resembles clusters of grapes and can attain a great size. Most of the moles are expelled in about the 20th week of pregnancy. The moler pregnancy is usually terminated by suction curettage. In a few cases, the mole spreads into the muscle of the uterus and causes bleeding. If this is severe, the obstetrician may remove the mole by surgery. In extremely rare instances, hydatidiform moles develop into choriocarcinomas, which are highly malignant tumours.

CHORIOCARCINOMA

Choriocarcinoma is a rare, extremely malignant type of tumour arising from the trophoblast. The reasons that normal chorionic cells undergo cancerous change, with exaggeration of their natural and potent tendency to invade the uterine muscle and break down blood vessels, are unknown. Choriocarcinoma occurs approximately once in 160,000 normal pregnancies. In approximately 50 percent of the cases the tumour develops from a hydatidiform mole, in another 25 percent after an abortion, and in 25 percent after a normal pregnancy. Occasionally, it appears after a tubal pregnancy, and it has been known to coexist with pregnancy. It is, for some unknown reason, more common in Asia. Choriocarcinoma developing as a teratoid tumour of the ovary (a tumour made up of a number of different tissues) is a rare entity unrelated to pregnancy and is not to be confused with the tumour discussed here.

As a rule, in the development of a choriocarcinoma there has been a normal pregnancy, an abortion, or the delivery of a mole, and the uterus has not returned to its normal size. The woman begins to bleed from the vagina. Blood loss may be modest or excessive in amount. Tissues obtained by a curettage (scraping) may be, but are not always, indicative of choriocarcinoma.

The tumour begins in the uterus, where it forms a spongy, bleeding mass of easily torn tissue or a shaggy ulcer. When examined microscopically, it is found to consist of both cytotrophoblast and syncytiotrophoblast. The cells spread rapidly by way of the bloodstream, producing secondary tumours in the lung, the brain, the liver, or elsewhere.

Formerly, choriocarcinoma was almost invariably fatal. Today an impressive (two out of three in some case series) number of patients have survived for many months after the administration of chemotherapeutic agents. Most workers in this field at this time are using methotrexate. The rapidly growing embryonic cells of the trophoblast need nucleic acids for growth and division. For the synthesis of nucleic acids, folinic acid is essential, and methotrexate, by preventing the conversion of folic acid to folinic acid, cuts off the supply of the latter. Many other cytotoxic drugs (drugs destructive to cells) also are used to treat choriocarcinoma, and other chemotherapeutic agents are being tested for effect on this type of tumour. Actinomycin D has been used successfully. Removal of the uterus is frequently, but not always, a part of the treatment of choriocarcinoma.

GESTATIONAL DIABETES

Gestational diabetes is a temporary condition in which blood sugar (glucose) levels increase during pregnancy and return to normal after delivery. A healthy pregnancy is characterized by increased nutrient use, increased insulin resistance, and increased insulin secretion. Blood glucose concentrations tend to be lower in pregnant women than in nonpregnant women because the mother supplies glucose to the growing fetus. All pregnant women have some degree of insulin resistance as a result of the normal secretion of several placental hormones, including placental growth hormone, placental lactogen, progesterone, and corticotropin-releasing hormone, which stimulates the production of adrenocorticotropic hormone (ACTH) in the pituitary gland and cortisol in the adrenal glands. In some cases, insulin resistance is increased by excessive weight gain during pregnancy. If insulin secretion does not increase sufficiently to counter the insulin resistance imposed by these changes, gestational diabetes occurs.

The worldwide frequency of gestational diabetes varies from about 1 to 15 percent of pregnant women. The large variability in frequency partly results from the fact that there is no widely agreed upon definition of gestational diabetes. However, no matter how it is defined, it is more common among obese women and African American and Asian women than among women of European descent. The outcomes of gestational diabetes also vary widely, ranging from large babies (fetal macrosomia), birth trauma, and neonatal hypoglycemia (abnormally low blood glucose levels) to maternal preeclampsia and increased perinatal morbidity.

Risk factors for gestational diabetes include older age, obesity, previous delivery of a large baby, and a family history of diabetes mellitus. Some physicians believe that all pregnant women should be tested for gestational diabetes at 24 to 28 weeks of gestation, whereas other physicians limit testing to women who have risk factors for gestational diabetes. The primary method used to diagnose the condition is an oral glucose tolerance test, in which blood glucose is measured hourly for several hours after ingestion of a large quantity of glucose (usually 75 or 100 grams). Although gestational diabetes is by definition transient, affected women have an increased risk of developing type II diabetes later in life.

PREECLAMPSIA AND ECLAMPSIA

Preeclampsia and eclampsia are hypertensive conditions that are induced by pregnancy. Preeclampsia, also called gestational edema-proteinuria-hypertension (GEPH), is an acute toxic condition arising during the second half of the gestation period or in the first week after delivery and generally occurs in young women during a first pregnancy. It is marked by elevated blood pressure (hypertension), protein in the urine (proteinuria), and swelling (edema) that is strikingly noticeable in the hands and face. Eclampsia, a more severe condition with convulsions, follows preeclampsia in about 5 percent of preeclamptic women and poses a serious threat to both mother and child.

The underlying causes of preeclampsia and eclampsia remain unclear. The primary clinical feature of elevated blood pressure may be attributed to malformed blood vessels feeding into the placenta from the uterus. Abnormal or damaged vessels can trigger the release of inflammatory substances and other molecules (e.g., angiotensin) that cause vessel inflammation or constriction. Other possible causes of preeclampsia and eclampsia include genetic defects, autoimmune disorders, and diet. One gene believed to be susceptible to defects that predispose some women to preeclampsia is catechol-*O*-methyltransferase (*COMT*), which produces an enzyme. Scientists suspect that the enzyme and its major metabolite called 2-methoxyestradiol (2-ME) are required for normal formation and function of placental vasculature. Lack of the *COMT* enzyme and therefore 2-ME has been linked with persistent placental hypoxia—a decrease in oxygen in placental tissue that is considered a hallmark of preeclampsia. Hypoxia, which stimulates the formation of new blood vessels, is normal in the first trimester of pregnancy and ensures sufficient delivery of nutrients and oxygen to the rapidly growing fetus. By the third trimester, the demand for new vessels drops and new vessel formation is halted—a process controlled by 2-ME. Prolonged exposure to hypoxia endangers the health of the fetus and the mother and is the primary reason premature delivery may be necessary in preeclamptic pregnancies.

Common symptoms of preeclampsia include headaches, visual disturbances, and stomach pain; however, it may be detected before the onset of symptoms by monitoring blood pressure and weight gain. Preeclampsia can often be controlled by special diets, medication, and limitation of activity. If it occurs late in pregnancy, there is the option of early delivery. Eclampsia can usually be avoided by these measures. If convulsions occur, they are treated with infusions of magnesium sulfate.

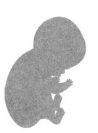

CHAPTER 7

ISSUES CONCERNING BIRTH CONTROL AND ABORTION

B irth control is the voluntary limiting of human reproduction, using such means as sexual abstinence,
contraception, induced abortion, and surgical sterilization.
It includes the spacing as well as the number of children
in a family. Birth control encompasses the wide range of
rational and irrational methods that have been used in the
attempt to regulate fertility, as well as the response of individuals and of groups within society to the choices offered
by such methods. It has been and remains controversial.
The U.S. reformer Margaret Sanger coined the phrase
in 1914–15 and, like the social movement she founded,
the term has been caught up in a quest for acceptance,
generating many synonyms: family planning, planned
parenthood, responsible parenthood, voluntary parenthood, contraception, fertility regulation, and fertility
control.

Human reproduction involves a range of activities
and events, from sexual intercourse through birth, and
depends as well on a series of physiological interactions,
such as the timing of ovulation within the menstrual cycle.
The visible events are central to the transmission of life
and have been subject to social and religious control. The
invisible factors in human reproduction gave rise early on
to speculation and in modern times have become the topic
of scientific investigation and manipulation. New knowledge relevant to birth control has diffused at different

rates through various social groups and has not always been available to those with the greatest need. Hence, the conflicts and controversies surrounding birth control have been complex and impassioned. The disagreement over birth control arises in part from the debate over what is natural and what is artificial (and, to some, unacceptable).

HISTORY OF BIRTH CONTROL

Written records of birth control methods survive from ancient times. Methods are mentioned among the various formulas and remedies recorded in the Ebers papyrus, a compilation of Egyptian medical texts dating from 1550 BCE. Classical writers, including Pliny the Elder, Pedanius Dioscorides (*De materia medica*, c. 77 CE), and Soranus of Ephesus (*On Midwifery and the Diseases of Women*, c. 100 CE), refer to contraception and abortion. Several authors from the flowering of Arabic medicine in the 10th century mention contraception, notably al-Rāzī (Rhazes; *Quintessence of Experience*), Ali ibn Abbas (*The Royal Book*), and Avicenna (Ibn Sīnā; *The Canon of Medicine*). The methods recommended by these early commentators fall into three groups: the reasonable but probably ineffective, such as wiping out the vagina after intercourse (Soranus); the reasonable and perhaps effective, such as using honey, alum, or lactic acid as spermicidal barriers (Ebers papyrus, Dioscorides, and Soranus); and the mystical and manifestly ineffective, for example suggesting that the woman jump backward seven times immediately after coitus (Soranus).

By 1900 all the methods of birth control now in use, with the exception of oral contraceptives, were understood and available in Europe and North America. The first to be developed was the condom. Folklore attributes the invention to a Dr. Condom, said to have been alarmed by the number of illegitimate offspring of Charles II of England. It is more likely, however, that the name derives from the Latin *condus*, for receptacle. The earliest published description is by the Italian anatomist Gabriel Fallopius in 1564. The first condoms were made from animal intestines and for the most part were used to prevent sexual transmission of disease. When Charles Goodyear discovered the process for vulcanization of rubber in 1839, he initiated a revolution in contraception, as well as transport, and condoms have been a popular choice for birth control since the second half of the 19th century. The use of vaginal barriers (diaphragms and caps, which are commonly used with spermicides) was recorded by the German physician F.A. Wilde in 1823. The medical forerunner of the intrauterine device was the stem pessary, first described and illustrated in 1868. By 1909, Richard Richter, a practitioner from near Breslau (Wrocław in present-day Poland), had described most of the advantages and disadvantages of this method of birth control. Vasectomy, or male sterilization, was practiced in the 19th century, and the first female sterilization by surgical occlusion of the fallopian tubes was performed by a U.S. surgeon in Ohio in 1881. The surgical techniques of induced abortion in use today were also known in the 19th century. In the 1860s an Edinburgh gynecologist, James Young Simpson, described a procedure for "dry cupping" the uterus. The procedure adumbrated vacuum aspiration, a method commonly used today for performing legal abortion.

The fact that conception was more likely to take place during certain phases of the menstrual cycle than others was suspected by classical authors. Adam Raciborski, a Paris physician, noted in 1843 that brides married soon after their menstruation often conceived in that cycle, while if the wedding occurred later in the cycle they commonly had another period before pregnancy occurred.

Hermann Knaus in Austria (1929) and Kyūsaku Ogino in Japan (1930) independently and correctly concluded that ovulation occurs 14 days prior to the next menstruation. In 1964 an Australian medical team, John and Evelyn Billings, showed how women could monitor changes in their cervical mucus and learn to predict when ovulation would occur.

"The greatest invention some benefactor can give mankind," wrote Sigmund Freud in the early years of the 20th century, "is a form of contraception which does not induce neurosis." Many of the elements to meet the goal of a new, more acceptable form of contraception were present about the time of World War I, yet two generations were to reach maturity before those elements were exploited. The role of hormones from the ovary was understood early in the 20th century by Walter Heape and John Marshall. The first extract of estrogen was produced in 1913, and the pure compound was isolated by the Americans Willard Allen and Alan Doisy in 1923. At this time Austrian physiologist Ludwig Haberlandt was carrying out experiments on rabbits to apply the new-found knowledge of hormones for contraceptive ends. By 1927 he was able to write, "It needs no amplification, of all methods available, hormonal sterilization based on biologic principles, if it can be applied unobjectionably in the human, is an ideal method for practical medicine and its future task of birth control." Hostile public attitudes made research on birth control virtually impossible, however, and Haberlandt's ideal was not realized until the 1960s.

EARLY ADVOCATES

In 1798 Thomas Malthus wrote *An Essay on the Principle of Population*. It posed the conundrum of geometrical population growth's outstripping arithmetic expansion in resources. Malthus, who was an Anglican clergyman, recommended late marriage and sexual abstinence as methods of birth control. A small group of early 19th-century freethinkers, including Jeremy Bentham, Francis Place (himself the father of 15 children), and John Stuart Mill, suggested more pragmatic birth control methods such as coitus interruptus, vaginal barriers, and postcoital douching. Robert Dale Owen, the son of a Scottish social reformer, helped spread these revolutionary ideas in North America, and in 1832 a Massachusetts physician and freethinker, Charles Knowlton, wrote a slim book called *The Fruits of Philosophy: or The Private Companion of Young Married People.* Although Knowlton's first edition was published anonymously, he was fined and imprisoned. The book appeared in England two years later and continued to be read for the next 50 years. In 1876 a Bristol publisher was prosecuted for selling *The Fruits of Philosophy.* Incensed, Charles Bradlaugh, the leader of Britain's National Secular Society and subsequently a member of Parliament, and Annie Besant reissued the pamphlet and notified the police. They were charged and tried, the public prosecutor claiming "this is a dirty, filthy book," but the conviction was quashed on grounds of a faulty indictment. The trial received wide publicity and, through the national press, brought birth control onto the breakfast table of the English middle classes at a time when, for economic reasons, they were eager to control their fertility. The Malthusian League, founded some years earlier by George Drysdale, began to attract wide public support. Similar leagues began in France, Germany, and the Netherlands, the latter opening the world's first family planning services, under Dr. Aletta Jacobs, in 1882.

But it was two women, Margaret Sanger in the United States and Marie Stopes in Britain, who were to make birth control the object of a national, and ultimately global, social movement. Both used the controversy that surrounded birth control as a ready way of attracting attention. Sanger, a trained nurse, encountered miserable conditions in her work among the poor. She was inspired to take up her crusade when she attended a woman who was dying from a criminally induced abortion. In 1914 she started a magazine, *The Woman Rebel*, to challenge laws restricting the distribution of information on birth

After attending to a woman who was dying from a criminally induced abortion, Margaret Sanger sought to make birth control a global cause. General Photographic Agency/Hulton Archive/Getty Images

control. She was indicted and fled to Europe, but when she returned to stand trial in 1916 the charges against her were dropped. Later that year she opened a family planning clinic in Brownsville, Brooklyn, New York, but the police immediately closed it, and Sanger was arrested and convicted on charges of "maintaining a public nuisance." After many vicissitudes, a compromise was struck and family planning clinics were allowed in the United States on the condition that physicians be involved in prescribing contraceptives. In 1936 a New York court, in a case known as *United States v. One Package of Japanese Pessaries*, ruled that contraceptives could be sent through the post if they were to be intelligently employed by conscientious physicians for the purpose of saving life or promoting the well-being of their patients.

In Britain the movement for birth control was led by Marie Stopes, the daughter of a middle-class Edinburgh family. She was one of the first women to obtain a doctorate in botany (from the University of Munich in 1904). In 1918 she published an appeal for sexual equality and fulfillment within marriage, *Married Love*, which at the time was considered to be a radical text. Margaret Sanger met Marie Stopes and persuaded her to add a chapter on birth control. Sanger's advocacy emphasized the alleviation of poverty and overpopulation, whereas Stopes sought as well to relieve women of the physical strain and risks of excessive childbearing. Her *Married Love* was followed by *Wise Parenthood* (1918), and in 1922 Stopes founded the Society for Constructive Birth Control and Racial Progress.

THE POPULATION EXPLOSION

In 1790 a Venetian monk, Gianmaria Ortis, concluded that human population growth could not continue indefinitely. Malthus' work a few years later stimulated more discussion and provided the intellectual clue that inspired Charles Darwin's theory of biological evolution through the survival of the fittest. The debate about human numbers remained academic, however, until the 1950s, when a surge in population occurred as a result of the comparative peace and prosperity following World War II.

In Malthus' time world population was less than 1,000,000,000, and when Sanger and Stopes opened the first birth control clinics population was still less than 2,000,000,000. In 1960 global population surpassed 3,000,000,000, and the next 1,000,000,000 was added in a mere 15 years. In the 19th century, the population of industrialized countries rarely grew by more than 1 percent per annum, but in the 1960s and '70s many developing countries exploded at a rate of 2 to 3 percent per year.

Rapid population growth has several economic consequences. It requires heavier investment in education, health, and transport merely to maintain these services at their previous level. Yet, the working population has a higher burden of dependence to support, making both individual and national saving more difficult. Although population growth is not the only problem dividing rich and poor countries, it is one important variable that has widened the gap in growth in per capita income between developed and developing nations. Advocates of birth control see it as a means to prevent the personal and social pressures that result from rapid population growth.

BIRTH CONTROL AND HEALTH

There is a marked relationship between patterns of reproduction and the risk of death to the mother and her child.

Maternal deaths and infant mortality are up to 60 percent higher among girls younger than age 15 than among women who have a child in their early 20s. The risk of death to the mother and her child rises again in the second half of the 30s. Maternal and infant mortality is lowest for the second and third deliveries. The risk of certain congenital abnormalities, such as Down syndrome, is also greater in older women. Therefore, patterns of sexual abstinence and birth control, which concentrate childbearing in the age group 20–35 and limit family size to two or three children, directly affect public health.

At the same time, it must be recognized that patterns of human reproduction have been finely tuned over millions of years of evolution and the postponement of childbearing until the later 20s or 30s also increases the risk of certain diseases. In particular, cancer of the breast is more common in women who postpone the first birth until the later 20s or older. In the Western world, the risk of death to women in childbirth is approximately one in 10,000, but in developing countries, where half the children born are delivered by traditional birth attendants, it is often 10 times as high. As the number of births worldwide rises, a greater number of women are likely to die having children. Simple access to birth control may be expected to reduce high death rates.

FAMILY PLANNING

National family planning movements have emphasized the right of the individual to determine family size as well as the contribution family planning can make to national and global population problems. Some methods of birth control, such as coitus interruptus and, in extreme cases, abortion, may involve no person other than the individual or couple. But most methods require manufacture, distribution, promotion, counselling, and in some cases financial subsidy.

The retail trade in contraceptives has been a major element in the spread of contraception and remains important in the developing world. In particular, social marketing programs, which adjust prices to people's needs, have allowed governments to make contraceptives available to large numbers of people quickly and at affordable cost. Private doctors may advise patients about the use of birth control on a confidential basis and may charge a fee.

The first altruistic attempts to offer direct family planning services began with private, pioneering groups and often aroused strong opposition. The work of Sanger and Stopes reached only a small fraction of the millions of couples who in the 1920s and '30s lived in a world irrevocably altered by World War I, crushed by economic depression, and striving for the then lowest birth rates in history. In 1921 Sanger founded the American Birth Control League, which in 1942 became the Planned Parenthood Federation of America. In Britain the Society for the Provision of Birth Control Clinics was to evolve into the Family Planning Association. As early as 1881 the British Malthusian League had brought together individuals from 40 nations to discuss birth control, and five genuinely international meetings had taken place by 1930. A conference was held in Sweden in 1946. The first birth control clinic in India opened in 1930, and in 1952 in Bombay, Margaret Sanger took the first steps toward creating what became the International Planned Parenthood Federation (IPPF).

The modern era in international family planning opened in the second half of the 1960s when governments, beginning with Sweden, gave money to support the worldwide work of the IPPF. William Draper lobbied with particular effectiveness in the United States to build up the IPPF and to put together the United Nations Fund for Population Activities (UNFPA), established in 1969. For several years the U.S. Agency for International Development helped to support the IPPF and the UNFPA. The United Nations held international conferences on population in Bucharest in 1974, in Mexico City in 1984, and in Cairo in 1994.

METHODS OF BIRTH CONTROL

There are several methods of birth control, and the basis of each of these approaches varies considerably. For example, whereas methods such as abstinence and condoms do not depend on medical intervention, hormonal contraceptives and intrauterine devices often require the oversight of a physician. In addition, there is a wide range in the effectiveness of these methods, with hormonal contraceptives having an exceptionally low failure rate relative to methods such as coitus interruptus.

ABSTINENCE

Abstinence is important in many societies. In the West, most individuals abstain from regular sexual intercourse for many years between puberty and marriage. Raising the age of marriage has been an important element in the decline of the birth rate in China, Korea, and Sri Lanka. Abstinence among couples with grown children is important in some traditional societies, such as certain Hindu groups.

BREAST-FEEDING

The role of breast-feeding in the regulation of human fertility can be illustrated by the following calculation: In

Pakistan breast-feeding is virtually universal, and many women breast-feed for two years or more. Fewer than 1 in 10 women use a modern method of contraception, but if breast-feeding were to decline to levels now found in Central America, four out of 10 women would have to use an artificial method of birth control just to prevent the fertility rate from rising.

Although the information is important to demography, there is no simple way to predict when an individual breast-feeding woman will become fertile again. If she seeks security against pregnancy, a woman may in fact have an overlap of several months between the time she adopts an artificial method and the end of her natural protection.

COITAL TECHNIQUES

Coitus interruptus, the practice by which the male withdraws the penis prior to ejaculation, has been an important method of birth control in the West and was used by more than half of all British couples until well after World War II. It is most common among Roman Catholic and Islāmic groups but is less used in Asia, where coitus reservatus (intercourse without ejaculation) may be more common. The failure rate for coitus interruptus (5 to 20 pregnancies per 100 women-years of exposure) overlaps with that of barrier methods of birth control.

Although frequently condemned by those promoting other methods of family planning, there is no evidence that coitus interruptus causes any physical or emotional harm. There may be preferable ways of controlling fertility, but for many couples coitus interruptus is better than no method. The belief that conception cannot take place unless the woman has an orgasm is widespread but untrue.

Postcoital douching is an ineffective method of birth control.

BARRIER METHODS

Modern high-quality condoms have the advantage of simplicity of use and anonymity of distribution. They are sold in pharmacies, in supermarkets, through the mail, and even in barber shops and at newsstands. Condoms have been used by more than half of British and American men at one time or another, and use is most extensive in Japan. The acceptance of condoms has been increased in recent decades by advances in packaging and lubrication and, more recently, by the addition of a spermicide. When used carefully, condoms can have a failure rate as low as some intrauterine devices (two to five per 100 women-years of exposure).

Many chemicals act as spermicides. One of the most widely used is a detergent, nonoxynol-9, found in most foams, pessaries, and dissolving vaginal tablets. Spermicides are either used alone, when they have a moderate failure rate, or in combination with a barrier method such as a diaphragm or a disposable sponge.

PERIODIC ABSTINENCE

Although a couple may make a private choice to use periodic abstinence, just as they might buy condoms, most modern methods of periodic abstinence require careful training by a trained counsellor. Awareness of human fertility can be valuable when a couple is attempting to conceive a child. The method makes considerable demands on the partners, but if well taught it may also enhance the marital relationship.

Several types of periodic abstinence, also known as the rhythm method or natural family planning, are practiced. The time of ovulation can be estimated from a calendar record of previous menstruation, but this method has low effectiveness. More reliable methods include keeping a daily record of body temperature or recording physical changes in the cervix (the neck of the womb) and cervical mucus (the mucous method, also called the Billings method). These methods may also be combined (symptothermic method). As with several methods of birth control, a wide range of failure rates has been recorded for the various types of periodic abstinence, extending from 1 pregnancy per 100 women-years of exposure to more than 20 per 100.

HORMONAL CONTRACEPTIVES

Hormonal contraceptives, widely known as birth control pills, are synthetic steroid hormones that suppress the release of follicle-stimulating hormone (FSH) and luteinizing hormone (LH) from the anterior lobe of the pituitary gland in the female body. FSH and LH normally stimulate the release of estrogen from the ovaries, which in turn stimulates ovulation—the release of a mature ovum from the female ovary. However, when FSH and LH are suppressed, the chances of ovulation and therefore fertilization by a male sperm cell are significantly reduced. When oral contraceptives are used correctly, they are between 92 and 99 percent effective in preventing an unintended pregnancy.

Although the principle of hormonal contraception was understood in the 1920s, it took another 30 years for American social reformer Margaret Sanger and American biologist and philanthropist Katharine McCormick to persuade reluctant scientists and physicians to create preparations of oral contraceptives. The first clinical report of the use of such preparations to suppress ovulation was published in 1956 by American endocrinologist Gregory Pincus and American gynecologist and researcher John Rock. Oral contraceptives were approved by the U.S. Food and Drug Administration in 1960, and marketing of the preparations in Britain began two years later.

There are many commercial preparations of oral contraceptives, but most of them contain a combination of an estrogen (usually ethinyl estradiol) and a progestin (commonly norethindrone). In general, oral contraceptives are taken in a monthly regimen that parallels the menstrual cycle. Protection from pregnancy is often unreliable until the second or third drug cycle, and during this time certain side effects such as nausea, breast tenderness, or bleeding may be evident. More serious side effects, including blood clots and a rise in blood pressure, are possible, especially in women older than age 34. However, the incidence of side effects from oral contraceptives has been significantly reduced by decreasing the amounts of estrogen and progesterone in the preparations. Normal ovulation usually commences two to three months after the drug is stopped.

Progestin-only preparations (the so-called Minipill) thicken the mucus lining the cervix and make it more acidic, thereby rendering it hostile to sperm. Progestin-only preparations are somewhat less reliable than the combination preparations but produce fewer side effects. Under certain circumstances, the progestin may be administered as an intramuscular deposit that gradually releases the hormone over the course of one to three months.

Levonorgestrel is a synthetic progestogen that is used as a form of contraception in women. Levonorgestrel is the mirror compound (enantiomer) of norgestrel, which was synthesized in the early 1960s by American scientist Herschel Smith at the U.S.-based company Wyeth Pharmaceuticals.

As a form of progesterone, levonorgestrel exerts its actions on the hypothalamus through a negative feedback mechanism, which causes a decrease in the secretion of LH and FSH and thereby inhibits ovulation. The drug also inhibits implantation and causes the mucus in the cervix to thicken, which blocks the ability of sperm to travel through the uterus and into the fallopian tubes, where fertilization of the ovum by a sperm normally takes place.

In the early 1980s levonorgestrel became widely used in a form of contraception marketed as Norplant. In this system levonorgestrel was implanted beneath the skin of the upper arm in six Silastic (silicone-plastic) capsules, which provided birth control for five years. However, this system has been replaced by Norplant II (Jadelle), which uses a different synthetic progestogen, called etonogestrel, implanted under the skin in specially designed rods the size of matchsticks.

Today levonorgestrel may be given alone or in a formulation that also contains estradiol. One of the primary uses of levonorgestrel is in intrauterine devices (IUDs), such as Mirena. This particular IUD, once inserted into the uterus, can remain there for up to five years, releasing about 20 micrograms of levonorgestrel daily. Levonorgestrel also is used in various formulations of oral contraceptives, including in combination with estradiol in Seasonale—an extended-cycle oral contraceptive, which enables an 84-day span between menstruations—and in a morning-after pill called Plan B. In 1999 Plan B became available by prescription in the United States. In 2006, after a long politically charged debate, the U.S. Food and Drug Administration approved the sale of Plan B to women (and men) aged 18 and older without a prescription. At least 40 other countries already sold such emergency contraceptives over the counter (Plan B is marketed internationally under a variety of other trade names, including Vikela, Postinor-2, and Imediat N). When a 0.75-mg tablet is taken within 72 hours of unprotected sex, followed by a second 0.75-mg tablet within the next 12 hours, the drug is about 90 percent effective in preventing pregnancy.

The efficacy of levonorgestrel in preventing pregnancy may be altered in the presence of certain substances, including phenytoin (an antiepileptic drug), nafcillin (a penicillin-derived antibiotic), and St.-John's-wort (an herbal supplement). Levonorgestrel taken orally sometimes causes changes in menstrual bleeding (i.e., heavier or lighter periods). Other common side effects include nausea, headache, fatigue, and abdominal pain.

Research on a male pill has been disappointing. Sperm production has been controlled under experimental conditions, and in China a substance called gossypol, derived from the cottonseed, has been used as an oral contraceptive for males. Most substances used in the control of male fertility, however, either have proved toxic or have depressed sexual drive as well as sperm count.

INTRAUTERINE DEVICES

Almost any foreign body placed in the uterus prevents pregnancy. Although intrauterine devices (IUDs) were invented in the 19th century, they only came into widespread use in the late 1950s, when flexible plastic devices were developed by Jack Lippes and others. The IUD, made in a variety of shapes, is placed in the uterus by passing it through the cervix under sterile conditions. Similar to hormonal contraceptives, IUDs probably act in several complementary ways. When the IUD is in place an abnormally high number of white blood cells pass into the

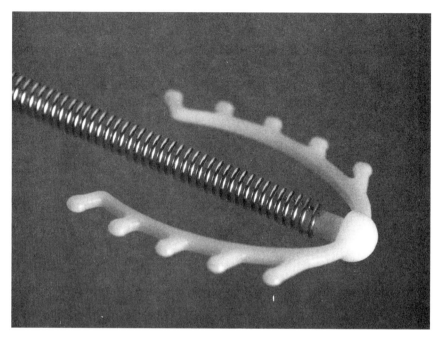

The intrauterine device works on the premise that any foreign object placed in the uterus prevents pregnancy. DEA/M. Fermariello/De Agostini/ Getty Images

uterine cavity, and the ovum, even if fertilized, is destroyed by the white blood cells before implantation. Nevertheless, one to three out of every 100 users per year will become pregnant with the IUD in place.

An intrauterine device can be inserted on any day of the menstrual period and immediately after a birth or abortion. The advantage of an IUD lies in its long-term protection and relative ease of use. The disadvantages include heavier menstrual flow and an increased risk of uterine infection. Approximately 60 million women worldwide use an IUD, with the largest use recorded in China. The devices are most satisfactory when used by older women who have had children and are recommended less frequently for young women, primarily because of the risk of pelvic infection.

In 1970 Jaime Zipper, a physician from Chile, added copper to plastic devices, thereby permitting designs that caused less bleeding and increased effectiveness. IUDs, including those that release contraceptive hormones (e.g., levonorgestrel-releasing IUDs), do not protect against sexually transmitted diseases, such as HIV/AIDS and herpes simplex.

VOLUNTARY STERILIZATION

Voluntary sterilization prevents more pregnancies each year than any other method of birth control. This approach has proved popular in both rich and poor countries, and the number of operations performed is likely to continue to rise. Wherever sterilization of the female (tubal sterilization) has been offered, it has proved popular. Fewer male sterilizations (vasectomies) than female sterilizations have been performed worldwide, but demand consistently grows wherever a reliable service is available.

Vasectomy is a quick, simple operation normally carried out under local anesthesia. The vas deferens, the tube carrying the sperm from the testicles to the penis, is blocked, and a number of ejaculations must be made after the operation to remove all the sperm capable of fertilization. Local bleeding and infection can occur after the operation, but no long-term adverse effects have been demonstrated in men. In some animals, however, disease of the blood vessels has been reported to be more common after experimental vasectomy.

The fallopian tubes, which carry the ovum from the ovary to the uterus, lie buried deep in the female pelvis. To perform sterilization a surgeon must either open the abdomen, in a procedure called laparotomy, and close the tubes under direct vision, or insert an optical instrument (laparoscope) to view the tubes so that a clip, ring, or electrocautery can be applied. The only proved side effects of female sterilization are those associated with any surgery and local or general anesthesia.

An individual seeking sterilization must accept the operation as irreversible while at the same time understanding that in rare cases, in either sex, the operation can fail even when properly carried out. In cases of extreme need, reversal of both female and male sterilization has been attempted, with more than 50 percent of patients later conceiving children. Surgical reversal is easier for male sterilization.

THE LEGALITY OF BIRTH CONTROL

In the 19th century, the law was used as an assertion of existing morality. In the United States Anthony Comstock lobbied to pass an Act for the Suppression of Trade in, and the Circulation of, Obscene Literature and Articles of Immoral Use. When asked why he classified contraception with pornography, Comstock answered, "If you open the door to anything, the filth will pour in." Anti-contraceptive and anti-sterilization clauses were added to the Napoleonic Code applying to France and French colonies. In Britain, however, the law never specifically condemned contraception or sterilization, and Bradlaugh and Besant were accused under the Obscene Publications Act.

The 20th century has seen statute laws used as a vehicle of social change and as a battleground of conflicting philosophies. The Nazi Third Reich invaded the bedrooms of its citizens before it moved its troops into the Sudetenland and Czechoslovakia. It forbade the display of contraceptives, which it condemned as the "by-product of the asphalt civilization." By contrast, the Proclamation of Teheran in 1968 (paragraph 16) provided, "Parents have a basic human right to determine freely and responsibly the number and spacing of their children." This concept was written into Yugoslavia's constitution, and China officially made family planning an obligation for each citizen. U.S. courts interpreted the constitutional right of privacy to include birth control choices when the Comstock Act was finally overthrown in the cases of *Griswold* v. *Connecticut* (1965) and *Eisenstadt* v. *Baird* (1972). In Ireland the case of Mary McGee (1973) reversed an Irish anti-contraceptive law of 1935, and in the Luigi deMarchi case in 1971 the Italian Supreme Court struck down the Fascist laws limiting the availability of contraception. At the other extreme, Singapore has passed legislation removing certain tax credits from couples with three or more children.

THE ETHICS OF BIRTH CONTROL

The ethics of birth control has always been a topic of debate. All the world's major religions endorse responsible parenthood, but when it comes to methods the consensus often dissolves. Hindu and Buddhist teachings are linked by a belief in reincarnation, but this has not been extended to an obligation to achieve maximum fertility. The Buddhist religion requires abstinence from any form of killing, and strict Buddhist groups have interpreted this requirement as support for opposition to contraception. At the same time, Buddhist scripture contains the phrase, "Many children make you poor," and the few prevailing constraints against birth control have been interpreted as affecting individuals, not state policy.

In the Muslim religion, the Prophet Muhammad endorsed the use of *al-azl* (coitus interruptus) for socioeconomic reasons and to safeguard the health of women. The Qur'ān instructs, "Mothers shall give suck to their offspring for two whole years if they desire to complete their term" (II,233). In general, modern methods of family planning have been accepted by Islāmic religious leaders, but sterilization is resisted as mutilation. Some fundamentalist Islāmic groups, most notably in Iran in the 1980s, have opposed family planning in general.

The Judeo-Christian tradition has been more divided in its approach to birth control, and Europe and North America have had a disproportionate role in medical research and practice. Until the Industrial Revolution in the West, artificial methods of birth control seemed irrelevant or even antagonistic to reproduction and to the spiritual goals of marriage. Christendom was slow to recognize new medical knowledge and new social needs, thereby retarding the development of birth control methods and diffusion of services. For example, in part because of religious objections, the U.S. National Institutes of Health were explicitly barred from research on contraception until 1961.

Historically, Jewish doctrines on marriage and procreation were related to the national struggle for survival and the traditions of a close-knit monotheistic community in which the individual was perpetuated through family. Judaism imposes an obligation to have children, but love and companionship are deemed an equally important goal of marriage. Orthodox sections of Judaism permit women to use certain methods of birth control, especially when necessary to protect the mother's health. Reformed and Conservative branches urge proper education in all methods of birth control as enhancing the spiritual life of the couple and the welfare of humankind. Many Jewish physicians and leaders, such as Alan Guttmacher, have joined in the advocating of birth control.

The early Christian Church reacted against the hedonism of the later Roman Empire and, believing that the

Second Coming of Christ preempted the need for procreation, held celibacy superior to marriage. Early Christians opposed the Gnostic movement that viewed the world as the creation of evil and procreation as the perpetuation of that evil. Instead they supported the Stoic argument that sexual passions distracted man from the contemplation of the One, the True, the Good, and the Beautiful. It was a short step for the 2nd-century theologian Clement of Alexandria to associate sexual intercourse with guilt and argue that it could only be justified by the obvious need to reproduce. Clement even argued that the human soul fled the body during a sexual climax. Augustine (354–430 CE), in his writings, especially in *Marriage and Concupiscence* (418 CE), laid the intellectual foundation for more than 1,000 years of Christian teaching on birth control. He concluded that the male semen both contained the new life and transmitted Adam's original sin from generation to generation.

Among the practices Augustine condemned were not only coitus interruptus (onanism) but also what today would be called natural family planning. Not surprisingly, the explicit justification of periodic abstinence by the modern church continues to come into conflict with remnants of Augustine's more pessimistic identification of sex with sin.

An important challenge to traditional Roman Catholic teaching arose in 1853 when the church's Sacred Penitentiary ruled that couples using periodic abstinence were "not to be disturbed." Among all Christian denominations, however, change was halting. Although in 1920 the Anglican Lambeth Conference condemned "any deliberate cultivation of sexual activity as an end in itself," by 1930 the Conference had taken some steps toward the moral justification of birth control. By 1958 its members concluded that "implicit within the bond of husband and

Augustine's association of sex with sin clashes with the overt valida-tion of periodic abstinence by the modern church. Time & Life Pictures/
Getty Images

wife is the relationship of love with its sacramental expression in physical union."

The Roman Catholic viewpoint developed even more slowly. The conservative theologian Arthur Vermeersch drafted much of Pope Pius XI's encyclical *Casti Connubii* (1930), condemning all methods of birth control except periodic abstinence as "grave sin." This teaching was reaffirmed by Pius XII in 1951. The Second Vatican Council (1962–65), however, described marriage as a "community of love" and the council's Constitution on the Church and the Modern World (*Gaudium et Spes*) exhorts parents to "thoughtfully take into account both their own welfare and that of their children, those already born and those which may be foreseen." Once the dual purposes of sexual relations to procreate and to express love had been accepted by the Second Vatican Council, however, some theologians and a great many Roman Catholic couples examined their own consciences and found it increasingly difficult to distinguish between intercourse during intervals of infertility brought about by the use of hormonal contraceptives and intercourse during the infertile intervals of the menstrual cycle. John Rock, who helped to develop the contraceptive pill and was himself a Roman Catholic, argued for just such a reassessment in his book *The Time Has Come* (1963). Gathering pressure led to the establishment of the Commission for the Study of Population and Family Life. It submitted its report to Pope Paul in 1966. Among the commission's members, the medical experts recommended by a vote of 60 to 4, and the cardinals by 9 to 6, to liberalize Roman Catholic teaching on birth control.

In 1968, however, Pope Paul restated the traditional teaching of *Casti Connubii* in his landmark encyclical *Humanae Vitae*, using papal authority to assert that "every conjugal act [has] to be open to the transmission of life."

Humanae Vitae came as a surprise to most church leaders and left many of the laity in a painful conflict between obedience and conscience. Six hundred Roman Catholic scholars signed a statement challenging *Humanae Vitae*, many episcopates attempted to soften the harsher aspects of the encyclical, a flood of priests left the church, and the number of U.S. Catholics attending mass weekly fell from 70 percent before the issuing of the encyclical to 44 percent a few years afterward. The total marital fertility (the number of children in a completed family) of U.S. Catholics (2.27 in 1975) became virtually the same as that of non-Catholics (2.17). At the same time a new movement began within the Roman Catholic Church, taking strength and inspiration from *Humanae Vitae*. Among lay organizations, the International Federation for Family Life Promotion was founded in 1974 and the Family of the Americas Foundation (formerly World Organization of the Ovulation Method—Billings; WOOMB) was founded in 1977.

The Eastern Orthodox Church maintains that parenthood is a duty. Although it considers the use of contraception to be a failure in spiritual focus, the church has not sought to hinder the distribution of birth control information or services.

Birth control, like other technologies, can be misused. In the 19th century, vasectomy was used for men judged to be compulsive masturbators, and a century later, during the state of emergency declared in India in 1975, the Indian government supported forcible sterilization of low-caste men as part of a population control program. In the not-too-distant past, unmarried women in the Western world who became pregnant faced such hostility from society in general that most felt they had no choice but illegal abortion, while in China today women are subject to intense social pressure to legally abort a second or subsequent pregnancy inside marriage. In contemporary Western society, conventional restraints on sexual experience prior to marriage are in turmoil. Vigorous debate centres on the question of whether the availability of birth control to young people encourages premarital sexual relations or avoids unplanned pregnancies that otherwise might occur. Certainly, similar patterns of availability of contraceptives may be observed in markedly different social settings with high and low incidence of premarital sex (e.g., the United States and China, respectively). There is no evidence that the availability of birth control either encourages or discourages particular patterns of sexual behaviour.

The debate over the ethics of induced abortion can arouse deep divisions even in otherwise homogeneous groups. At one extreme abortion is deemed the moral equivalent of murder and the life of the fetus is held to take precedence over that of the pregnant woman. At the other extreme it is argued that a woman has an absolute right over the pregnancy within her body. Surveys of opinion show that most people find abortion to be a sad and complex topic. The majority would prefer not to experience abortion but nevertheless feel that abortion is justified in certain cases, such as when tests show evidence of congenital abnormality, when pregnancy results from sexual crimes, or when the parents live in extreme poverty. The embryological discoveries of the past century cannot solve the metaphysical questions posed in the past. The U.S. Supreme Court decision on abortion in 1973 concluded, "We need not resolve the difficult question of when life begins. When those trained in the respective disciplines of medicine, philosophy, and theology are unable to arrive at any consensus, the judiciary, at this point in the development of man's knowledge, is not in a position to speculate as to the answer." In short, the definition individuals give to the beginning of life determines their judgment about the acceptability or licitness of abortion, and those definitions remain in the sphere of wholly human judgment.

THE SIGNIFICANCE OF BIRTH CONTROL

Modern humankind can never return to the way of life that characterized most of human evolution. Settled agriculture and, to an even greater extent, urban living have irrevocably altered natural, finely tuned patterns of human reproduction. New social and artificial restraints on fertility must replace high infant mortalities and the invisible but important physiological controls that once limited family size. The variables that encourage small families are still not fully understood, but they include urbanization, educational and employment opportunities for women, and easy access to family planning services. In a traditional agricultural society, children bring hope of economic rewards to their parents at an early stage by sharing in the work that is necessary to support the family, whereas in modern industrial societies the care and educating of children represent long years of heavy expenditure by the parents. This switch in the cost of children may be the most important factor determining the adoption of family planning.

Western societies took more than a century to reach zero population growth and adjust to the rapid expansion of population that accompanied their industrialization. Most changes that occurred in patterns of family planning took place before public family services were established and at considerable emotional and physical costs to many couples. By contrast, nearly all governments of contemporary Third World countries have established national family planning policies and actively encourage the use of public family services. The World Fertility Survey shows that more couples in developing countries desire small families than actually achieve their goals.

The significance of the choices facing policymakers and individual families can be illustrated by reference to trends in family planning in the People's Republic of China. For a generation after the Revolution of 1949, national leaders maintained that a Communist economy could accommodate any rate of population growth, and family planning services, while available, were not emphasized. As a result of the rapid population growth in the 1950s and '60s, however, the number of marriages in China exceeds by 10,000,000 each year the number of fertile partnerships broken by death or by the onset of menopause. In an attempt to stabilize the population, the Chinese government recommended that 50 percent of rural couples and 80 percent of urban couples have only one child. The application of this type of policy had an ironic effect on individual women: Older women belonged to a generation that could not always obtain birth control services, and younger women were encouraged or, in some cases, even forced to abort pregnancies they wanted to keep.

Consensus has not been reached on the range of birth control methods society should offer to individual members. The right of couples to determine the number and spacing of their children is almost universally endorsed, whereas the possibility of coercive family planning is almost as widely condemned. Throughout the world, awareness of the advantages and disadvantages of specific methods of birth control, thoughtful judgments about ethics, and further evolution in medical and scientific knowledge will continue to be important to the welfare of the family, of individual countries, and of the entire world.

ABORTION

Abortion is the expulsion of a fetus from the uterus before it has reached the stage of viability (in humans, usually about the 20th week of gestation). An abortion may occur spontaneously, in which case it is also called a miscarriage, or it may be brought on purposefully, in which case it is often called an induced abortion.

Spontaneous abortions, or miscarriages, occur for many reasons, including disease, trauma, genetic defect, or biochemical incompatibility of mother and fetus. Occasionally, a fetus dies in the uterus but fails to be expelled, a condition termed a missed abortion.

Induced abortions may be performed for reasons that fall into four general categories: to preserve the life or physical or mental well-being of the mother; to prevent the completion of a pregnancy that has resulted from rape or incest; to prevent the birth of a child with serious deformity, mental deficiency, or genetic abnormality; or to prevent a birth for social or economic reasons (such as the extreme youth of the pregnant female or the sorely strained resources of the family unit). By some definitions, abortions that are performed to preserve the well-being of the female or in cases of rape or incest are therapeutic, or justifiable, abortions.

PROCEDURES

Numerous medical techniques exist for performing abortions. During the first trimester (up to about 12 weeks after conception), endometrial aspiration, suction, or curettage may be used to remove the contents of the uterus. In endometrial aspiration, a thin, flexible tube is inserted up the cervical canal (the neck of the womb) and then sucks out the lining of the uterus (the endometrium) by means of an electric pump.

In the related but slightly more onerous procedure known as dilatation and evacuation (also called suction curettage, or vacuum curettage), the cervical canal is enlarged by the insertion of a series of metal dilators while the patient is under anesthesia, after which a rigid suction tube is inserted into the uterus to evacuate its contents. When, in place of suction, a thin metal tool called a curette is used to scrape (rather than vacuum out) the contents of the uterus, the procedure is called dilatation and curettage. When combined with dilatation, both evacuation and curettage can be used up to about the 16th week of pregnancy.

From 12 to 19 weeks the injection of a saline solution may be used to trigger uterine contractions. Alternatively, the administration of prostaglandins by injection, suppository, or other method may be used to induce contractions, but these substances may cause severe side effects. Hysterotomy, the surgical removal of the uterine contents, may be used during the second trimester or later. In general, the more advanced the pregnancy, the greater the risk to the female of mortality or serious complications following an abortion.

In the late 20th century, a new method of induced abortion was discovered that uses the drug RU 486 (mifepristone), an artificial steroid that is closely related to the contraceptive hormone norethnidrone. RU 486 works by blocking the action of progesterone, which is needed to support the development of a fertilized ovum. When ingested within weeks of conception, RU 486 effectively triggers the menstrual cycle and flushes the fertilized ovum out of the uterus.

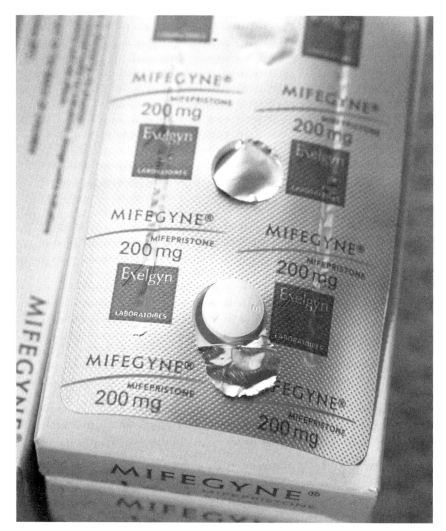

RU 486 blocks progesterone action, which is crucial for the support of a developing ovum. Phil Walter/Getty Images

Legality of Abortion

By the end of the 19th century, almost every country in the world had passed antiabortion legislation. In the United States restrictive laws were propelled not so much by moral considerations as by the desire of the medical profession to regulate the practices of unqualified doctors.

The 20th century saw the pendulum swing in the opposite direction, and in the first decade of the 21st century, roughly 60 percent of the world's population lived in countries where abortion was legally available. The Soviet Union (1920) became the first country in the 20th century to permit legal abortion, and the Scandinavian and most Eastern European countries had liberal abortion laws by the late 1960s. In Britain the Offenses Against the Person Act of 1861 was reversed by the 1967 Abortion Law, and by 1970 Canada and several U.S. states (including New York State) had passed abortion reform legislation. Arguments usually centred on hard cases, such as that of a woman carrying an abnormal fetus or living in extreme poverty. On January 22, 1973, the U.S. Supreme Court struck down as unconstitutional all antiabortion laws remaining in the United States. The Court argued "that the right of personal privacy includes the abortion decision." India, China, Australia, Italy, France, the Netherlands, and many other countries decided to permit abortion under statute law or following individual case precedents. It has always been difficult to harmonize statute law with biological processes, and several new therapies, such as the use of drugs to induce delayed menstruation, and even the use of IUDs, have not been clearly defined as falling under the category of either contraception legislation or abortion legislation.

In this most controversial aspect of birth control, legal positions have oscillated, depending on circumstance and on government. In 1935 Joseph Stalin reversed Lenin's liberal abortion law in the Soviet Union, and the Nazis declared abortions to be "acts of sabotage against Germany's racial future." In 1942 a woman was guillotined in Nazi-dominated France as a punishment for abortion, and in 1943 the government of the Third Reich introduced the death penalty for abortionists who "continually impaired the vitality of the German people." After the defeat of the U.S. antiabortion laws in 1973, a strong drive was undertaken by antiabortionists in the United States to limit the interpretation of the Supreme Court ruling and, if possible, to reverse that ruling by congressional action, constitutional amendment, or the appointment to the Supreme Court of justices who were against abortion.

The law, by defining marriage age, regulating medical practice, and controlling advertising and such factors as the employment of women, also affects many other variables that determine the size of a family. For example, Section 4(5) of the 1954 British Television Act prohibits the advertising of matrimonial agencies, fortune-tellers, and contraceptives.

A DIVISIVE ISSUE

Whether and to what extent induced abortions should be permitted, encouraged, or severely repressed is a social issue that has divided theologians, philosophers, and legislators for centuries. Abortion was apparently a common and socially accepted method of family limitation in the Greco-Roman world. Although Christian theologians early and vehemently condemned abortion, the application of severe criminal sanctions to deter its practice became common only in the 19th century. In the 20th century such sanctions were modified in one way or another in various countries, beginning with the Soviet Union in 1920 and with Japan and several eastern European and Scandinavian countries in the 1950s. The unavailability of birth-control devices was a factor in the acceptance of abortion in some countries. In the late 20th century, China used abortion on a large scale as part of its population-control policy. Some jurisdictions with large Roman Catholic populations, such as Portugal and Mexico City, decriminalized abortion in the early 21st century, despite strong opposition from the church, while others, such as Nicaragua, increased restrictions on it.

A broad social movement for the relaxation or elimination of restrictions on the performance of abortions resulted in the passing of liberalized legislation in several states in the United States during the 1960s. The U.S. Supreme Court ruled in *Roe* v. *Wade* (1973) that unduly restrictive state regulation of abortion was unconstitutional, in effect legalizing abortion for any reason for women in the first three months of pregnancy. A countermovement for the restoration of strict control over the circumstances under which abortions might be permitted soon sprang up, and the issue became entangled in social and political conflict. In rulings in 1989 and 1992, a more conservative Supreme Court upheld the legality of new state restrictions on abortion, although it proved unwilling to overturn *Roe* v. *Wade* itself. In 2007 the court also upheld a federal ban on a rarely used abortion method known as intact dilation and evacuation.

The public debate of the issue has demonstrated the enormous difficulties experienced by political institutions in grappling with the complex and ambiguous ethical problems raised by the question of abortion. Opponents of abortion, or of abortion for any reason other than to save the life of the mother, argue that there is no rational basis for distinguishing the fetus from a newborn infant; each is totally dependent and potentially a member of society, and each possesses a degree of humanity. Proponents of liberalized regulation of abortion hold that only a woman herself, rather than the state, has the right to manage her pregnancy and that the alternative to legal, medically supervised abortion is illegal and demonstrably dangerous, if not deadly, abortion.

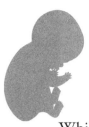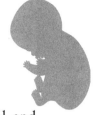

CONCLUSION

While issues surrounding the use of birth control and abortion will likely persist for decades to come, significant progress continues to be made concerning scientists' basic knowledge of the human reproductive system and how it functions in health and disease. One of the most intense areas of research in modern reproductive medicine is the development of improved assistive reproductive technologies. A significant challenge in this area of research centres on finding new ways to reduce the risk of multiple births while ensuring the success of procedures such as in vitro fertilization.

Modern reproductive science is also concentrated on the elucidation of the basic cellular activities that contribute to human embryological development as well as to day-to-day function of the reproductive organs. Of particular importance is achieving a better understanding of how environmental factors, such as maternal and paternal diet and exposure to harmful chemicals, affect gamete (sperm and ova) motility and function, the processes of fertilization and implantation, and the early steps of embryonic growth. With the aid of powerful microscopes and techniques enabling the molecular study of cells, scientists are able to explore complex topics, such as the contribution of oxidative stress (the presence of excess reactive oxygen molecules in cells) to sperm and ova malfunction and infertility in men and women.

Identifying the basic cellular processes that underlie embryonic development has numerous implications in terms of improving scientists' knowledge of human diseases ranging from congenital abnormalities to neurobiological conditions such as autism spectrum disorders. In the latter case, establishing associations between embryological markers (e.g., the appearance of certain proteins or changes in gene expression during different embryological stages) and the later development of autism and similar conditions may help researchers identify biological factors that contribute to these complex disorders. The placenta is a tissue of significant interest for the identification of embryological markers. Studies of stored placental samples and of the children of the mothers from whom the samples were collected have allowed scientists to form correlations between specific placental abnormalities and the subsequent development of autism spectrum disorders in the children. The data, however, are preliminary, and further investigation is required before scientists will be able to establish clear associations.

Finally, as reproductive medicine advances further into the 21st century, researchers continue to work toward finding new ways to prevent the spread of sexually transmitted diseases, particularly AIDS. Entities such as the World Health Organization (WHO) and the Joint United Nations Progamme on HIV/AIDS (UNAIDS) play fundamental roles in supporting international efforts to raise global awareness of AIDS. To support this work, WHO established World AIDS Day in 1988. This observance, which occurs annually on December 1, encourages the global dissemination of information about AIDS. The event is especially important for making this information available to people in developing countries, where lack of financial means and organized health care may otherwise prevent its distribution. In addition, scientists are generating and testing new drugs for the treatment of AIDS and other sexually transmitted diseases. Thus, although the annual loss of life from this group of diseases remains substantial, scientists and health officials are hopeful that their efforts will reduce the incidence and severity of these conditions in the coming years.

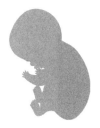

GLOSSARY

amenorrhea Failure to menstruate.

androgens Hormones that primarily influence the growth and development of the male reproductive system.

azoospermia A condition marked by the absence of sperm in the ejaculate.

dizygotic (DZ) twins Fraternal twins who develop from different zygotes.

endometrium Glandular lining of the uterus.

epididymides A system of ductules that holds maturing sperm and forms a tangled mass before combining into a single coiled duct that is continuous with the vas deferens.

erythroblastosis A disease that occurs when the infant's blood and the mother's blood are incompatible.

follicle-stimulating hormone (FSH) One of two gonadotropic hormones concerned with the regulation of the activity of the gonads, or sex glands.

gametes The sperm and ova (eggs), referred to also as sex cells.

gonadotropin-releasing hormone (GnRH) A neurohormone that stimulates the synthesis and secretion of the luteinizing hormone and follicle-stimulating hormone by the anterior pituitary gland.

gonadotropin Hormone secreted from the anterior pituitary gland that acts on the ovaries and the testes.

human chorionic gonadotropin (HCG) Gonadotropin that increases significantly following implantation of the fertilized ovum in the uterine wall and forms the basis of pregnancy tests.

hypopituitarism Deficiency of one or all pituitary hormones caused by damage to the pituitary gland.

idiopathic A condition that occurs spontaneously or that results from an unknown cause.

labia majora Two marked folds of skin that form the lateral boundaries of the vulval or pudendal cleft, which receives the openings of the vagina and urethra.

labia minora Two small folds of skin inside the labia majora. On each labia minora, the upper part crosses over the clitoris to create the prepuce, and a lower portion passes beneath the clitoris to form its frenulum.

luteinizing hormone (LH) One of two gonadotropic hormones that is concerned with the regulation of the gonads.

menarche An individual's first menstrual period marked by the maturation of the hypothalamus, pituitary, and ovaries.

menopause End of menstruation caused by the cessation of ovarian function, representing the end of a woman's reproductive life.

monozygotic (MZ) twins Twins who both developed from a single zygote.

oligospermia Low sperm count.

ovulation Release of a mature egg from the female ovary.

pituitary gland Secretes hormones directly into the bloodstream.

progesterone Hormone secreted by the female reproductive system that regulates the condition of the endometrium.

prostatic utricle In the male, a short diverticulum or pouch lined by mucous membrane.

seminal vesicles Either of two elongated saclike glands the secretions of which form the bulk of semen.

steroid hormones Hormones belonging to the class of chemical compounds known as steroids that are secreted by the three steroid glands: adrenal cortex, testes, and ovaries.

symptothermic method Natural family planning method that involves a combination of keeping a daily record of body temperature or recording physical changes in the cervix and cervical mucus.

BIBLIOGRAPHY

The characteristics of human reproduction and reproductive organs are reviewed in **Robert H. Williams** (ed.), *Textbook of Endocrinology*, 6th ed. (1981), covering in detail the endocrine aspects of the male and female reproductive systems; **Richard E. Jones**, *Human Reproductive Biology* (1991); **Ralph M. Wynn** and **William P. Jollie** (eds.), *Biology of the Uterus*, 2nd ed. (1989), a useful summary of modern research on many aspects of uterine anatomy and physiology; **Ethel Sloane**, *Biology of Women*, 3rd ed. (1993); and **Claude Gompel** and **Steven G. Silverberg**, *Pathology in Gynecology and Obstetrics*, 4th ed. (1994), which contains a chapter on each organ of the female genital tract and one on the breast. Reproductive technologies are explained in **Lori B. Andrews**, *New Conceptions* (1984); **Arthur L. Wisot** and **David R. Meldrum**, *New Options for Fertility* (1990); and **Sherman J. Silber**, *How to Get Pregnant with the New Technology* (1991).

Information on menstruation may be found in **Doreen Asso**, *The Real Menstrual Cycle* (1983); **John G. Gruhn** and **Ralph R. Kazer**, *Hormonal Regulation of the Menstrual Cycle* (1989); and **Linda R. Gannon**, *Menstrual Disorders and Menopause: Biological, Psychological, and Cultural Research* (1985).

Diseases of the human reproductive system are treated in **James B. Wyngaarden, Lloyd H. Smith, Jr.,** and **J. Claude Bennett** (eds.), *Cecil Textbook of Medicine*, 19th ed. (1992); *Campbell's Urology*, 6th ed. edited by **Patrick C. Walsh** *et al.*, 3 vol. (1992), one of the most complete textbooks in the field of urology; **Donald R. Smith**, *General Urology*, 11th ed. (1984), well written; **Robert W.**

Kistner (ed.), *Gynecology*, 4th ed. (1986), a detailed work; *Novak's Textbook of Gynecology*, 11th ed. by **Howard W. Jones III, Anne Colston Wentz,** and **Lonnie S. Burnett** (1988); **Stephen C. Rubin** and **Gregory P. Sutton** (eds.), *Ovarian Cancer* (1993); **Charles E. Rinear,** *The Sexually Transmitted Diseases* (1986); and **L.C. Parish** and **Friedrich Gschnait** (eds.), *Sexually Transmitted Diseases: A Guide for Clinicians* (1989).

General texts include *Human Embryology*, 4th ed. by **W.J. Hamilton** and **H.W. Mossman** (1972); and *Williams Obstetrics*, 19th ed. by **F. Gary Cunningham** *et al.* (1993), a standard textbook in the field. Additional information may be found in the following specialized texts: **Irwin R. Merkatz** and **Joyce E. Thompson** (eds.), *New Perspectives on Prenatal Care* (1990); **Robert K. Creasy** and **Robert Resnik** (eds.), *Maternal-Fetal Medicine: Principles and Practice*, 3rd ed. (1994); *Burwell and Metcalfe's Heart Disease and Pregnancy*, 2nd ed. by **James Metcalfe, John H. McAnulty,** and **Kent Ueland** (1986); and **Richard S. Abrams,** *Handbook of Medical Problems During Pregnancy* (1989).

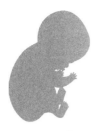

Index

A

abdomen, 20, 21, 22, 39, 47, 111, 112, 121, 127, 164, 184, 194, 196, 199 229

abdominal cavity, 29, 43, 47, 105, 122, 182, 184

abdominal pain, 172, 196, 204, 227

abdominal wall, 23, 161, 204

abortion, 110, 132, 160, 161, 168, 180, 193, 194, 195, 196, 206, 211–219, 228, 236–245

abstinence, 157, 211, 215, 219, 221, 223–224, 231, 233–235

accessory organs, 35–38

acquired immune deficiency syndrome (AIDS), 151, 152, 154, 155–157, 229, 247

adolescence, 19, 30, 48, 52, 53, 59, 67–69, 72, 133, 143, 148, 165

adrenal
   abnormalities, 57, 124
   cortex, 53, 63
   glands, 52–53, 56, 57, 61, 79, 84, 124, 146, 207
   hormones, 139
   steroids, 52
   tumours, 57, 119, 125, 135

afterbirth, 97, 100, 160, 194

aging
   female fertility and, 83, 85, 180–181
   old age, 31, 45, 60, 147, 186

alcohol consumption, 99, 110, 164, 178, 179, 199

alpha-fetoprotein screening, 112–113

amenorrhea, 56, 136, 138, 141–142

amniocentesis, 111–112, 199

amnion, 102

amniotic fluid, 97, 102, 111, 202, 203, 204, 205

amniotic sac, 98, 204

ampulla, 34, 47, 48, 194

androgens, 20, 27, 29, 30, 31, 37, 49, 50, 52–57, 58, 65, 69, 88, 124–128, 130, 131, 135, 136, 137, 142, 146, 147, 148, 174

anemia, 139, 150

anorexia nervosa, 143

anovulation, 146, 147

anterior pituitary gland, 51, 55, 62, 63, 65, 135

anus, 26, 152

aorta, 23

aromatase, 58, 136

arrhenoblastoma, 142

artery
   to the cremaster muscle, 27
   femoral, 27
   internal iliac, 26, 42
   internal pudendal, 26
   testicular, 32
   uterine, 47, 78, 100, 101
   vaginal, 42

artificial insemination, 186–191

autism, 246, 247

azoospermia, 185

B

bacteria, 59, 104, 140, 162, 164, 165, 166, 167, 168, 170, 171, 201, 202
balanitis, 162
barrier methods (contraceptive), 223
barriers (contraceptive), 212, 213, 215, 222
benign prostatic hyperplasia, 173
birth control
    controversies, 186, 190, 211, 212, 216, 243
    early advocates of, 214–217
    ethics of, 190–191, 231–238
    and health, 218–219
    history of, 212–214
    legality of, 230–231
    methods of, 221–230
    significance of, 238–239
birth control pills, 224
birth defects, 99, 110, 112, 118, 119–133
bladder, 26, 33, 34, 35, 37, 40, 41, 43, 119, 123, 124, 149, 150, 153, 173
blastocyst, 19, 46, 94, 97–98, 178, 188, 192
bleeding, 80, 82, 84, 86, 132, 134, 137, 138, 139, 140, 141, 142, 143, 173, 177, 183, 192, 193, 194, 196, 197, 198, 199, 200, 202, 205, 206, 225, 227, 229
blood cells, 53, 104, 140, 171, 227, 228
blood supply, 26, 32, 40, 42, 75, 98, 106, 122, 162, 203
blood vessels, 22, 26, 36, 44, 45, 47, 49, 60, 84, 101, 102, 104, 105, 106, 132, 201, 202, 203, 204, 206, 209, 229

brain
    effect on, 30, 56, 59, 63, 75, 78, 79, 80, 145
    anomolies, 203
    disorders, 135
    injuries, 135
    tumours, 135, 206
breasts
    milk production, 56, 59, 62, 108, 109, 141, 169, 171
    soreness, 82
bulbourethral (Cowper) glands, 21, 35, 37–38, 40, 68

C

cancer
    breast, 86, 170, 171
    cervical, 140, 155, 159, 172, 175–176
    ovarian, 176–177
    prostate, 172, 174–175
    of the reproductive system, 151, 172–177
    testicular, 122, 174
    uterine, 86, 147, 176–177
    vulvar, 175
candidiasis, 158, 166
cell division, 92, 94
cervical canal, 38, 40, 41, 42, 43, 44, 45, 88, 168, 241
cervicitis, 168–169
cervix, 40, 41, 42, 43, 44, 59, 104, 112, 127, 140, 141, 159, 164, 165, 168, 169, 171, 175, 176, 177, 180, 182, 183, 188, 191, 192, 193, 199, 200, 203, 204, 224, 225, 226, 227

cesarean section, 200

chancroid, 151, 159

chemotherapy, 139, 174, 175, 176, 177

childbirth, 39, 44, 160, 219

Chlamydia trachomatis (chlamydia), 158, 159, 168, 171, 182

choriocarcinoma, 205, 206–207

chorionic villi sampling, 112

chromosome disorders, 124, 131–133, 136, 141, 188

chromosomes, 29, 90, 94, 95, 96, 124, 129, 130, 131, 132, 133, 136, 141

cilia, 32, 48

clitoris, 26, 38, 39, 56, 69, 88, 96, 123, 128, 133, 166

coital techniques, 222–230

coitus interruptus, 215, 219, 221, 222, 231, 233

collagen fibres, 36

colostrum, 108

conception, 22, 97, 100, 102, 105, 186, 191, 192, 194, 213, 222, 240, 241

conceptus, 47, 87, 97, 98, 100, 101, 102, 178, 192, 194, 195, 198

condoms, 154, 155, 157, 212, 213, 221, 223

contraceptives
hormonal, 221, 224–227, 235
intrauterine, 168, 227–229
oral, 61, 79, 138, 143, 147, 154, 212, 227
prescribing of, 217, 237
types of, 154, 155, 157, 165, 212, 213, 221, 223, 224–229

corpus albicans, 50

corpus cavernosum, 24

corpus luteum, 46, 50, 57, 61, 64, 77, 78, 79, 81, 98, 99, 100, 105, 181

corpus spongiosum, 24, 25, 149

cortex, 49, 50, 52, 53

cotyledons, 102

Cowper glands, 21, 35, 37–38, 40, 68

cramps, 138, 139, 144

Cushing syndrome, 57

cystic fibrosis, 112, 189

cystoscopy, 173

cysts, 44, 119, 140, 146, 199, 201, 205

cytomegalovirus, 159

D

Darwin, Charles, 218

delayed puberty, 136–137

deoxyribonucleic acid (DNA), 56, 58, 188, 189

depression, 35, 85, 144, 145, 220

diabetes
gestational, 130, 178, 202, 203, 207–208
type II, 146, 208

diaphragm, 43, 105

diaphragm barrier (contraceptive), 154, 165, 213, 223

diet, 109, 145, 209, 210

dilation, 26, 47, 84, 106, 108, 183, 245

disorders
congenital, 99, 118–133
during pregnancy, 192–210
gynecological, 165
of menstruation, 57, 138–148
of the placenta, 199–202
reproductive, 118–133
of sexual maturity, 66, 133–137
of the testes and penis, 148–150

dizygotic (DZ) twins, 114–116
Down syndrome, 112, 113, 180, 219
ductus deferens, 20, 21, 27, 30, 31,
    32–34, 37, 54, 96
ductus epididymidis, 32
dysmenorrhea, 138–139

E

eclampsia, 208–210
ectopic pregnancy, 47, 172, 192–197
egg (ovum)
    and artificial insemination,
        186–191
    fertility phase of, 80–81, 114
    and infertility, 178–181
    and the reproductive cycle, 19,
        38, 46, 48, 49, 57, 59, 61, 62,
        69, 87–98
ejaculation, 20, 22, 26, 30, 32, 37,
    68, 89, 90, 164, 222, 229
ejaculatory ducts, 20, 21, 31,
    34–37, 96
embryo, 19, 50, 54, 92–94, 96,
    97–104, 114, 190–191, 197
epididymis, 20, 23, 30, 31–32, 33,
    96, 162, 163, 188
epididymitis, 162
erectile dysfunction, 65, 148
erection, 23–26, 88, 148, 149
estradiol, 49, 54, 57, 58, 75, 76, 77,
    78, 225, 226
estriol, 57, 58
estrogen, 38, 49, 50, 51, 52, 54, 56,
    57–60, 63, 64, 75, 77–86, 98,
    100, 108, 125, 127, 132,
    133–137, 139, 140, 142, 145,
    166, 176, 214, 224, 225
estrone, 49, 54, 57, 58

ethical issues
    and birth control, 231–238,
        239, 245
    and IVF, 190–191
excretory duct, 34
exercise, 86, 136, 143, 145, 147
external genitalia, 21–31, 38–42

F

fallopian tubes, 20, 40, 43, 47–48,
    50, 59, 61, 64, 77, 81, 91, 92,
    96, 141, 164, 171, 172, 179,
    182–183, 187, 189, 193, 196,
    213, 226, 229
falloposcopy, 182–183
family planning, 211, 215, 216,
    219–221, 222, 223, 231, 232,
    233, 238, 239
fertility drugs, 116, 181
fertilization, 92–94
    artificial, 117, 186–190
    of the egg (ovum), 46, 47, 48,
        50, 61, 87, 116, 226, 186
    problems with, 130, 141, 169,
        181, 196, 224
fetal alcohol syndrome, 110
fetus
    abnormalities and disorders, 180,
        197, 198, 200–205, 207, 209
    development, 29, 57, 87, 88, 97,
        98, 99, 100, 102, 105, 108,
        110, 125, 128, 179
    tests, 110, 111, 112
fibres
    muscle, 33, 38, 44, 47, 53, 105
    nerve, 23, 29, 47
fibroid, 139, 183
fibrous sac, 22

fibrous tissue, 25, 27, 35, 43, 49,
    83, 136, 150, 171
flagellum, 90
folic acid, 99, 207
follicle-stimulating hormone
    (FSH), 31, 50, 55, 83, 91, 130,
    180, 224
frenulum, 25, 39
fusion, 92, 121, 123, 131

G

Galen, 153
gametes, 20, 89, 94, 189
genetic abnormalities, 112,
    118–133, 145, 189, 209, 240
genital herpes, 152, 154–155,
    167, 229
genitalia
    external, 21–31, 38–42
    female, 38–51
    internal structures, 31–38,
        40–51, 121, 124, 132, 162
    male, 20–38
genital warts, 158–159
gestational edema-proteinuria-
    hypertension (GEPH), 208
glands
    anterior pituitary, 51, 55, 62, 63,
        65, 135
    bulbourethral (Cowper), 21, 35,
        37–38, 40, 68
    mammary, 59
    pituitary, 30, 31, 46, 50, 52, 59,
        61, 62, 63, 64, 65, 75, 79, 81,
        91, 108, 118, 119, 121, 134, 142,
        185, 207, 224
    prostate, 31, 34, 35–37, 54, 119,
        120, 150, 162, 173
    sebaceous, 27, 39, 54, 60, 69, 108

sweat, 39, 54, 69
thyroid, 79, 84, 85, 130, 139
glans clitoridis, 39
glans penis, 24, 88, 119, 158, 162
gonadal dysgenesis, 131, 136, 141, 180
gonadotropin-releasing hormone
    (GnRH), 30, 50, 51, 55, 134,
    137, 185
gonadotropins, 30, 50, 51, 62–64,
    75, 122, 134, 135, 137, 141, 181
gonads, 20, 29, 38, 65, 96, 125, 132,
    133, 136
gonorrhea, 151, 152–154, 158, 171,
    172, 182, 195
granuloma, 159
granulosa cells, 29, 49, 50, 77
growth hormone, 79, 132, 207
growth hormone deficiency,
    136, 137

H

heart, 84, 85, 88, 104, 111, 132,
    152, 204
hemorrhage, 47, 194, 196, 197,
    203, 204
hepatitis B, 159
hermaphrodite, 124–125, 128–129
hermaphroditism, 96, 124–125,
    128–129
herpes simplex virus type 2
    (HSV-2), 152, 154–155, 167, 229
hormones
    female, 20, 38, 48, 49, 50, 52,
        57–65, 68, 75, 78–86, 99, 108,
        125, 137, 139, 142, 207, 214, 224
    male, 20, 27, 29, 30, 52–57, 75,
        88–89, 137, 146
    steroid, 49, 52, 55, 56, 57, 63,
        125, 135, 224, 241

human immunodeficiency virus
(HIV), 152, 155, 157, 229
hydatidiform mole, 205, 206
hydramnios, 203–204
hydrocele, 148–149
hymen, 38, 40, 123, 142
hyperinsulinemia, 147
hyperplasia, 57, 125, 135, 172–173
hypogonadism, 131
hypopituitarism, 136, 137
hypoplasia, 119
hypothalamus, 51, 52, 55, 63, 65,
75, 76, 79, 80, 83, 127, 133, 134,
135, 146, 226
hysterectomy, 86, 139, 201

I

imaging tests, 99
immune system, 152, 157, 188
implantation, 19, 46, 61, 87,
97–102, 109, 124, 178, 179, 180,
181, 183, 186, 188, 189, 190–
196, 198, 199, 200, 202, 226,
228
impotence, 148, 163, 164
infections, 59, 123, 139, 140, 150,
151–172, 182, 195, 198, 201,
202, 228
infertility
causes of, 146, 147, 172, 178–186
female, 178–185
male, 185–186
treatment for, 79, 186–191
insulin, 146, 147, 207
interactions
behavioral, 71–73
physical, 71–73, 85
psychological, 67, 85, 134
intersexuality, 124–133

interstitial cells, 29, 36, 49, 57, 62,
64, 83, 127
interstitial pregnancy, 194, 197
intrauterine devices (IUD),
171, 213, 221, 223, 226,
227–229, 243
in vitro fertilization (IVF),
116–117, 131, 181, 186–191

K

Kallmann syndrome, 65, 136, 137
kidney
arteries (renal), 23, 203
damage, 120, 173, 205
development of, 53
disease, 149
Klinefelter syndrome, 124,
129–131, 137

L

labia majora, 27, 38, 39, 166, 175
labia minora, 39, 40, 123, 175
labour
childbirth, 39, 44, 160, 219
premature, 117, 179, 199, 210
lactogenic hormone, 108
laparoscopic surgery, 147, 189
laparoscopy, 184, 229
leukorrhea, 164–165
Leydig cells, 29, 55, 127
libido, 56, 65, 84, 85, 121, 131
ligament pregnancy, 194, 197
ligaments, 43, 44, 47, 49, 107
Lippes, Jack, 227
lumen, 30, 50
lutein cells, 77
luteinizing hormone (LH), 50, 55,
63, 83, 91, 127, 130, 135, 181, 224

lymphatic system, 27, 162, 169, 170, 171, 174
lymphogranuloma venereum, 158, 159
lymph vessels, 23, 27, 29, 44, 49, 105, 106, 161

M

malnutrition, 137
mammary glands, 59
mastitis, 169–171
menarche, 69, 70, 72, 73, 76, 81–82
menopause, 82–86
menorrhagia, 139
menstrual cycle, 76–82
menstrual disorders, 138–148
menstruation
  definition of, 74–75
  hormonal control of, 78–80
  normal, 82
  phases of, 76–78
mesoderm, 100
metrorrhagia, 140–141
miscarriage, 160, 178, 180, 188, 189, 197–199, 240
monozygotic (MZ) twins, 114, 116
mons pubis (mons veneris), 38, 39
mucous membrane, 33, 35, 36, 37, 40, 42, 44, 45, 59, 74, 94, 120, 140, 168, 169
mucus plug, 104, 183
multiple births, 79, 113–117, 179, 186, 189, 190, 191
muscle, 25, 27, 32, 35–39, 42, 45, 54, 56, 59, 60, 71, 88, 107, 121, 139, 146, 183, 205, 206
muscle fibres, 33, 38, 44, 47, 53, 105
mutations, 65, 124, 134, 137, 145, 189

N

nerve fibres, 23, 29, 47
neurons, 63
newborn, 29, 48, 124, 165, 245
nonoxynol-9, 223
nucleic acids, 207
nucleus, 23, 29, 55, 59, 90, 91, 92, 94
nutrition, 66, 73, 83, 86, 91, 99, 118, 145, 147

O

obesity, 208
oligohydramnios, 205
orchitis, 162–164
ovaries
  and disease, 57, 143, 145, 148, 206
  and hormones, 29, 46, 47, 75, 79, 107, 124, 214, 224
  and infertility, 180
  and reproduction, 20, 77, 80, 81, 91, 92, 98, 105, 192, 194
  structure of, 48–50
ovulation, 46, 50, 57, 61, 64, 75, 76, 77, 78, 79, 80–81, 91, 114, 116, 133, 138, 144, 211, 214, 224, 225, 226
ovulation diorders, 181–184

P

pelvic examination, 109, 142, 196
pelvic inflammatory disease (PID), 139, 158, 171–172, 181
penicillin, 154, 227
penis, 20, 21, 23–26, 37, 39, 40, 66, 67, 68, 87, 88, 89, 96

penis, abnormalities and disorders, 119–123, 131, 133, 148–150
perineal membrane, 25
perineum, 26, 39, 175,
periodic abstinence, 223–224, 233–235
peritoneum, 41, 43, 44
peritonitis, 161
pituitary glands, 30, 31, 46, 50, 52, 59, 61, 62, 63, 64, 65, 75, 79, 81, 91, 108, 118, 119, 121, 134, 142, 185, 207, 224
placenta
    development of, 99–103
    disorders, 199–202
placenta accreta, 199, 200–201
placentae abruptio, 199, 200
placental cysts, 199, 201
placenta praevia, 199–200
polyps, 139, 140, 141, 169
population, 73, 179, 214–215, 217–218, 219, 221, 235, 236, 238, 239, 241, 244
posthitis, 162
preeclampsia, 203, 208–210
pregnancy
    development of the placenta, 99–104
    disorders during, 118–124
    ectopic, 47, 172, 192–197
    gestation, 19, 20, 29, 98–113, 128, 194, 208, 240
    prenatal care and testing, 109–113
    tests, 109
premature birth, 117, 179, 199, 210
premenstrual syndrome (PMS), 78, 82, 138, 143–145
prenatal care and testing, 109–113, 199

preovulatory surge, 64, 181
priapism, 149–150
progesterone, 46, 50, 57, 61–62, 64, 75, 76, 77, 78, 79, 81, 98, 100, 108, 125, 132, 137, 145, 176, 181, 185, 188, 198, 207, 225, 226, 241
pronucleus, 94
prostate gland, 31, 34, 35–37, 54, 119, 120, 150, 162, 173
pseudohermaphroditism, 96, 119, 124, 125–128, 129
pseudopuberty, 134, 135
puberty
    delayed, 133, 136–137
    normal, 20, 36, 39, 45, 50, 52, 53, 54, 60, 63, 65–73, 118, 123, 124, 128, 129, 132, 147, 170
    precocious, 119, 126, 133–135
pubic hair, 53, 67, 68, 69, 70, 71, 82, 127, 134, 147
pubic lice, 151, 160
puerperal fever, 160–161

Q

quadruplets, 114, 116

R

recto-uterine pouch, 41
rectum, 37, 40, 41, 43, 44, 121, 124, 152
red blood cells, 53
reproductive disorders
    delayed puberty, 133, 136–137
    in females, 122–124
    genetic and congenital, 118–133

hermaphroditism, 96, 124, 128–129

intersexuality, 124–133

Klinefelter syndrome, 129–131

in males, 119–122

precocious puberty, 119, 126, 133–135

pseudohermaphroditism, 125–128

Turner syndrome, 131–133

reproductive system

female, 38–51

male, 20–38

ribonucleic acid (RNA), 56

Roe v. Wade, 245

Roman Catholic Church, 190, 233, 235, 236, 245

RU 486 (drug), 241

S

salpingoscopy, 182

Sanger, Margaret, 211, 215, 216, 217, 218, 220, 224

scrotal sac, 27, 33, 148

scrotal septum, 26

scrotum, 20, 21, 22, 26–27, 29, 39, 67, 96, 121, 149, 161, 163

sebaceous glands, 27, 39, 54, 60, 69, 108

secondary sex characteristics, 20, 51, 66–70, 112, 121, 125, 126, 132, 137

semen, 20, 21, 23, 26, 34, 35, 36, 37, 38, 88, 89, 185, 186, 191, 233

seminal vesicles, 21, 30, 34, 35, 37, 54, 68, 96, 119, 164

seminiferous tubules, 23, 29, 30

Sertoli cells, 29, 30, 55, 64

sex cells, 48, 89, 92

sex hormones

androgen, 20, 27, 29, 30, 31, 37, 49, 50, 52–57, 58, 65, 69, 88, 124–128, 130, 131, 135, 136, 137, 142, 146, 147, 148, 174

estrogen, 38, 49, 50, 51, 52, 54, 56, 57–60, 63, 64, 75, 77–86, 98, 100, 108, 125, 127, 132, 133, 137, 139, 140, 142, 145, 166, 176, 214, 224, 225

gonadotropin, 30, 50, 51, 62–64, 75, 122, 134, 135, 137, 141, 181

progesterone, 46, 50, 57, 61–62, 64, 75, 76, 77, 78, 79, 81, 98, 100, 108, 125, 132, 137, 145, 176, 181, 185, 188, 198, 207, 225, 226, 241

testosterone, 29, 30, 31, 52, 53, 54, 55, 56, 58, 64, 68, 125, 127, 128, 135, 138, 185, 186

sexual intercourse, 20, 64, 84, 87–89, 150, 152, 155, 164, 175, 183, 211, 212, 221

sexually transmitted diseases (STDs)

AIDS, 151, 152, 154, 155–157, 229, 247

candidiasis, 158, 166

chancroid, 151, 159

chlamydia, 158, 159, 168, 171, 182

cytomegalovirus, 159

genital herpes, 152, 154–155, 167, 229

genital warts, 158–159

gonorrhea, 151, 152–154, 158, 171, 172, 182, 195

granuloma, 159

hepatitis B, 159
HIV, 152, 155, 157, 229
lymphogranuloma venereum, 158, 159
pubic lice, 151, 160
syphilis, 150, 151, 152–154, 159, 162, 171, 202
trichomoniasis, 158, 166
urethritis, 153, 158
single embryo transfer (SET), 191
smoke (cigarette), 86, 99, 110, 178, 179
sperm
canal, 31–35
motility, 92, 179, 185, 186
structures of, 89–91
spermatic cords, 22, 23, 26, 27, 34, 121, 148, 162
spermatogenesis, 30, 31, 54, 135
spermatogonia, 22, 30
spermatozoa, 19, 22, 29, 64, 89, 92
sperm canal, 31–35
spermicides, 212, 213, 223
spina bifida, 113
Stein-Leventhal syndrome, 57, 142, 143, 145–148
sterility, 69, 148, 162, 163, 191
sterilization, 211, 213, 214, 229–230, 236
steroid hormones, 49, 52, 55, 56, 57, 63, 125, 135, 224, 241
stillbirth, 117, 199
Stopes, Marie, 215, 217, 218, 220
stress
emotional, 80, 142, 143, 145
physical, 85, 125, 138, 204
sweat glands, 39, 54, 69
Swyer syndrome, 141

symptothermic method, 224
syphilis, 150, 151, 152–154, 159, 162, 171, 202

T

Tay-Sachs disease, 112, 189
temperature (body), 78, 84, 181, 224
testes
cancers and infections, 122, 162, 163, 164, 174
disorders, 118, 121, 122, 125, 126, 127, 128, 130, 131, 135, 137, 148–150
function, 20, 21, 26, 27–31, 33, 34, 37, 48, 52, 54, 55, 62, 64, 67, 89
testosterone, 29, 30, 31, 52, 53, 54, 55, 56, 58, 64, 68, 125, 127, 128, 135, 138, 185, 186
thyroid, 79, 84, 85, 130, 139
toxoplasmosis, 202
trichomoniasis, 158, 166
tuberculosis, 161–162, 171, 202
tumours
benign, 172, 174, 183, 201
detection of, 175, 207
growth of, 124, 128, 135, 139, 195, 202, 206
malignant, 57, 65, 125, 133, 134, 142, 143, 148, 150, 174, 205, 206
tunica albuginea, 22, 27, 29
tunica vaginalis, 22
tunica vasculosa, 22
Turner syndrome, 124, 131–133, 136, 141

twins
conjoined, 92, 114
fraternal, 91, 114, 115
identical, 92, 114

U

ultrasound, 99, 110–111, 113, 173,
174, 175, 181
umbilical cord, 97, 98, 100, 102,
178, 198, 202, 293
urethra
female, 39, 40, 123, 124
male, 23, 24, 25, 31, 34, 35, 36,
38, 68, 119, 120, 121, 149
urethritis, 153, 158
urine, 23, 35, 54, 60, 77, 78, 82,
109, 120, 123, 149, 153, 167,
181, 209
uterine arteries, 47, 78, 100, 101
uterine cavity, 45, 77, 94, 101, 183,
188, 192, 193, 197, 228
uterine fibroids, 183
uterus
abnormalities of, 192, 193,
194, 195, 197, 198, 199, 200,
201, 203, 204, 205, 206, 207,
213, 216
and abortion, 240, 241
disorders of, 123, 124, 127, 137,
139, 141
during pregnancy, 87, 88, 91,
92, 94, 96, 97, 98, 102, 104,
105, 106, 107, 111, 112, 113
infections and cancers of, 160,
171, 172, 176
and infertility, 178, 179, 180,
182, 183, 186, 188, 190

and mestruation, 74, 75, 76,
77, 82
reproductive system, 19, 20, 35,
38, 40, 59, 61, 64, 69
structure of, 38, 40, 41, 42–47,
48, 50

V

vagina, 20, 35, 38, 39, 40–42,
43, 44, 59, 69, 88, 89,
92, 96, 106, 179, 199,
200, 201
vagina, diseases and abnormalities, 123, 124, 127, 142, 154,
158, 164, 165, 167, 168, 169,
172, 175, 206
vaginal bleeding, 74, 75, 84, 86,
132, 134, 137, 140, 192, 193,
196, 197, 198, 199
vaginitis, 165–166, 167
vas deferens, 31, 32, 54, 229
vasectomy, 213, 229, 236
Vatican Council (Second), 235
veins, 23, 26, 27, 33, 80, 101, 108,
150, 185
venereal disease (VD), 151–160
vesiculitis, 164
villi, 100, 101, 102, 112
vulva, 38, 39, 96, 106, 161, 166,
167, 175
vulvitis, 166–168

W

weight
at birth, 110, 179–180
gain during pregnancy, 84, 98,
207, 210

of infants, 110
loss, 147
white blood cells, 140, 171, 227, 228

X

X chromosomes, 94, 124, 129,
130, 131, 132, 141
X-ray, 72, 83, 173, 182

Y

Y chromosomes, 29, 90, 94, 129,
130, 131, 132, 133, 141
yolk sac, 29, 91, 101, 112

Z

zygote, 94, 114, 116, 190